Improving Learning by Widening Participation in Higher Education

Improving Learning by Widening Participation in Higher Education presents a strong and coherent rationale for improving learning for diverse students from a range of socio-economic, ethnic/racial and gender backgrounds within higher education, and for adults across the life course.

Edited by Miriam David, the Associate Director of the ESRC's highly successful Teaching and Learning Research Programme, with contributions from the seven projects on *Widening Participation in Higher Education* (viz Gill Crozier and Diane Reay; Chris Hockings; Alison Fuller and Sue Heath; Anna Vignoles; Geoff Hayward and Hubert Ertl; Julian Williams and Pauline Davis; Gareth Parry and Ann-Marie Bathmaker), this book provides clear and comprehensive research evidence on the policies, processes, pedagogies and practices of widening or increasing participation in higher education. This evidence is situated within the contexts of changing individual and institutional circumstances across the life course, and wider international transformations of higher education in relation to the global knowledge economy.

Improving Learning by Widening Participation in Higher Education also considers:

- the changing UK policy contexts of post-compulsory education;
- how socio-economically disadvantaged students – raced and gendered – fare through schools and into post-compulsory education;
- the kinds of academic and vocational courses, including maths, undertaken;
- the changing forms of institutional and pedagogic practices within higher education;
- how adults view the role of higher education in their lives.

This book, based upon both qualitative studies and quantitative datasets, offers a rare insight into the overall implications for current and future policy and will provide a springboard for further research and debate. It will appeal both to policy-makers and practitioners, as well as students within higher education.

Miriam David is Professor of Sociology of Education and Associate Director (Higher Education) of the ESRC's Teaching and Learning Research Programme at the Institute of Education, University of London.

Improving Learning TLRP

Series Editor: Andrew Pollard, Director of the ESRC Teaching and Learning Programme

Improving Learning in College
Roz Ivanic, Richard Edwards, David Barton, Marilyn Martin-Jones, Zoe
Fowler, Buddug Hughes, Gregg Mannion, Kate Miller, Candice Satchwell
and June Smith

Improving Working as Learning
Alan Felstead, Alison Fuller, Nick Jewson and Lorna Unwin

Improving Disabled Students' Learning
Mary Fuller, Jan Georgeson, Mick Healey, Alan Hurst, Katie Kelly,
Sheila Riddell, Hazel Roberts and Elisabet Weedon

Improving Learning in Later Life
Alexandra Withnall

Improving the Context for Inclusion
Andrew Howes, Sam Fox and Heddwen Davies

Improving Learning in a Professional Context
James McNally and Allan Blake

Improving Literacy at Work
Alison Wolf and Karen Evans

Improving Mathematics at Work (forthcoming)
Celia Hoyles, Richard Noss, Phillip Kent and Arthur Bakker

Improving Research through User Engagement (forthcoming)
Mark Rickinson, Anne Edwards and Judy Sebba

Improving What is Learned at University (forthcoming)
John Brennan

Improving Teaching and Learning in Schools (forthcoming)
Mary James and Andrew Pollard

Improving Learning through the Life-course (forthcoming)
Gert Biesta, John Field, Ivor F. Goodson, Phil Hodkinson and
Flora J. MacLeod

Improving Learning by Widening Participation in Higher Education

Edited by
Miriam David

with Ann-Marie Bathmaker,
Gill Crozier, Pauline Davis,
Hubert Ertl, Alison Fuller,
Geoff Hayward, Sue Heath,
Chris Hockings, Gareth Parry,
Diane Reay, Anna Vignoles and
Julian Williams

Routledge
Taylor & Francis Group
LONDON AND NEW YORK

First published 2010
by Routledge
2 Park Square, Milton Park, Abingdon, Oxon OX14 4RN

Simultaneously published in the USA and Canada
by Routledge
270 Madison Avenue, New York, NY 10016

Routledge is an imprint of the Taylor & Francis Group, an informa business

© 2010 Miriam David, Ann-Marie Bathmaker, Gill Crozier,
Pauline Davis, Hubert Ertl, Alison Fuller, Geoff Hayward, Sue Heath,
Chris Hockings, Gareth Parry, Diane Reay, Anna Vignoles and Julian Williams
for editorial selection and material; individual contributions, the authors

Typeset in Charter ITC and Stone Sans by
Keystroke, Tettenhall, Wolverhampton
Printed and bound in Great Britain by
TJ International Ltd, Padstow, Cornwall

British Library Cataloguing in Publication Data
A catalogue record for this book is available from the British Library

Library of Congress Cataloging in Publication Data
Improving learning by widening participation in higher education/
[edited by] Miriam E. David . . . [et al.].
    p. cm.
    1. People with social disabilities—Education (Higher)—Great Britain.
    2. Educational equalization—Great Britain. I. David, Miriam E.
    LC4096.G7I66 2010
    379.2'60941—dc22   2009015150

ISBN 10: 0–415–49541–5 (hbk)
ISBN 10: 0–415–49542–3 (pbk)
ISBN 10: 0–203–86797–1 (ebk)

ISBN 13: 978–0–415–49541–7 (hbk)
ISBN 13: 978–0–415–49542–4 (pbk)
ISBN 13: 978–0–203–86797–6 (ebk)

Contents

Appendices 202

Illustrations

Figures

Tables

Contributors

Miriam David, AcSS, FRSA is Professor of Sociology of Education and Associate Director (Higher Education) of the ESRC's Teaching and Learning Research Programme at the Institute of Education University of London. She has a world-class reputation for her research on social diversity, gender and inequalities in education, including lifelong learning and higher education. She is chair of the Council of the Academy of Social Sciences (AcSS), a member of the ESRC's Research Grants Board and the Governing Council of Society for Research in Higher Education (SRHE). She is co-editor (with Philip Davies) of *21st Century Society* journal of the Academy of Social Sciences and an executive editor of *British Journal of Sociology of Education*. Her most recent publications include (with Pam Alldred) *Get Real About Sex: The Politics and Practice of Sex Education* (2007, London: McGraw Hill/Open University Press), (with Diane Reay and Stephen Ball) *Degrees of Choice: Social Class, Race and Gender in Higher Education* (2005, Stoke-on-Trent: Trentham Books). She edited a special issue of *Research Papers in Education* 23, 2, 2008, based on the TLRP's work on widening participation in Higher Education.

Ann-Marie Bathmaker is Professor of Further Education and Lifelong Learning at the University of the West of England, Bristol. Her particular area of interest is the transformation of policy as espoused into policy as experienced, especially in relation to the changing experience of learning, education and training, amongst those who do not follow traditional smooth learning trajectories. She worked on the National Research and Development Centre for Adult Literacy and Numeracy Project entitled 'Impact of Skills for Life on Learners' from 2003 to 2007. Recent publications include: Bathmaker, A.M, Brooks, G., Parry, G. and Smith, D. (2008) Dual-Sector Further and Higher Education: Policies, Organizations and Students in Transition, *Research Papers in Education*, 23, 2, 125–137; Bathmaker, A.M. and Avis, J. (2007) 'How do I cope with that?' The challenge of 'schooling' cultures in further education for trainee FE lecturers, *British Educational Research Journal*, 33, 4, 509–532.

Gill Crozier is Professor of Education and Assistant Dean (Research) in the School of Education, Roehampton University. She is a sociologist of education and her work has focused on 'race' and its intersection with social class and gender. She has researched extensively issues relating to parents and schools, and young people, and is also concerned with education policy, and the socio-cultural influences upon identity formation and learner experiences. She recently directed a two-year ESRC-funded research project (R000239671) *Parents, Students and the School Experience: Asian Families' Perspectives*.

Pauline Davis is Senior Lecturer in Education at the University of Manchester. She has a longstanding interest in hybrid and qualitative social research methodologies in the context of socio-cultural theories of learning and identity, and in inequality, social and educational inclusion. In addition, she has a keen interest in mathematics education following on from an earlier career as a mathematics lecturer in the further education sector. Pauline has directed a number of research projects in inclusive education and financial education for the Economic and Social Research Council, Nuffield Foundation, DfES and others. She is currently a co-investigator on the ESRC-funded project *Mathematics Learning, Identity and Educational Practice: The Transition into Higher Education*. She also recently directed a three-year research project funded by the School of Finance, *Becoming Financially Literate, 16–19 Education*.

Hubert Ertl is Lecturer in Higher Education at the Department of Education, University of Oxford. He directs the Department of Education's MSc in Higher Education and convenes the Higher Education and Professional Learning Research Group. He is Fellow of Linacre College, Oxford. After completing his training in the German dual system of vocational education, Hubert did his first degree in business studies, vocational education and English at the Ludwig-Maximilians-Universität (LMU) in Munich. Recent publications include: Hölscher, M., Hayward, G., Ertl, H. and Dunbar-Godet, H. (2008) The Transition from Vocational Education and Training to Higher Education: a successful pathway? *Research Papers in Education* 23, 2, 139–151; Ertl, H. and Kremer, H. (2006) Curricular reform and college-based Innovation in vocational education and training in England and Germany, *Research in Comparative and International Education*, 1, 4, 351–365; Ertl, H. (2006) Educational standards and the changing discourse on education: the reception and consequences of the PISA study in Germany, *Oxford Review of Education* 32, 5, 619–634; Ertl, H. (2006) European Union policies in education and training: the Lisbon agenda as a turning point?, *Comparative Education* 42, 1, 5–27; Ertl, H. (2005) Higher Education in Germany: a case of 'uneven' expansion? *Higher Education Quarterly*, 59, 3, 205–229.

Alison Fuller is Professor of Education and Work and Head of the Post Compulsory Education and Training Research Centre in the School of Education at the University of Southampton. Her work and publications focus on four main areas: education–work transitions; patterns of adult participation in education; vocational education and apprenticeship; and learning in the workplace. Her book *Improving Working as Learning* (co-authored with Alan Felstead, Alison Fuller, Nick Jewson and Lorna Unwin) has recently been published in the Routledge, TLRP Gateway Series.

Geoff Hayward is Lecturer in Education based at Oxford University's Department for Education. He is the Associate Director of the ESRC Research Centre on Skills, Knowledge and Organisational Performance (SKOPE), a director of the Nuffield 14–19 Review, co-director of the Oxford Centre for Socio-cultural and Activity Theory (OSAT) and co-convenor of the Higher Education and Professional Learning research group. After a period of secondment to the University of Bath as part of the ground-breaking Macmillan post-16 science education project, Geoff returned to higher education as a teacher educator, first at the Liverpool Institute of Higher Education and then at the University of Oxford. Recent and forthcoming publications include: Hayward, G. (forthcoming) VET and the school to work transition, in *The Elsevier International Encyclopaedia of Education*; Ertl, H. and Hayward, G. (forthcoming) Modularity, in *The Elsevier International Encyclopaedia of Education*; Hayward, G. and McNichol, J. (2007) Modular mayhem? The reform of the A level science curriculum in England, *Assessment in Education: Principles, Policy and Practice*, 14, 3, 335–351; Hayward, G. (2007) Vocationalism and the decline of vocational learning in England, in Bechel, J.J. and Fees, K. (eds) *Bildung oder Outcome?* Herbolzheim: Centaurus, pp. 91–112; Leney, T., May, T., Hayward, G. and Wilde, S. (2007) *International Comparisons in Further Education*, London: DfES.

Sue Heath is Professor of Sociology in the School of Social Sciences at the University of Southampton. She is a co-director of both the ESRC National Centre for Research Methods and the ESRC-funded Centre for Population Change. Sue's substantive research interests lie within the sociology of education and the sociology of youth, with a particular interest in the changing nature of transitions to adulthood.

Chris Hockings is Professor of Learning and Teaching at the University of Wolverhampton and is a Senior Researcher within the University of Wolverhampton's Institute of Learning Enhancement. She is also a National Teaching Fellow. She plays a key capacity-building role within the university, creating institutional frameworks to ensure learning and teaching research influences policy and is embedded in practice. Her research interests range from the learning and teaching of mathematics in higher education to her recent work on widening participation. She is currently leading a HEFCE/ESRC-funded project in collaboration with Sandra Cooke, looking at the learning, teaching and academic engagement of university students from diverse social, cultural and educational backgrounds.

Gareth Parry is Professor of Education at the University of Sheffield. After working in further education colleges in London, he moved to research and teaching positions at City, Warwick and Surrey Universities as well as the Institute of Education University of London. He was an academic consultant to the Dearing inquiry into higher education in the United Kingdom and the Foster review of further education colleges in England. He was elected a Fellow of the Society for Research into Higher Education in 2002.

Diane Reay is Professor of Education in the Faculty of Education, University of Cambridge with particular interests in social justice issues in education, Pierre Bourdieu's social theory, and cultural analyses of social class. She has researched extensively in the areas of social class, gender and ethnicity across primary, secondary and post-compulsory stages of education. Recent funded research projects include primary-secondary school transfer, choice of higher education, pupil consultation and voice, working-class students in higher education, and the white middle classes and comprehensive schooling. Her book on higher education choice and access, *Degrees of Choice* (with Miriam David and Stephen Ball), was published in 2005 by Trentham Press.

Anna Vignoles is Professor in the Economics of Education at the Institute of Education and a deputy director of the Centre for the Economics of Education. Her research interests include issues pertaining to equity in education, school choice, markets in education and the economic value of schooling. She is an adviser to both the HM Treasury and the Sector Skills Development Agency, and has undertaken extensive research for the Departments for Children, Schools and Families and Innovation, Universities and Skills. Recently, she has provided advice to the House of Commons Education and Skills Committee investigation of higher education funding, the House of Lords Economic Affairs Select Committee, as part of their inquiry into education and training opportunities for young people, and Lord Leitch's Review of Skills.

Julian Williams is Professor of Mathematics Education and Director of Post-Graduate Research studies at the University of Manchester. He led the ESRC-TLRP-WP project on mathematics and is currently engaged in a study of students' transition into higher education. His main research interests are in mathematics education, socio-cultural and activity theory, and generally in learning, teaching and assessment.

Additional contributors

Laura Black   University of Manchester

Marion Bowl   University of Birmingham

John Clayton   University of Sunderland

Sandra Cooke   University of Birmingham

Claire Crawford   Institute of Fiscal Studies, London

Paul Hernandez-Martinez   University of Manchester

Michael Hölscher   University of Heidelberg, Germany

Graeme Hutcheson   University of Manchester

Su Nicholson   University of Manchester

Maria Pampaka   University of Manchester

Nattavudh Powdthavee   Institute of Education, University of London

Geoff Wake   University of Manchester

Series editor's preface

The *Improving Learning* series showcases findings from projects within the Economic and Social Research Council's Teaching and Learning Research Programme (TLRP), the UK's largest ever coordinated educational research initiative.

Books in the *Improving Learning* series are explicitly designed to support 'evidence-informed' decisions in educational practice and policy-making. In particular, they combine rigorous social and educational science with high awareness of the significance of the issues being researched.

Working closely with practitioners, organisations, and agencies covering all educational sectors, the Programme has supported many of the UK's best researchers to work on the direct improvement of policy and practice to support learning. Over seventy projects have been supported, covering many issues across the life course. This book is the result of collaboration between seven projects concerned with widening participation in higher education. We are proud to present the results of this work.

Each book provides a concise, accessible and definitive overview of innovative findings from a TLRP investment. If more advanced information is required, the books may be used as a gateway to academic journals, monographs, websites, etc. On the other hand, shorter summaries and research briefings on key findings are also available via the programme's website at www.tlrp.org.

We hope that you will find the analysis and findings presented in this book are helpful to you in your work on improving outcomes for learners whether in government, in college or university concerned with policies, pedagogies or institutional practices.

Andrew Pollard
Director, TLRP
Institute of Education, University of London

Acknowledgements

We would like to thank the Higher Education Funding Council for England (HEFCE) and the Economic and Social Research Council (ESRC) for their generous support for the seven projects in the widening participation in higher education suite of projects as part of the Teaching and Learning Research Programme (TLRP). We would also like to thank and acknowledge all the help and support for the principal investigators of their research teams. The seven ESRC projects are as follows, and compose the following teams of principal investigators, and research associates and assistants, without whose help these seven projects would not have been completed. We list the projects below in the order of their ESRC research number for ease of reference here.

Socio-Cultural and Learning Experiences of Working-Class Students in Higher Education
RES-139–25–0208
Gill Crozier, Diane Reay, John Clayton, Lori Colliander and Jan Grinstead

Learning and Teaching for Social Diversity and Difference in Higher Education
RES-139–25–0222
Chris Hockings, Sandra Cooke, Marion Bowl, Hiromi Yamashita and Samantha McGinty

'Non-participation' in Higher Education: Decision-making as an Embedded Social Practice
RES-139–25–0232
Alison Fuller, Sue Heath, Martin Dyke, Nick Foskett, Ros Foskett, Brenda Johnston, Felix Maringe, Karen Paton, Patricia Rice, Laura Staetsky, John Taylor and Marie Kenny

Widening Participation to Higher Education: A Quantitative Analysis
RES-139–25–0234
Anna Vignoles, Alissa Goodman, Claire Crawford, Haroon Chowdry, Nick Powdthavee, Steve Machin, Sandra McNally, Iftikar Hussain, Steve Gibbons and Shqiponja Telhaj

Degrees of Success: Learners' Transitions from Vocational Education and Training to Higher Education
RES-139–25–0238
Geoff Hayward, Hubert Ertl, Harriet Dunbar-Goddet and Michael Hölscher

Keeping Open the Door to Mathematically Demanding Programmes in Further and Higher Education
RES-139–25–0241
Julian Williams, Laura Black, Pauline Davis, Graeme Hutcheson, Su Nicholson, Geoff Wake, Paul Hernandez-Martinez and Maria Pampaka

Universal Access and Dual Regimes of Further and Higher Education
RES-139–25–0245
Gareth Parry, Ann-Marie Bathmaker, Greg Brooks, David Smith, Diane Burns, Cate Goodlad, Liz Halford, Karen Kitchen, Sammy Rashid, Anne Thompson, Will Thomas and Val Thompson

Part I

What are the issues?

Chapter 1

Introduction to the dilemmas of widening participation in higher education

Miriam David

1 Introduction

The aim of *Improving Learning by Widening Participation in Higher Education* is to provide clear and comprehensive research evidence on attempts to extend access to and participation in post-compulsory and higher education in the twenty-first century. Specifically our concern is with widening participation to a diversity of individuals comprising the economically, educationally and socially disadvantaged, in terms of poverty or social class, and also age, ethnicity or race and by gender. These may also now be seen as under-represented social groups although we will consider changing definitions and concepts in this respect. We will cover an array of English policies, processes, pedagogies and practices. We will bring together our views on appropriate teaching and learning strategies as well as institutional policies and practices. Our collective evidence is drawn from a set of social science research projects which were commissioned by the Higher Education Funding Council for England in 2005 to consider what was happening in England and to evaluate the evidence about policies, practices and pedagogies.

These projects were, of course, situated within the *context* of wider UK and international transformations of higher education in relation to the global knowledge economy. In presenting our research we will, inevitably, have to consider the changing policy contexts of post-compulsory education and how these have developed out of policy and practice initiatives over a long historical sweep. This will take into consideration the second half of the twentieth century as a backdrop to these particular policy shifts towards mass higher education (and indeed massive universities) and wider economic and labour market changes with demographic implications. These changes were also entwined with the more international and global economic transformations, often considered as part of globalisation.

A linked consideration will be *conceptual*: how educational or learning opportunities were transformed, increased or widened for men and women as individuals across the life course and through changing institutional policies and practices, nationally and internationally. We will consider how economically and socially disadvantaged (classed or poor, raced and gendered) students fare through primary and secondary schools and into post-compulsory education, whether in colleges or universities. What contribution, in particular, do prior educational or learning experiences have to continued educational participation, or the desire to return to educational opportunities as adult men and women, and over the life course? This research takes into account the changes in both individual identities and institutional circumstances. The processes of transforming post-compulsory and higher education into a mass or universal system will be taken into consideration. We will also focus on the specific kinds of subjects or disciplines studied, through the kinds of academic or vocational courses undertaken and what the different future employment and other prospects are for either academic or vocational pathways. One focus will be on the criticality of mathematics education for some subjects and forms of higher education, especially in relation to courses in science, technology, engineering and mathematics itself or medicine, often known as STEM subjects. We will also review changing forms of institutional and pedagogic practices within higher education to cope with new and diverse students rather than those previously considered traditional students in universities, namely, conventional 18 year olds. Forty years ago a conventional undergraduate student was typically white, male and from the middle or upper classes. We will also evaluate how adult men and women, mostly over the age of 21, think about higher education in their lives and across the life course, in relation to families, friends, employment, work or leisure.

As part of a series of books emanating from the Teaching and Learning Research Programme (TLRP), and whose overall aim is to draw from research findings about how to improve learning and teaching across the life course, our aim is to present a strong and coherent rationale for improving learning for diverse students. Here we will focus on the meanings of widening access to, or participation in, higher education for students from a range of socio-economic, ethnic/racial and gender backgrounds within different higher education settings and across the life course. In our concluding section, having presented and reviewed the evidence in part two of the book, we will therefore address the question of what are appropriate policy contexts and changes for the post-compulsory sectors of education to ensure a more consistent and equitable system for diverse students and across a diversity of subjects and institutions. We hope to contribute to current policy debates about equity and diversity in student access, successes in and outcomes from diverse educational and learning opportunities and different institutional practices and across the life course, including family and employment.

Indeed, to anticipate our conclusions, the central core of our findings is that educational or learning opportunities have been massively increased in the twenty-first century, and for an increasingly diverse array of students, from diverse families and disadvantaged socio-economic backgrounds. However, *these policies have not led to fair or equal access to equal types of higher education or outcomes in the labour market*. For example, whilst more women and people from ethnic minorities now participate in some kinds of higher education, their opportunities and successes in the subsequent labour market are not necessarily equal to those of men from white and middle-class families. The diverse educational or learning opportunities that are on offer may not lead to equal benefits in graduate or professional labour markets. Indeed with recent and significant economic downturns in wider global contexts many opportunities may not lead to economic benefits although social benefits may well accrue and be extensive for some previously disadvantaged people. Social mobility on a widespread basis is not demonstrated through these projects; diverse instances of individual mobility and involvement in educational opportunities across the life course are revealed.

The projects also show that some UK policies have provided the opportunities for the development of potential new institutional practices and pedagogies to engage diverse students for the twenty-first century. We can see how influential critical pedagogies have been, and what the potential for further developments in inclusive and personal pedagogies might be. This potential could only be achieved however if the policies and practices that limit progressive developments were to be changed. If post-compulsory and higher education in *all* subjects and institutions is to be more equitable we raise questions about relevant national policy contexts, and institutional practices, as well as the appropriate pedagogies to ensure social justice across disadvantaged, gendered and ethnic minority students.

2 Higher education policy debates in a changing global knowledge economy

Given the global as well as local changes in higher education, and the expansion to mass or universal post-compulsory or higher education in the context of transformations in global and international knowledge economies, the question of how to transform policies on *fair access and participation*, pedagogies or teaching and learning, and practices becomes an urgent one. Access, diversity and equity are key *concepts* in relation to expansion of higher education nationally and internationally and changing *contexts* especially labour markets and economic globalisation. In policy terms, ideas about increasing 'access' for various socio-economic groups have gone beyond a simple issue of entry into institutions of higher learning. They have been translated into questions of 'widening participation' in higher education or post-compulsory learning for the socially or economically disadvantaged, or social class and gender. The term 'diversity' has achieved common currency in both policy and research circles, and no longer only as race/ethnicity but as a more all-embracing yet contested term about *learners* not simply students.

The recent expansion of post-secondary educational opportunities and their differential structuring internationally into diverse forms of college, university or higher education plays out very differently from a global or European perspective with many individuals, institutions and systems at a significant disadvantage compared to others. The experiences of individuals and institutions existing at the margins of mainstream higher education developments are diverse as they are often overlooked in identifying institutions and systems at the leading edge of development. Poverty, war, violence and diaspora can affect opportunities for and attitudes towards learning in fundamental ways, while cultural attitudes and practices at school can also create or reinforce disadvantage even in developed or advanced systems and practices of higher education.

Moreover, political, social and cultural globalising tendencies are influencing policy-makers and institutions to address issues such as social justice and equity, including questions of not only 'access' to institutions but inclusive participation, pedagogies and practices within them. There are a variety of diverse, expanding and changing educational contexts, particularly global higher education as it is changing in the twenty-first century, and learning in forms of formal education such as in schools, colleges, university or higher education and the relations between formal education and employment.

Growing socio-political awareness of the central importance of innovation in universities, colleges and post-compulsory learning makes these fundamental questions. Recent research agendas in globalising higher education have highlighted the problematic nature of the exchange and transfer of knowledge, through rapidly changing forms of digitalisation, understanding and skills between different institutional contexts and their implications for pedagogies and practices between forms of learning, work and employment. These raise questions about equity in learning and work across the life-course and not only in higher education itself. The development of a social scientific understanding of teaching and learning in different settings and of how diverse learning occurs over the life course and across contexts is therefore critical to these questions. Research on diverse learning after the compulsory stage of schooling in a variety of diverse, expanding and changing educational contexts is a vital element of global, regional and national forms of higher education today. This book builds upon precisely these manifold developments in social scientific ways of studying these complex questions.

Several key themes around *access, diversity and equity* can be identified as a basis for researching these questions from the perspectives of education and social research, namely aspects of the rapidly changing *contexts* of higher education, state or local policies and institutional forms of higher education and post-compulsory learning; how this expansion of post-compulsory learning and higher education plays out differently from a global perspective with many individuals, institutions and systems at a significant disadvantage compared to others; and *conceptual* in teasing out and mapping the diverse pathways and transitions individuals follow into higher education, with their origins in differentially structured and inequitable opportunities for education, training or employment; the interaction of learning and identities for adults following different gendered paths through the life course after leaving compulsory education; and new ideas for pedagogies and educational futures for the twenty-first century.

These themes relate not only to the twenty-first century expansions of higher education but also to the historical developments of higher education in relation to globalisation and economic competitiveness in the twentieth century, diverse stakeholders in transforming higher education in the twenty-first century, including national policy-makers and their focus on access and equity policies for widening participation in higher education, and also pedagogies and practices for the future of higher education in the twenty-first century. These then provide the broad context for conceptual understandings of the policies on access, diversity and equity in expanding English higher education relative to other countries in the UK, in Europe, Australasia and the Americas.

3 Origins and meanings of the widening participation in higher education research projects in UK policy context

The UK government, during the first half of the first decade of the twenty-first century, has been eager to develop and extend learning opportunities for both young people and adults, across their life course, to ensure that the education and skills base of the UK economy is internationally competitive. This emphasis in educational policy has built upon previous initiatives in the twentieth century to extend and enhance the UK economy through developments in its skills and knowledge base, including with computer and digital technologies. In keeping with many other industrial countries and in relation to developments in the knowledge industries and economies, this has led to new emphases on how to expand and enhance educational opportunities beyond secondary or compulsory education, and into new and traditional forms of higher education. Deploying new ideas about forms of governance and what have been called new managerialism or neo-liberalism has meant that a variety of new and innovative approaches to education and individual or personal learning opportunities have been tried and tested.

These various policy and governance initiatives have also been associated with new and innovative subjects, disciplines and the uses of new technologies, including education and digital or computer-based, in forms of teaching and learning, as well as in the kinds of appropriate resources and forms of organisation to achieve these developments. Indeed, the pace of developments in the balances between transformations in what has been called 'the knowledge economy' and new forms of teaching or learning regimes has become known in some contexts as new forms of 'academic capitalism' (Slaughter and Rhoades 2004). In other contexts, economic globalisation is often attributed to these manifold processes.

Widening participation in higher education was not a new policy mantra in the twenty-first century. Indeed, ideas about how to make educational opportunities more equal for various groups such as those in poverty, economically and socially disadvantaged, or on the basis of being working class, from an ethnic or racial minority, and according to gender, had been a policy theme throughout the second half of the twentieth century. Initially, though, it was a theme applied to reconstructing secondary and compulsory education, rather than access to, or participation in, higher education. This was mirrored in policy developments in other countries such as Australia, Canada and the USA, as well as developing countries, such as Brazil, India and Tanzania. The ideas were linked to broad political and democratic campaigns for citizen, civil, social or human rights, including ethnicity, race or gender and played out differently in different national contexts. In the UK a key emphasis was on social class or disadvantage whereas in the USA, given different demographics and governance questions, ideas about race or ethnicity becoming defined as diversity became more prevalent.

In the 1960s UK higher educational opportunities were extended from a very low base of less than 10 per cent of the age cohort of 18 year olds (largely white middle-class men) through, first, the creation of new universities in the wake of the Robbins Committee report of 1963 and, second, the implementation of what became known as a 'binary policy'. This policy for higher education built upon a previous policy for secondary education of creating targeted opportunities for either traditional academically oriented students in universities, or more focused technological and vocational opportunities in a separate group of institutions, known as polytechnics from 1970. These thirty polytechnics were created out of the system of technological or technical colleges, largely based in metropolitan areas, whereas the new universities were from a mix of the elite colleges of advanced technology (i.e. Aston, Bath, Bradford, Brunel, City, Salford) or entirely new creations on green field sites (e.g. East Anglia, Kent, Sussex, Warwick and York). A system of structured higher educational opportunities, around types of academic or technological courses, and linked to socio-economic status was thus embedded within UK policies and practices for expanding higher education from their inception.

Several attempts were made to change these systematic inequalities. For instance, in the 1980s, attempts were made to increase opportunities of mature and mainly female students in new provisions, through a Conservative government drive entitled 'Higher education: meeting the challenge' (Cmnd 114, 1987). The funding of higher education was also changed through the 1988 Education Act of a Conservative government.

Four years later, through the Further and Higher Education Act, 1992, a more radical measure of abolishing the binary policy and creating new universities in place of polytechnics was achieved.

As we shall see, some began to refer to pre-1992 and post-1992 universities as ways of referring to structured types. The traditional or pre-1992 universities were created from medieval times, and include what are now considered elite universities such as Cambridge and Oxford, to those from the nineteenth century (often referred to as Victorian or red-brick) such as Birmingham, Leeds, Manchester and Sheffield, and those of the twentieth century such as Keele and Warwick; whilst the new or post-1992 universities include Sunderland, West of England and Wolverhampton. These two groups around legislative notions are, however, not sufficiently fine-grained to accommodate all the nuances between and within institutions of higher education, although broad patterns may be discerned. In particular, social distinctions over time may have related to size and quality of subjects taught and forms of quality research and its type of funding.

Through the 1992 Act, the funding base was changed so that institutions had to be more transparent in the balances between teaching and research activities. A major committee was set up by the then Conservative government under the chairmanship of Lord Ron Dearing to consider new forms of 'higher education in the learning society'. Reporting in 1997, on the cusp of an incoming Labour government committed to 'education, education, education', it addressed the broad question of funding of both institutions and individual students over the question of the costs of tuition and maintenance and the longer-term social and economic benefits from employment and labour market participation. The Labour government took the unusual step for the UK of imposing top-up tuition fees for full-time undergraduate students in universities on the basis of the Dearing Report's mixed recommendations (2007). Paying for higher educational expansion became a major dilemma towards the end of the twentieth century linked to the complex question of individual or social beneficiaries. This dilemma was not only one for the UK but had international ramifications, given the expanding opportunities in distance and digitalised learning.

Building upon these complex developments, in 2003 the UK Labour government published a white paper on the future of higher education (Cm 5735, 2003) to initiate debate about how to expand the institutions of higher education, including universities, and other possible colleges, to ensure an expansion of places for young people. The express UK policy emphasis in 2003 was the aim to ensure that 50 per cent of the relevant age cohort (18–30 year olds) participated in some form of higher education, as then defined, by 2010. In other words, the UK government was eager to ensure a more educated and trained labour force, building upon its previous economic and social developments in learning and educational opportunities. At that time over 30 per cent of the age cohort was already participating in what were defined as forms of higher education.

In November 2003, during the course of this lively but vexed debate, the then UK Government Department for Education and Skills (DfES) responsible at the time for extending and measuring educational opportunities decided to change the basis on which to administer and judge progress in achieving what it referred to as 'fair access'. Thus it changed the administrative basis for collecting evidence about extending participation rather than merely access or entry. It decided that the figures should measure participation rather than entry (with those enrolled on a course for over six months being included in the tally). The Higher Education Initial Participation Rate (HEIPR) was created as an administrative device for evaluating how higher educational institutions were making progress towards increasing 'access'. This slightly extended definition became the new basis for thinking about not only access or entry but also 'participation in higher education' (HERO 2006). Significantly, it did not take the issues beyond undergraduate students' first year nor give consideration to fine-grained notions of fairness or equity in participation.

Nevertheless, these administrative and policy measures laid the foundation for the 2004 Higher Education Act, around which there was a very lively and indeed acrimonious public debate around undergraduate student access and participation in different types of higher education, and the so-called benefits accruing in the labour market or the 'graduate premium'. The public and media debates focused upon the specific balances between types of university and types of undergraduate (or first degree) student, as well as the funding mechanisms to ensure increased participation of new types of student and new kinds of institution. Given public policy arguments about the beneficiaries of educational expansion on an individual and social basis, the Labour government proposed a major change in policy to the introduction of fees for university tuition. It was argued that the chief beneficiaries of university expansion, in terms of both educational and economic benefits, would be the individual (and full-time undergraduate) students, rather than the wider social and economic benefits. Albeit that it was also argued that extending higher educational opportunities was necessary for the international competitiveness of the UK economy. The parliamentary decision about these questions hung on a thread, despite the Labour government's huge majority of over 100: only five votes made it a majority decision. This demonstrates how contested the questions about equity and fairness in higher education participation had become. Debates centred on public finances versus private and personal benefits in an expanding and yet diverse system of learning opportunities.

The new form of university finances that the Labour government ushered in for England limited the size of fees to be charged by each university up to a maximum of £3,000 p.a. and the government was to decide on how many students each university could admit. It also opened up opportunities for individual students to have either loans or bursaries from each university in order to finance the fees to be paid (and to pay back the loans from subsequent participation in the labour market). This system of fees was also complicated in that it was only introduced for English universities (whether those created before or in the 1992 Further and Higher Education Act) and not higher or further education colleges. It was also only for full-time student participants. Universities and colleges could continue to expand other educational opportunities on a part-time basis. In order to monitor university or higher education provision and progress towards the continuing aim of 'fair access', the government also proposed a new administrative system of regulation of individual and institutional 'access' of types of students from economically and socially disadvantaged families and schools. It set up both an official Access Regulator and an administrative Office of Fair Access (known as OFFA) to set targets for individual institutions in their progress to extending access, but without strong financial means to ensure this.

This kind of debate raises questions about political judgements about the purposes of, and end results, or successful outcomes from types of higher education. Some would argue that the best or most successful results from universities are linked to what has been called the graduate or wage premium accruing, whether over a life-time or a more specific period. We shall indeed address the evidence about the social and economic benefits accruing to particular pathways into and through diverse forms of higher education. Policy debates have also altered and shifted around what is meant by higher or post-compulsory education, including raising serious policy debates about the age of compulsion itself. Most recently there has been a white paper (2008) about the raising of the school leaving age (age of compulsion) to 18 years old. This kind of debate is also linked to the question of education or training for particular skills for employment, as compared with a more traditional form of 'liberal-humanist' academic education of the variety traditionally found in liberal arts colleges and universities.

Debate has often also centred on whether concerns for equity and fair access are diluting a commitment to academic excellence. Transitions into universities or higher education are challenging for many groups and there is still a strong presupposition that the academic path is the 'royal road' into higher education against which all other pathways are compared. Our research on social, ethnic and gender identities in relation to following different pathways and the subsequent opportunities they may enable, contributes to problematising these issues. Transitions into higher education may be particularly challenging for groups such as the disabled, disadvantaged and black and minority ethnic students and those from backgrounds that have traditionally seldom participated in higher education, as well as for individuals and groups who have followed routes other than the 'royal (academic) road' into universities.

It is taken for granted, though, that students in the UK and North America must pass through rigorous admission procedures before enrolling at HE institutions. However, many HE systems have completely different ways of admitting students; some countries have no admission procedures at all. For example, in some European countries, it is not the university (the receiving institution), but the school (the delivering institution) that decides on access to HE. Certificates of selective secondary schools often grant a kind of 'entitlement' to enrol at universities. Access and admissions policies at Asian HE institutions also have their own unique qualities. To challenge the preconceptions and embedded normative assumptions, how different education systems organise the transition from school to HE needs to be problematised. In an age of globalisation, a comprehensive international comparative analysis of access and admission is essential in understanding the different ways in which access and related admission policies and procedures could be conceptualised and enacted.

For example, the Sutton Trust (an independent educational charity and pressure group set up in the early twenty-first century) has been campaigning to ensure that 'the best and the brightest' get into what have been nicknamed the 'Sutton 13', namely elite and traditional or old universities, created largely before the twentieth century, rather than ensuring improvements in learning and teaching across all forms of post-compulsory and higher education as expanded by the twenty-first century (Sutton Trust 2007). In other words, this organisation remains firmly committed to the 'royal road' and a narrow and academic definition of universities, including a focus on 'blue skies' research, and through the Research Assessment Exercises (RAE) since 1986. They focus largely upon academically able but economically disadvantaged students, often defined as working class, and attending some form of state secondary education, whereas other pressure groups, such as Action on Access, focus on access to and participation within an array of diverse educational institutions, from colleges to universities.

In the immediate aftermath of the passing of the 2004 Act, the UK Labour government set in train a major review, chaired by Lord Leitch, of the expansion and extension of skills and training in view of the potential demographic decline in the number of 18 year olds available for higher education. A major factor focusing attention on adult participation across the life course was the projected demographic decline in the number of young people. It was predicted that between 2010 and 2020, there would be a reduction by 100,000 or 15 per cent of 18 year olds. The government thus accepted the recommendation of the Leitch Report (2006) that at least 40 per cent of adults (aged 19–65) should be qualified to level 4 (HE level) by 2020, up from a rate of 31 per cent in 2008.

A lively policy debate ensued from this point about the precise balances between types of universities and backgrounds as well as types of student. The question of how to define extending education or learning opportunities beyond compulsory education and for different types of students on the basis of academic abilities or merit versus vocational education and/or training became an increasingly vexed one. As we have already argued, this theme or thread had been there from its origins in the expansion of educational opportunities in the twentieth century. By the early twenty-first century, such post-compulsory educational or learning opportunities were far more extensive than had ever been imagined or thought possible.

Questions about how to provide access to higher education or skills became the regular subject of popular and political debate in ways that were unheard of only a few decades previously. For instance, in the 1960s there was virtually no popular or public debate about entitlement to university access or participation. The expansion of higher education, in the aftermath of the Robbins Report (Cmnd 2154 1963) was of only esoteric interest. Perhaps this was because well under 10 per cent of the age cohort of 18 year olds participated in universities (and the vast majority were young white and middle-class men).

Over the ensuing forty years, the vicissitudes of UK policy developments in relation to equality of educational opportunities, and the individual or social factors underpinning them, became subject to major changes, in relation to wider changes in economic and social developments. Moreover, the question of how to 'measure' and evaluate such complex developments became the subject of social and educational research. Indeed, participatory or policy action research within education has become a key aspect of many of these developments. As part of the changing process there has been the involvement of more social science and educational researchers, including also more women researchers, taking either an equality or a gender focus.

Indeed, over the last forty years, the overall numbers of undergraduate students participating in some form of higher education has quadrupled from half a million in 1965, to two million in 2005–6 (HEFCE 2005a). As Hayward and colleagues go on to argue: 'educational participation beyond the compulsory school age has increased in the UK since 1945, with a massive increase in participation in full-time provision between 1985 and 1994'. Moreover, over the years from 1996–7 to 2005–6, in absolute terms, women have outnumbered men and are 60 per cent of full-time student population in UK universities with some variations in English, Northern Irish, Scottish and Welsh forms of access and participation. By 2006–7, men remained the majority in overseas undergraduate and postgraduate enrolments, with these kinds of international enrolments increasing year on year. (Unfortunately, as we shall see, our projects did not enable us to pursue these kinds of issue of UK-wide and international access and participation.)

There are also variations according to age, so that young participation (namely undergraduate students under the age of 21) is no longer the norm (in part attributable to demographic decline). The participation rate in higher education (i.e. universities and higher education colleges) of young people (aged 18 or 19) in England is around 30 per cent at the end of the period studied (HEFCE 2005a). The report goes on to show that almost 54 per cent of first-year undergraduates were aged 21 or over or so-called mature students. Overall the report argues that:

> Inequality of the sexes in *young* [my emphasis] participation has risen steadily: by the end of the period studied, young women in England are 18 per cent more likely to enter higher education than young men. This inequality is more marked for young men living in the most disadvantaged areas, and is further compounded by the fact that young men are less likely than young women to successfully complete their higher education courses and gain a qualification.

The kinds of questions raised in this brief review of the UK policy context for determining 'fair access' and how to widen participation in higher education are clearly heavily debated and contested around economic and social values of expanding education, and what is meant by equity or fairness in access, entry or participation and possibly success and outcomes. We turn now to the detailed specification of these research projects upon this wider canvas.

4 The specific research commissioning and the seven individual projects

In early 2005, during the course of this major public debate about the form of higher educational expansion and how to widen or increase access to and participation within higher education, at the behest of the UK government through its Higher Education Funding Council for England (HEFCE) the Economic and Social Research Council (ESRC) with its major educational research programme – the Teaching and Learning Research Programme (TLRP) – put out a call for research proposals. HEFCE had committed approximately £2 million funding for research on the topic of widening participation in and fair access to higher education. Given it was HEFCE funding, only 'researchers based at higher education institutions in England, in collaboration with other partners as appropriate' were invited to submit proposals for a small number of projects (approximately 5–8). The call for proposals detailed both the aims and the definitions of 'widening participation' and higher education itself:

Aims and Scope of the Competition

1. The aim of this competition is to support high quality innovative research with the potential to enhance understanding, and inform and/or underpin future policy, practice and outcomes relating to widening participation in, and fair access to, higher education (HE) in

England. In order to ensure capacity building and the widest possible impact upon policy, practice and learning outcomes, proposals should build and strengthen links between researchers, learning and teaching staff and widening participation practitioners.

2. Widening participation is taken to mean extending and enhancing access to and experience of HE, and achievement within HE, of people from so-called under-represented and diverse social backgrounds, families, groups and communities and positively enabling such people to participate in and benefit from various types of HE. These could include people from socially disadvantaged families and/or deprived geographical areas, including deprived remote, rural and coastal areas or from families that have no prior experience of HE. Widening participation is also concerned with diversity in terms of ethnicity, gender, disability and social background in particular HE disciplines, modes and institutions. In addition it can also include access and participation across the ages, extending conceptions of learning across the life course, and in relation to family responsibilities, particularly by gender and maturity.

3. Higher Education is also to be conceptualised broadly in terms of pedagogies or practices of learning and teaching and may include delivery of HE programmes from sub-degree to doctoral level. These may be delivered in various types of institution, including teaching-intensive universities, research-intensive universities, Further Education colleges offering higher education, HE institutions offering further education, and HE colleges and various forms of distance learning. In other words, this covers HE across the spectrum.

4. The research studies can also be broadly conceptualised to give consideration to various innovative aspects of policy and practice around developments to widen engagement, participation and retention in HE. International comparisons of experience in widening participation, including HE pedagogies, policies and practices or developing programmes within and across higher education locally, nationally or internationally will also be considered.

5. This new phase will support theoretically informed, carefully designed and grounded studies of widening participation in HE (February 2005).

The TLRP then set up a process both to explain the social scientific perspectives underpinning the call to potential researchers and to consider the proposals that were submitted under this very broad and all-encompassing brief for quality in educational and social scientific research. The brief, however, focused upon specific conceptions of 'equity' or 'diversity' and especially in relation to socio-economic disadvantage.

Similarly the brief was theoretically and methodologically eclectic and did not specify a particular educational or social scientific approach.

The TLRP Directors' Team reviewed all the proposals around its broad conceptual framework (see Figure 1.1) developed for analytical and policy impact purposes. The proposals were also peer reviewed through the usual ESRC peer-review process and, on this basis, the team made recommendations to the TLRP's Steering Committee, made up of social science academics and representatives of UK-wide research and user organisations within higher education. The Steering Committee made the decisions about which seven projects to support, aiming to balance theoretical and methodological approach with different substantive approaches to types of access to, or participation within, higher education.

The seven projects that were chosen were to provide complementary theoretical and methodological approaches within the above conceptual framework. The aim was to build up collaborative and yet complementary robust findings around these themes and outcomes. The seven projects were deliberately chosen with these conceptual notions in mind and for this purpose:

a) *Universal Access and Dual Regimes of Further and Higher Education.* This project team was led by Professor Gareth Parry and based at Sheffield University. It included Professors Ann-Marie Bathmaker, Greg Brooks and David Smith as Directors, with Diane Burns, Cate Goodlad, Karen Kitchen, Sammy Rashid, Anne Thompson and Val Thompson as researchers. It was to focus on the political, economic and cultural contexts, with an especial focus on

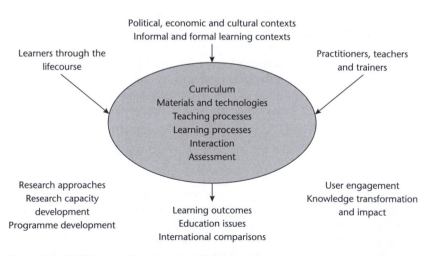

Figure 1.1 TLRP's overall conceptual framework

developing an analysis of the policy contexts or regimes for and organisational development of further and higher education. Changing governance policies around differentiation and binaries of further and higher education were to be the main focus, together with collecting evidence from dual systems about 'disadvantaged students' and their progress through a sample of institutions with a mix of further and higher education.

b) *Widening Participation to Higher Education: A Quantitative Analysis*. This project team was led by Professor Anna Vignoles of the Institute of Education, University of London, with Alissa Goodman at the Institute of Fiscal Studies, London. Other researchers included Claire Crawford and Haroon Chowdry both of the Institute of Fiscal Studies, London, and Nick Powdthavee of Institute of Education, University of London with Steve Machin, Sandra McNally, Iftikar Hussain, Steve Gibbons and Shqiponja Telhaj all of the Centre for Economic Performance, London. The team was to provide a statistical mapping of the evidence about learners going through different educational stages from schools into higher education. It was to be based upon a cohort study using official administrative datasets around types of students, defined in terms of socio-economic characteristics and types of institutions including universities, classified according to teaching and research quality. The focus was to be policy-oriented about the successes of a cohort of diverse students and the implications for higher education institutes (HEIs) and policy-makers of educational provisions for outcomes in the labour market and graduate premia.

c) *Socio-Cultural and Learning Experiences of Working-Class Students in Higher Education*. This team was led by Professor Gill Crozier then of Sunderland University and now Roehampton University, with Professor Diane Reay at Cambridge University. The two researchers were John Clayton at Sunderland University and Lori Colliander of University of Cambridge. This theoretically important and policy-relevant project was to address a key policy question about how working-class students fared into and through four different types of higher education. The project also was to address questions of socio-economic disadvantages in relation to learning processes and learners and learning processes in types of higher education, attempting to develop a theoretical understanding and substantive evidence about working-class students learning how to learn in different types of higher education.

d) *Degrees of Success: Learners' Transitions from Vocational Education and Training to Higher Education*. This team based at Oxford University was led by Dr Geoff Hayward with Dr Hubert Ertl and included Drs Harriet Dunbar-Goddet and Michael Hölscher. This project was chosen because of its fit with other projects in terms of its mixed forms of data analysis and policy developments around economic benefits. It was to focus on institutional practices around academic versus vocational studies in a variety of HEIs and individual subjects, including identities of learners and learning processes in types of subjects into and through different institutional forms of higher education.

e) *Keeping Open the Door to Mathematically Demanding Programmes in Further and Higher Education.* This team was based at the University of Manchester and led by Professor Julian Williams, with co-investigators Drs Laura Black, Pauline Davis, Graeme Hutcheson, Su Nicholson and Geoff Wake. The research assistants were Drs Paul Hernandez-Martinez and Maria Pampaka. This project was chosen because it gave consideration to the twin theoretical and methodological issues of the identities of disadvantaged students in relation to the question of pedagogical practices around mathematics education in colleges as a prelude to higher education. The question of learners' identities and dispositions in relation to learning processes in types of higher education and teachers/types of teaching was to be the focus using two different pedagogies for mathematics education.

f) *Learning and Teaching for Social Diversity and Difference in Higher Education.* This project team was led by Professor Chris Hockings of the University of Wolverhampton, with Ms Sandra Cooke and Dr Marion Bowl of the University of Birmingham. Their researchers were Hiromi Yamashita and Samantha McGinty. This project was to focus centrally on curriculum, learning and teaching within higher education amongst diverse students and their teachers in two different higher education institutions and across a range of subjects, including new and traditional subjects. A key question was: how do teachers engage and encourage participation among groups of diverse students? Teaching and learning processes to engage diverse students were to feature uppermost.

g) *'Non-participation' in Higher Education: Decision-making as an Embedded Social Practice.* This project team was based at the University of Southampton and led by Professors Alison Fuller and Sue Heath. The team also included Martin Dyke, Nick Foskett, Ros Foskett, Brenda Johnston, Felix Maringe, Karen Paton, Patricia Rice, Laura Staetsky, John Taylor and Marie Kenny. This project was chosen to widen our understandings about how adults think about their educational and social identities in relation to participating in higher education, given that they are qualified to do so. Taking the notion that not all qualified adults choose to participate in higher education, this team focused on the social networks, or so-called networks of intimacy, that influence individuals' decisions about whether to participate in higher education across different stages of the life course

The seven projects commenced in late 2005 or 2006 and all were completed by 2008. Whilst the projects were commissioned by the English Higher Education Funding Council to address specific questions about the evidence for the relations between increasing or widening access to and participation in higher education and learning outcomes, the projects' findings have more general application. They not only address specific policy issues about the system of post-compulsory education and the obstacles and opportunities to participation for individuals and institutions, but also the broader questions of the links between prior educational and social experiences and learning through the life course.

The projects also continue to contribute to what remains a lively public debate about the evidence base for widening access to and participation in higher education. For example, the *Times Higher Education* (24 July 2008) asked a range of academics and practitioners to comment on whether investing in widening participation (can) achieve the best results, or whether the government should spend on 'improving performance among working class students in schools'. Several of those questioned mentioned difficulties with defining working-class status and disadvantage, and in setting out the appropriate evidence or policies. Some cited some of our evidence about evaluating prior educational experiences, as we shall see, and others raised the difficult question of political judgement about what constitutes equity or fairness in educational opportunities and outcomes. We turn now to how the seven projects begun to develop their research questions and appropriate analysis for policies, pedagogies and practices around diversity and equity.

5 How the projects addressed the issues of fair access to and widening participation within HE

We now give more detailed consideration as to how the projects developed their individual and collective approaches to the questions of access to and participation within higher education. The approaches used linked to a range of theories and methodologies within the social sciences. They involved different methods – both quantitative and qualitative – approaches, and different ways of selecting individuals as learners or teachers and other 'stakeholders' in institutions for their studies. In the first place, it is important to give some consideration to broad theoretical and methodological approaches as a basis for seeking to address the overall research questions.

5.1   *Theoretical and methodological frameworks*

Three of the project teams (Hayward, Parry and Vignoles) drew on political and economic theories as a key to their analytical approaches. They took issues of the official UK policy frameworks around economic competitiveness and how to organise higher education provisions around questions of academic merit versus questions of vocational or skills training as being essential to policy developments for equity and fair access or participation. The question of student successes and outcomes from forms of higher education, in terms of forms of graduate employment, and thus the notion of the graduate premium across the life course were also of significance in framing two of these projects (Hayward and Vignoles) whilst Parry's team was more interested in wider economic policies and practices for framing institutional policy developments around forms of further and higher education or dual regimes of policy, contrasted with system-wide forms of competition. Fuller's team, having taken the changing policy context of developing skills and an employment agenda into account through especially the use of the Labour Force survey, then moved clearly into a more sociological framing of the research.

Whilst the three teams (Hayward, Vignoles and Parry) focused on policy analysis as an overarching theoretical framing, this did not necessarily translate into the same methodological approaches. Parry's team deployed detailed analysis of national and local institutional policy and practice developments, largely through interviews and documentary analysis. Hayward's team was also interested in developing an overarching analysis of institutional developments with respect to academic versus vocational education and training (VET). Thus they too engaged with policy interviews at the institutional level. However, in addition Hayward's team also used administrative datasets on student transitions into forms of higher education (drawing on the Universities Central Admissions Service (UCAS)) for these statistical data on academic versus vocational education pathways. Third, this team also interviewed individual students at several different higher educational institutions about their identities and perspectives across their courses which were mainly vocational courses. Parry's team similarly conducted interviews with groups of students within their colleges and higher education institutions.

Vignoles' team's methodology mirrored that of Hayward's team in that it devised a unique dataset from administrative data from both Higher Education Statistics Agency (HESA) and the government department (now the Department for Children, Schools and Families and formerly the Department for Education and Skills) responsible for monitoring student progress through schools and into higher education. Thus, Vignoles' team produced a detailed mapping of all state school pupils in one cohort over their educational trajectories. This is from a census of all students in a cohort from 2004–5, following their trajectories into higher education, and studying their previous educational experiences and subsequent outcomes from higher education and into the labour market.

These three teams were concerned to consider the different economic and social values accruing to different studies within and across higher education and into employment. Similarly, Williams' team, studying mathematics education in forms of further education colleges, became interested in the values attributed to different approaches to and forms of maths education for future participation in higher education and employment. However, the concept of value has been differently deployed by this team from Hayward's and Vignoles' and here it centres on personal and social values rather than economic or an outcome in terms of salary.

Indeed, Williams' team, like Hockings' and Crozier's teams, use sociological, social and/or cultural theories to understand and analyse forms of student learner and teacher participation within different institutional contexts of higher education, either for access to or participation within different universities.

Four of the teams (Crozier, Fuller, Hockings and Williams) drew on social or sociological and cultural theories to frame their research questions and approaches. Whilst they all tend towards social rather than economic theories to underpin their research, there are differences in their particular frameworks. Crozier's team has extended and developed earlier work, using Bourdieu's sociological theories. Fuller and Hockings' teams have similarly been interested in how these theories have provided a framework for study. However, Fuller's team has foregrounded qualitative social network analysis and the role of social capital within networks. Hockings' team has drawn on social as well as psychological theories of learning, teaching and ways of knowing in their attempt to understand how students from diverse backgrounds engage and participate in different subjects. Williams' team has incorporated cultural and psychological perspectives with actor network theories, namely cultural, historical activity theories (CHAT) as the basis for their interpretations.

This diversity of theoretical and methodological perspective is a great strength in offering a range of insights across the complementary issues. All the teams were interested in teasing out, from a theoretically informed perspective, the ways in which individuals, as learners, students, adults and potential students, or teachers and other administrators involved in higher education, expressed their identities and concerns about learning and learning opportunities. They have each provided a complementary and in-depth study of how a range of students approach and decide about higher education participation.

5.2 Conceptualising diversity and equity

Given that all the projects were funded and largely based within England, definitions of fairness or equity in access or widening participation focused chiefly upon socio-economic disadvantage or social class and diversity rather than more multi-cultural questions about ethnicity, race or the relatively recently emerging policy issues concerning international students, whether from Africa, Asia, Europe or the other nations of the UK.

However, it should also be noted how these seven diverse teams also included a diversity of researchers. Interestingly the research teams comprised a significant number of equity, feminist and critical researchers, with four of the main grant-holders being senior women researchers, and each of the teams including several well-known women as diversity, equity, gender and feminist researchers. This represents a significant shift in the demography of social science research grant holders in the UK over the past decade. It also provides an example of how transformations in the demography of social science research have been occurring with changes in higher education.

How each project team defined and selected the individuals it would study thus revolved around particular definitions of equity and socio-economic disadvantage in relation to family or parental backgrounds or individual circumstances, and in relation to different types of educational institution. The teams led by Hayward, Vignoles and Williams used relatively broad notions of 'poor' versus 'wealthy' family or parental backgrounds drawing on official datasets and in relation to state schools (rather than independent schools) and colleges. Parry's team similarly used broad and official notions of socio-economic disadvantage within the local further and higher education colleges studied. All of these teams also linked the socio-economic data to gender and ethnicity. The Fuller and Hockings' project teams used more dynamic evidence of family and social backgrounds associated with social networks as well as parental backgrounds, including, in the case of Hockings, data drawn from official university sources. Crozier's team made use of a traditional social class parental educational and occupational split between working-class and middle-class students within different forms of higher education.

The age of students also was a concern to several of the projects. Whilst Vignoles' study mapped of one cohort of young people as they passed through state schools and into higher education, all the other projects had more of a variation in terms of age. Williams' students, based as they were in further education colleges and undertaking access and A-level courses for higher education, also tended to be under 21. Students for the studies by Crozier, Hayward, Hockings and Parry were drawn from different types of higher education institution and thus ranged over conventional and mature students. Indeed it is the linkages with particular types of contrasting universities and other higher education colleges that show the diversity of age of students. Fuller's team focused upon adults, that is, over 21, and therefore potentially mature students as the core of the study.

Thus the diversity of institutions and the subjects studied within these institutions reflected the diversity of the students selected. There was therefore a dynamic interplay between the students and their institutions and subjects. Parry's and Williams' teams, for instance, deliberately selected local further education colleges where the students were more likely to be disadvantaged. Crozier's, Hayward's and Hockings' teams chose to compare and contrast different types of higher education institution and the students within them. Williams' and Hayward's teams chose to study students pursuing particular subjects or topics, namely either maths education or vocational education and training. Whilst maths is a prerequisite for the study of science, technology, engineering and medicine (STEM) at the more research-intensive universities, it may also be important for other vocationally oriented courses. By contrast, some vocationally oriented courses such as social work or nursing may also be taught now in research-intensive universities, making the distinctions between types of university complicated and related to the rapidly changing and expanding system of higher education.

Crozier's and Hockings' teams focused upon choosing the contrasting institutions before deciding on how to select within them. However, both did then choose students from across an array of subjects, largely but not only within the humanities and social sciences. (Hockings' team studied biosciences, business, computing, history, health and social care.) Both also considered pedagogical practices within these subjects and institutions. Fuller's team, by contrast, chose not to study students within higher education, but rather the perceptions of non-participants.

5.3 Conceptualising and contextualising higher education

Given the different theoretical and substantive approaches, how the different types of higher education institution are defined and described is relatively problematic. However, this issue is only a dilemma with respect to presenting the research evidence within the individual chapters that follow. It does not affect our overall argument about the ways in which equity and fairness within and between institutions and individuals are distributed over the life course, as forms of systematic inequalities. The question remains one of reaching out to so-called under-represented groups. For instance the National Audit Office (25 June 2008) in publishing a review of the funding of new strategies intended to widen participation remains concerned with this as a dilemma (NAO 2008).

For the purposes of the presentation of our studies we shall refer to different types of university by reference first to the broad categories established by the 1992 Further and Higher Education Act, namely *old universities* established before 1992, or *new universities* established by or after 1992. Parry's team will, however, provide a much more detailed and nuanced contextualisation of the multitude of changes that took place both before and after 1992. The focus will particularly be on the creation of a variety of further and higher education institutions since 1992, and most especially in the twenty-first century.

Some of our project teams (Crozier, Hayward, Hockings and Vignoles) have used more fine-grained distinctions about these old and new universities. Crozier's team chose two different and distinctive old universities (namely a so-called red-brick and an elite) whereas Hayward's team reflected on the differences through the lens of the subjects, namely academic versus vocational. As the team points out, these may overlap in particular instances. Vignoles' team chose a more differentiated distinction for the purposes of analysing fairness in relation to student success and outcomes in the labour market. Her team has distinguished between old universities with respect to research quality and intensity. (These specific universities tend to map onto the Sutton 13 – referred to earlier). Hockings' team chose a traditional old and a new university for study.

In our conclusions we will return to the question of equity and fairness in the distribution of opportunities for socio-economically disadvantaged or under-represented groups to participate in these different types of university and other forms of higher education. We shall draw further policy recommendations on the basis of these detailed and nuanced studies of widening participation in higher education at a particular moment in English higher education policy.

6 Organisation of the book

Having set the scene in this introduction, in the second part of the book we move into a detailed presentation of the seven research studies. What does all our research tell us about equity or fair access and widening participation in higher education? Whilst each chapter draws primarily on the individual project teams' studies, we have organised the material so that we can draw together our evidence, first, about policy contexts and development and, second, about how diverse students go through a range and diversity of educational institutions. What are the key features of their educational experiences and how are they related to different institutions and individual characteristics? Third, we present evidence about different teaching and learning practices and pedagogies for a diversity of students, and across a diversity of subjects. Finally, we present our evidence about how men and women make choices about education in relation to family and employment.

In Chapter 2, Parry and his team set out to provide a detailed and nuanced contextualisation of the ways in which English policies and practices for higher education have evolved from the twentieth century and into the twenty-first century. Drawing on both the project material about the origins and rationale for differentiation in policies for further and higher education and the views of stakeholders in policy and administration, a comparison and contrast is drawn with other UK and European countries in the evolution of higher education and in relation to economic as well as social policies. The chapter also brings in other evidence from both TLRP research and the other projects detailed below to provide a clear map of systemic and systematic differentiation in higher education. This leads away from equalising opportunities and outcomes towards different regimes of practice.

Chapter 3 provides our detailed research evidence about individual students and their progress and pathways through schools and their transitions into and through higher education. It has four separate sections. First, Vignoles' team provides a clear mapping of the ways in which disadvantaged students in state schools fare in relation to higher education. This is based upon the cohort analysis of state school pupils in 2004–5. In particular, the question of how socio-economically disadvantaged and ethnic minority men compared with their female counterparts fare is amply demonstrated. Quite simply, the team argues that the issue of equal or fair access to and participation within types of higher education, and particularly in old and research-intensive universities, does not have its origins in higher education entry. Rather prior educational experiences in different types of state schools contribute to the inequalities in participation in higher education.

Crozier's team then go on to show how working-class students in different types of higher education, ranging from a further education college to a new and two different old universities, have very diverse educational experiences. Despite the differences in both pedagogies and practices within and across these four different types of higher education, the team argues that the working-class students learn how to learn and become resilient learners. Nevertheless, they too argue that prior educational experiences affect these learners and learning processes and leave systematic differences.

Hayward's team argues similarly that trajectories into and through higher education are systematically different for students who have embarked upon academic subjects by contrast with those on vocational education and training courses. Their evidence is both quantitative and qualitative and demonstrates another facet of how diversity and differences are reinforced through the educational processes leading up to and within higher education institutions.

The final section in this chapter provides further evidence of how students in a selection of further and higher education colleges feel about and succeed in their studies. This final section draws upon another aspect of the work of Parry's team and has been written by Ann-Marie Bathmaker.

In Chapter 4 we move on to consider our evidence from the perspective of pedagogies and practices around diverse students and their access to or participation within higher education. This chapter contains two sections. Hockings' team focused specifically on diverse pedagogies within six subjects within an old and a new university. Here they demonstrate how complicated notions of diversity are in relation to student learning and pedagogical practices.

This argument is followed by a similar and complementary study by Williams' team. This study is specifically about how students studying mathematics in further education, and undertaking contrasting types of learning and teaching fare. This team focuses upon how the students evaluate the different pedagogical approaches and the uses of mathematics in their potential future lives and whether in forms of higher education requiring maths or not.

Chapter 5 moves into a discussion about our evidence on different outcomes of higher education in terms of age-based participation. Again there are two sections. Vignoles' team provides us with another statistical mapping of progress through higher education as a prelude to the labour market. In particular, the focus is on administrative evidence about retention and 'drop out' or 'staying on' in different types of higher education institution. The team again demonstrates how socio-economically disadvantaged students suffer and are indeed at a disadvantage with respect to how they fare in relation to their higher education progress. The team also shows, however, that this is not necessarily linked to age and that mature students tend to be more motivated and gain better degrees than conventionally aged students.

In this respect, the research evidence of Fuller's team becomes very important indeed. They were concerned about the wider factors underpinning decisions about whether or not and, if so, when, to participate in higher education. Through their network analysis they demonstrate the range and variety of pathways and conceptions of the value of higher education held by their research participants. Choices are clearly related not only to employment or economic benefits but also to the fit with family lives and circumstances.

In the concluding part of the book (Part III), in Chapter 6 we draw together these various themes and threads to provide evidence about how to extend and increase equitable or fair access to and participation within higher education for disadvantaged groups. We discuss here the complex and constantly changing definitions about both the conceptualisation and the contextualisation of diversity of individuals and institutions. We suggest that innovatory policies and practices that take account of the changing global and international contexts for higher education need to be taken into consideration. We also argue for policies that are sensitive to the diversity of practices and pedagogies within and across institutions and for a reconsideration of the policy framing around only notions of economic benefits and beneficiaries.

In Chapter 7 we address the question of how to improve learning by widening participation in higher education. We argue for the centrality of educational opportunities across the life course to align to men and women's changing socio-economic and family circumstances. We also therefore suggest an array of inclusive and personal pedagogies that might engage students of the future in educational courses and new or innovative subjects, going beyond the conventional and known subjects of the twentieth century. We aim to imagine futures for higher education that go beyond the conventional boundaries of possibilities. Thus we address the current policy concerns about social mobility and how to change circumstances for under-represented groups in an entirely new light, and yet in keeping with the intricate and detailed evidence produced from these seven unique projects on widening participation in higher education.

In the appendices we include a section on the methodologies of each project.

Part II

What does the research tell us?

The 'key findings' from across the seven projects are presented in four separate chapters, starting with an analytical historical policy context in Chapter 2, followed by four separate sections in Chapter 3 on different facets of policy and practice in relation to equity and diversity in fair access and participation in higher education. In Chapter 4 we consider two different facets of teaching and learning with respect to student diversity. In Chapter 5 we present evidence about student outcomes on the one hand, and non-participation in higher education on the other.

Chapter 2

Policy contexts

Differentiation, competition and policies for widening participation

Gareth Parry

1 Introduction

Government policies to reduce the disparities in participation between social groups in English higher education are emphatic, ambitious and contentious. Along with targets for growth, they intersect with measures to change the pattern of demand for, and supply of, undergraduate education. More specifically, they are coupled with reform of the system of funding and student support. They accompany efforts to foster competition, collaboration and a diversity of institutional mission. They extend to all providers of higher education, they reach into schools, communities and the workplace, and they bear on the social, economic and intellectual conditions for learning and teaching.

In this chapter, the context for contemporary policies on widening participation is reviewed and the forms taken by these interventions are outlined. The distinctive features of this policy enterprise are highlighted, including its genesis and politics. Its debates and directions are described, especially those that require each university and college to demonstrate a commitment to widening participation as a condition of public funding. The purpose is to expand on some of the themes introduced by Miriam David in the opening chapter and so set the scene for the contributions that follow.

In the second part of the chapter, a closer examination is made of the relationship between policies addressed to widening participation and those concerned with the future size, structure and shape of the higher education system in England. Drawing on the findings of the project on *Universal Access and Dual Regimes of Further and Higher Education* (the FurtherHigher Project), the rationale for a two-sector system of further and higher education is examined and the impact of this division on widening participation is assessed. In so doing, the role of further education colleges in increasing and broadening participation in undergraduate education is analysed using frameworks derived from differentiation and stratification theory.

Findings from this project are presented in two places in this volume. Our research at the system and organisational levels is reported in this chapter. Our investigation of student transitions in case study institutions is discussed by Ann-Marie Bathmaker in Chapter 3, Section 4.

2 Widening participation as a policy enterprise

Although many individual institutions had long-standing access involvements and commitments, it was not until the report of the National Committee of Inquiry into Higher Education (the Dearing Committee, 1996–97) that a system-wide approach to widening participation was recommended (NCIHE 1997) and then adopted. Following the election of a new Labour government in 1997 and its broad acceptance of the Dearing proposals (DfEE 1998a), the Higher Education Funding Council for England (HEFCE) was given responsibility for developing, funding and monitoring the bulk of activity in this area. Under three successive Blair governments and into the Brown administration, widening participation emerged as a major policy enterprise and a regular source of political controversy.

2.1 Mass expansion and its characteristics

For Dearing, as for policy-makers in other national systems, the guiding assumption was that growth opened higher education to a wider range of students. Expansion over the previous decade, when numbers grew dramatically and the participation rate for young people doubled from 15 to 30 per cent, had indeed been associated with increased participation by a range of social groups.

That by women was probably the most striking, as noted by Anna Vignoles in Chapter 5, Section 1. Their percentage of the undergraduate education had doubled since the time of the last inquiry into higher education (the Robbins Committee, 1961–63) and women were now a majority of the student population, in line with their demographic representation. Nevertheless, like other groups, they were unevenly distributed across subjects and levels of study, especially in research degrees. The growth years had also seen expanded participation by adult students, by those from the middle and higher socio-economic groups, by individuals with new kinds of entry qualifications (such as access courses), and by students from ethnic minorities. What had not changed significantly was the ratio of participation between social classes (Coffield and Vignoles 1997; Robertson and Hillman 1997).

The inquiry was also exercised by institutional patterns of participation. In large part, these reflected the policies and purposes of the binary division between university and non-university higher education which was finally abandoned in 1992. Over 80 per cent of students in the old universities entered with traditional A-level (academic) qualifications compared to less than 60 per cent in the new universities. Mature students, those from ethnic minorities and working-class students were more strongly represented in the former polytechnics that became universities following binary abolition in 1992.

The new universities and other colleges that joined the older universities in the unified sector of higher education offered more of their courses in part-time modes and, along with further education colleges, provided undergraduate programmes at levels below the bachelor degree. Access by older students to part-time programmes was generally on the basis of a broader set of entry requirements, including relevant work and life experience. In the case of the Open University, for long the only open-access provider of undergraduate education in the English system, entry to its credit-based and modular courses by distance learning was subject only to payment of a part-time fee.

Similarly, admission to the full-time higher national diploma (HND) and the part-time higher national certificate (HNC) might demand specific vocational qualifications (sometimes linked to local employment) or a pass in one A-level subject. These vocationally oriented programmes were originally free-standing qualifications but, as a result of their integration into the modular systems of polytechnics during the 1980s, they and other short-cycle programmes also came to function as intermediate or transfer qualifications to the bachelor degree. According to the inquiry report, black students in particular were more likely to study for degree qualifications part-time. They, together with students from the Indian sub-continent, were more likely to study for 'sub-degree' qualifications than the population as a whole.

The spectacular growth of the late 1980s and the early 1990s that influenced these patterns was secured by government policies based on competition for public funds and 'efficient expansion' (DES 1991). However, this shift to a mass scale of higher education was achieved at the expense of a further lowering of the unit of public funding for higher education and with little attempt to plan or coordinate the rapid increase in numbers. As a result of growing pressure on the public purse, especially in relation to the costs of student support, growth was brought to an abrupt halt in 1994. The deepening crisis of funding that followed was the trigger for the setting-up of the national committee of inquiry, with the agreement of the governing and main opposition parties.

To limit the damage to the quality and effectiveness of higher education in the short term as well as provide for renewed growth, the committee recommended that students contribute to the costs of full-time undergraduate education. Less noticed and discussed amid the clamour surrounding this proposal was the recommendation that government should have a long-term strategic goal of expanding higher education at the sub-degree levels:

> The balance of demand between full-time and part-time, and between young and mature learners will be influenced by the extent of public

and employer support, and how far individuals are expected to contribute to the costs of higher education. At least initially, we see a large part of the growth taking place at sub-degree level. This is likely better to reflect the aspirations of many of those who may enter this expanded system, large numbers of whom are likely to have non-standard entry qualifications and more diverse aspirations. It will also address the UK's relative international disadvantage at these levels.

(NCIHE 1997: 100)

Less anticipated again was the recommendation that, in the medium term, priority in growth in sub-degree provision should be accorded to further education colleges:

In many cases, local requirements for sub-degree higher education can be met particularly well by further education colleges, whether as direct providers or in a partnership with a higher education institution. Delivery throughout the UK of higher education by further education colleges is extensive and important in many communities. It is predominantly sub-degree and often of a vocational nature. It can be especially important for students regarded as 'non-traditional' to higher education institutions many of whom need to be able to study near their homes.

(ibid.: 259)

Here were a set of proposals intended to respond to future demand from wider parts of society and the economy for local, accessible, flexible, diverse and distributed forms of higher level education. At the same time, they were a counter to, and rejection of, many of the features that characterised the English transition to mass higher education. They were also recommendations much influenced by the example of Scotland where the wide scope to study sub-degree higher education in further education colleges had contributed to a much higher participation rate (42 per cent) in that country (Gallacher 2002; Parry 2005).

English expansion had not only focused on full-time higher education leading to the honours degree at establishments of higher education. Growth had altered the balance of enrolments between institutions, with the former polytechnics and major colleges accounting for nearly two-thirds of the additional students recruited. The universities recruited most of the remainder and the colleges of further education attracted the smallest proportion of numbers and experienced the slowest rate of growth. In addition, expansion affected the shape of the system, with growth at the bachelor level matched by a reduction in the proportion enrolled at the other undergraduate levels. Whether provided by new universities or further education colleges, these were the levels where most students studied part-time for short-cycle vocational qualifications and where, historically, the social base of participation was broader and older.

2.2 Buoyant demand and early policies on widening access

The growth and access policies of the Thatcher and Major governments that drove this expansion were very different from the retrenchment imposed on higher education at the beginning of this period of Conservative rule. Nevertheless, it was during this time that a reformulation of the Robbins principle on access to higher education was accepted so that qualification for entry might be interpreted more broadly. Instead of 'qualified by ability and attainment' (Committee on Higher Education 1963), the revised principle asserted that courses should be available to all those who 'can benefit from them' (DES 1985).

The change to a policy of growth was prompted by an economic concern about future requirements for highly qualified workers ahead of a demographic decline in the size of the school-leaver population. The modest amount of expansion countenanced by this new policy turned into an unexpected and unprecedented wave of growth, propelled by buoyant student demand and the willingness or need of institutions to increase their numbers in order to maintain their levels of funding.

In advance of this surge in numbers, the government had invited 'all those with relevant responsibilities to consider carefully the steps to secure increased participation by both young and older people, and to act accordingly' (DES 1987). For the first time, three routes into higher education were officially recognised: traditional A-level qualifications, vocational qualifications ('best for some of those who might not in the past have entered higher education') and access courses ('for those, mainly mature, entrants who hold neither traditional sixth form nor vocational qualifications'):

> The changes should not be underestimated; it will be necessary both to adjust the balance of provision to match the needs of the economy and to accommodate students with a wider range of academic and practical experience than before, many of whom will not have the traditional qualifications for entry. Not only will entry requirements and procedures have to be changed; institutions of higher education will have to adapt their teaching methods and the design of their courses to accommodate new types of student.
>
> (ibid.: 9)

Moreover:

> It [the government] believes that increased participation in higher education need not be at the expense of academic excellence; indeed the stimulus of change should help to sharpen awareness of the different types of achievement that properly form part of the output of higher education.
>
> (ibid.)

When the polytechnics and higher education colleges were removed from the ownership and control of the local authorities in 1988, a commitment to widening access was one of the three aims of the new Polytechnics and Colleges Funding Council (PCFC) as well as a specific objective for this sector (PCFC 1992). Formally, however, the same goal was not prominent in the mission statement of the funding council established for the new unified higher education sector in 1992. With a cap on student numbers introduced soon after its inception, it was left to a HEFCE advisory group on access and participation to consider the approaches to widening access being taken by institutions and how these might be enhanced by the funding council. In anticipation of the Dearing recommendations, the group proposed that access-related missions be recognised in the funding of individual establishments (HEFCE 1996).

2.3 Renewed growth and larger policies on widening participation

While renewed expansion was expected to broaden participation, as it had done in the recent past, the Dearing Committee believed that progress would be greater still if widening participation was made 'a necessary and desirable objective of national policy'. At the same time, it believed that institutions were 'even-handed between one student and another in their selection and admission against policies and criteria that reflect their missions'. The latter was soon questioned by ministers who were not convinced that some universities – the most research-intensive in particular – were doing enough to address issues of participation by students educated in state schools and from less advantaged backgrounds.

The implementation of the Dearing recommendations was the first of four policy phases or moments in a concerted effort, over ten years, to reduce the social class gap in participation. In welcoming the inquiry proposals, the newly elected Labour government placed increasing and widening participation at the heart of its policies for creating a learning society.

> Our priority is to reach out and include those who have been under-represented in higher education, including young people from semi-skilled or unskilled family backgrounds and from disadvantaged localities, and people with disabilities.
>
> (DfEE 1998a: 11)

In this first phase of activity, the cap on expansion was removed and priority in the allocation of additional funded numbers given, among other criteria, to institutions that could widen access for under-represented groups and expand sub-degree provision. Such establishments were expected to have a participation strategy in place, a mechanism for monitoring progress, provision for the governing body to review achievement and a track record of successful activity.

Within its mainstream funding method for teaching, the HEFCE already provided a premium for part-time and mature students to recognise the additional costs of providing for them. Along with a funding supplement to support the learning of students with disabilities, it introduced what became known as a 'postcode premium' or 'widening participation allocation' to cover the additional costs of recruiting and retaining students from disadvantaged localities. This allocation accounted for up to 9 per cent of the teaching grant for some institutions. The aim was not just to increase participation from under-represented groups but also to help all such students succeed in their studies:

> Our research shows how non-completion . . . correlates with a number of factors, particularly entry qualifications and social class. We must be sure that wider participation in HE [higher education] does not simply result in more students failing. Within our proposed funding programme we seek to support institutions in establishing and improving structures that help students from non-traditional backgrounds to succeed.
>
> (HEFCE 1998: 3)

Within its special funding programme, the funding council also allocated funds to build partnerships between higher education institutions and other organisations, including further education colleges and schools, to address low expectations and achievement and to promote progression into and within higher education. The government also funded its own programme aimed at 'bright young students from poor backgrounds' and spanning a range of outreach activities, including summer schools, campus visits, mentor schemes and marketing targeted at 'families and communities who do not have a tradition of entering HE' (DfEE 2000a). These two schemes were eventually brought together in 2004 under the banner of Aimhigher, so extending the role and profile of the HEFCE in this area of policy.

The slow rate of growth in higher education achieved since 1997 was the context for a second evolution of national policy for widening participation. In an effort to stimulate demand the government announced an ambitious target for participation in higher education and launched a new short-cycle undergraduate qualification, the foundation degree. Doubtful that existing forms of sub-degree provision would deliver further significant growth, the foundation degree was introduced as a flagship qualification that would redress the under-performance of the education and training system at the intermediate levels. Although the new target and the new degree were keyed to economic imperatives, the expansion generated linked to a social agenda in which 'education must be a force for opportunity and social justice, not for the entrenchment of privilege' (DfEE 2003).

A third and politically contested episode in the career of widening participation policy was the decision to allow variable fees to be charged (up to a maximum level) for full-time undergraduate education. To ensure that higher tuition fees did not have a detrimental effect on widening participation, those institutions wishing to charge variable fees were required to submit 'access agreements' to an independent regulator. Approved and monitored by the Office for Fair Access, these agreements set out (with milestones) how institutions would safeguard and promote fair access – in particular for low income groups – through bursary and other financial support and outreach work. If a serious and wilful breach of an access agreement was found, the regulator could impose financial sanctions.

Apart from the acceptability of fee deregulation, which brought the government close to defeat during its passage through parliament, these proposals reignited earlier controversies about the fairness of admissions and their need for transparency. In 2004, the Schwartz review identified five main principles for 'fair admissions' and made a number of recommendations for good practice to underpin the assessment of applicants to higher education (Admissions to Higher Education 2004). The prospect of access agreements also rehearsed long-standing arguments about whether higher education could or should play a part in tackling problems beyond its immediate reach; and, if so, where and how these efforts might best be applied.

The fourth and current phase of policy activity arose in response to evidence suggesting that progress in widening participation had stalled. The HEFCE was asked to look again at its support for widening participation, the effectiveness of interventions and the options 'for going further still' (DfES 2006a).

In its report to the government on these matters, the funding council pointed to the difficulty in distinguishing the costs of widening participation from those attached to a host of related activities undertaken by an institution. It was not just that funding for widening participation came in a block grant which an institution was free to allocate 'largely as it sees fit'. The evidence for the impact of interventions was notably weak given the difficulties of establishing relationships (let alone casual connections) in the evidence collected (HEFCE 2006c). Nor was academic research a ready or reliable guide to 'what works' (HEFCE 2006b).

A subsequent independent assessment also concluded that too little was known about widening participation activities but not before highlighting institutional variations in the recruitment of students from under-represented groups. Around one-fifth of institutions performed significantly better than expected in recruiting from these groups whilst a similar proportion achieved significantly worse than expected. New universities generally performed at or significantly above their benchmarks. However, the majority of institutions recognised widening participation in their high-level strategies and no breaches of access agreements had yet been identified by the access regulator (NAO 2008).

3 Democratisation and diversion in a post-binary system

English policies for widening participation reach back to the compulsory years of schooling and this is where some see their proper place. Nevertheless, many directives are pointed at higher education itself and, its near-neighbour, further education. In England, higher education and further education are separate territories in a two-sector system of tertiary education and training. The modern architecture of sectors was created at the same time that higher education underwent its most rapid and recent expansion. The same basic structure is expected to do service for the next wave of growth yet this division has been simultaneously undermined and reinforced by measures to increase the proportion of higher education taught in further education colleges.

At present, the 130 universities and other establishments in the higher education sector account for the great majority of students enrolled at each of the main levels of postgraduate, bachelor and sub-bachelor under-graduate education. The 400 or so further education institutions in the learning and skills sector include 300 general and specialist colleges that teach most of the other higher education students in the English system. Higher education is usually a small – sometimes very small – part of the work of these colleges, the bulk of which is at the secondary or equivalent levels. All the same, these small pockets of activity and the larger numbers found in some colleges represent around one in ten of the domestic student population in higher education.

How societies arrange their post-secondary systems and which sectors, institutions and programmes take the growth in enrolments are matters debated by scholars and policy-makers alike. Relationships between expansion, diversification and differentiation are central concerns of theory and research in higher education, especially how they serve to reduce or reproduce patterns of social and institutional inequality (Shavit *et al.* 2007). In particular, where growth has occurred mainly through hier-archical differentiation, as in a tiered system of institutions running from the most selective (research intensive) to the least selective (teaching intensive), questions arise about the complementary or contradictory functions performed by the teaching-mainly and teaching-only establishments (Dougherty 1994).

For institutions such as community, vocational and further education colleges in mass systems of higher education, arguments continue about whether the growth taken by these lower-rank institutions should be viewed as a process of democratisation or diversion. If the former, then students qualifying for, or entering into, higher education from these establishments share in some of the same opportunities made available to individuals on other pathways. If the latter, then less advantaged and non-traditional students (who commonly populate these institutions) find themselves steered into lower-status programmes, routes and outcomes.

Rather than bringing new populations into higher education, the effect of expansion is diversion, so reducing the recruitment pressures on elite establishments and relieving them of responsibilities for widening participation (Brint and Karabel 1989).

For many policy-makers, the key issue is how to reconcile pressures for greater diversity – a diversity of mission, costs or standards – with demands for access, inclusion and equity. While some governments do not hesitate to use intervention or the market to accelerate or accommodate rates of growth, few are willing to accept the double stratification – social and institutional – that might result from such policies.

In England, such considerations surrounded the access mission of the polytechnics and colleges in the (then) non-university sector of higher education (Cheung and Egerton 2007; Pratt 1997). Today, they attach to the same institutions in their role as post-1992 universities and university colleges. Increasingly too, they apply to the higher education contribution of further education colleges, especially since 1997 when these institutions were brought into a radical policy programme to change the pattern of provision and demand in higher-level education and training.

The pursuit of this goal – 'the English experiment' (Parry 2007) – and its implications for widening participation, for institutional differentiation and the continuation of a two-sector system were core research questions investigated by the FurtherHigher Project. Once the province of historians (Sharp 1987; Silver and Brennan 1988), the distinction between further and higher education is now of growing interest to philosophers and sociologists (Barnett 1990; White 2009; Young 2006). Although focused on England, our study is informed by comparative and contextual studies of developments in analogous systems, including jurisdictions where the higher education role of the college sector (or segment) is changing and where new combinations and configurations of higher and post-secondary education are evident (Gallacher and Osborne 2005; Garrod and Macfarlane 2009; Moodie 2008).

3.1 Reassembling further and higher education

The present-day separation of institutions into sectors of higher education and further education has its origins in legislation passed in 1988 and 1992. Before that, higher education was provided by an autonomous sector of universities (funded by central government) and by institutions that were part of a local authority system of further education (funded through local government). The creation of the polytechnics in the 1960s was part of a general policy to concentrate the future development of full-time higher education within the further education system in a limited number of major institutions (DES 1966). Despite regular attempts by central government to see more advanced (higher education) work move into the larger and strongest establishments, the general colleges of further education still accounted for roughly one in five of all higher education students in the non-university sector at the beginning of the 1980s (Parry 2003).

One of the principles justifying the local authority stake in higher education was the importance of maintaining links ('a seamless robe') between advanced and non-advanced further education. The local authority presence in higher education ensured that issues of access and progression were not ignored. In so doing, it was often chided by central government for presiding over scattered and isolated provision and for resisting the amalgamation or closure of whole institutions:

> The total provision required is not necessarily as well deployed across colleges as it could be. There is a need for a substantial geographical spread in the interests of access . . . But there is also evidence that degree work is so much better done where there is a fair concentration of it, that this consideration should prevail over the claims of easy access.
>
> (DES 1985: 37)

After a decade of struggle between local and central government for control of this sector of higher education, and at the height of political conflicts between Labour-controlled metropolitan authorities and the Thatcher government, the polytechnics and other major colleges were removed from local authority control. Existing national planning arrangements were declared 'unsatisfactory' and, in place of a system that gave undue weight to local interests, a more effective lead was required 'from the centre' (DES 1987).

Following the Education Reform Act of 1988, all institutions 'of substantial size' (with 350 full-time equivalent higher education students) and 'engaged predominantly in higher education' (with more than 55 per cent of their activity in higher education) were transferred to a new polytechnics and colleges sector under its own funding council (the PCFC). On the other side of the binary line, the universities also came under a new Universities Funding Council (UFC). The colleges mainly concerned with non-advanced further education remained with local government and, even though these institutions continued to offer courses of higher education, the local authority interest in higher education was now regarded as 'residual'.

Beyond this, the legislation and accompanying policy texts had little or nothing to say about the place of higher education outside the PCFC and UFC sectors. Nor was there an overall plan or rationale for a system differentiated along these lines. Rather, the new divisions and territories produced by this reform owed more to specific and immediate priorities. Nor was a redefined purpose provided for a further education sector shorn of its senior institutions. In the absence of a larger vision or argument for the 1988 settlement, it was left to lone individuals to recover a mission for further education (Stubbs 1988).

When, in 1992, further education colleges were themselves removed from local government and equipped with their own funding council, there was once again no overarching argument for a two-sector tertiary structure. Neither the division between the two sectors nor the relationships between their peak bodies and constituent institutions were a major policy concern. Whatever else they might stand for, sectors were there to limit the overlap of courses and qualifications, and to contain and control the movement of institutions between their territories. Transfers might be desirable in principle but such cases were likely to be rare. Furthermore, the direction of movement was from further education to higher education. Although theoretically possible, there was no process for reverse transfer to the further education sector.

In short, such arrangements assumed that higher education and further education stood for different levels of learning and, for this reason, should be provided by separate types of tertiary organisation. Except for the part-time HNC, responsibility for the funding of all the main qualifications in higher education rested with the HEFCE. In 1999, the funding of the HNC also passed to the HEFCE, leaving the Further Education Funding Council (FEFC) and its successor, the Learning and Skills Council (LSC), with responsibility for a collection of higher-level courses whose status as higher education was unclear. Responsibility for the funding of any further education courses in the higher education sector lay with the FEFC and was inherited by the LSC.

3.2 Changing supply and demand

When, after 1997, this assumptive and administrative structure was disturbed, if not challenged, by policies to expand higher education in the further education sector, neither an overhaul of two-sector arrangements nor their imminent demise were entertained. Instead, governments requested that ways be found to make it easier for institutions to work with the funding, quality and reporting bodies of another sector. In practice, the remits, interests and priorities of the sector agencies have afforded limited scope (and little appetite) for joint or coordinated action. On the one side, this has resulted in the failure to develop a coherent and consistent policy for a college-based higher education, as acknowledged in a recent review of this activity (HEFCE 2006a). On the other, it has continued a policy of no policy in respect of the further education offered by higher education sector institutions, even though cross-sector mergers have changed the balance of work in some universities (LSC 2007).

In their origin as well as their reformulation, the Dearing recom-mendations on a 'special mission' for further education colleges reflected the divisions of responsibility laid down in 1988 and 1992 and, more

critically, the asymmetries of influence and power underlying these relationships. As a higher education body making policy for the further
education sector, the Dearing inquiry was a supreme example of this
division of labour. While there was scope for more cooperation between
the two funding bodies, the inquiry concluded that a single body (as later
established in Scotland) would be 'too large to work properly or to
represent the range of interests adequately' (NCIHE 1997).

The committee also rejected the option that all sub-degree provision in
the colleges should be funded by the further education funding body. Its
preference was for all higher education, irrespective of its location, to be
funded by the higher education funding council. Only this could 'force a
consideration of the relative costs of similar provision across all the providing institutions' and, only within a higher education context, could there
be the development of 'the sort of sub-degree qualifications with value'.

Not reported by the inquiry was the larger amount of sub-degree
education in England found in the higher education sector than in the
college sector. In a situation in which higher education institutions and
further education colleges competed in some of the same markets for
higher education students, the Dearing recommendations on 'growth and
transfer' to the colleges were unlikely to enjoy the support of all institutions
in the higher education sector, including the funding council. Limiting the
expansion of sub-degrees to the colleges was likely to 'damage or restrict
opportunities' and yield to the view (implicit in the recommendation) that
this was 'a cheaper option' (HEFCE 1997).

From the beginning, a combination of weak demand for sub-degree
courses, unfilled places allocated to further education institutions and
doubts about quality in a minority of colleges served to derail the Dearing
proposals for a discrete or specific role in higher education. Rather than rely
on the colleges to lead any future expansion on the basis of existing sub-
bachelor qualifications, the Blair government turned to other ways of
stimulating demand and securing growth. First, a target was set to increase
the participation rate to 50 per cent of all 18 to 30 year olds by the year
2010; and, second, the foundation degree was invented to invigorate and
carry the future expansion in undergraduate education.

At the centre of the English experiment to 'break the traditional pattern
of demand' was the work-focused foundation degree (DfEE 2003). Taught
in colleges and universities, awarded by the latter, and designed and
developed with employers, the new degree was intended to be highly
valued in the labour market and to appeal to a broad mix of students:

> For all these reasons – to meet the shortage of people with technician
> level qualifications, to develop in students the right blend of skills
> which employers need, and lay the basis for widening participation and
> progression – we need a new qualification.

> (DfEE 2000b: 8)

Although a qualification in its own right, arrangements for progression to the third year of a designated bachelor degree would be guaranteed. Over time, the foundation degree was expected to become the standard two-year (or part-time equivalent) qualification in English higher education. With additional funded places offered in preference to bachelor degrees and development funding available for institutions and employers, the goal of 100,000 students by 2010 was likely to be met.

Underlying this growth strategy was the argument that saturation had been reached with regard to traditional students. To fulfil the 50 per cent participation target institutions would need to recruit and retain students from non-traditional backgrounds, including those holding or studying for vocational qualifications. Ahead of turbulence in the market for students following the introduction of variable fees, further education colleges and higher education institutions were funded to come together as lifelong learning networks – across a city, area or region – to offer new progression opportunities for vocational students (HEFCE 2004).

The networks were the one major outcome of a partnership between the HEFCE, the LSC and the relevant government department to advance vocational and workplace progression. As before, it was the funding council for higher education that led this initiative and the extent of the collaboration between the two sector bodies was less effective and productive than ministers had wished.

3.3 Enduring and diverging regimes

At each of the levels of data collection and analysis in the FurtherHigher Project there is evidence to suggest that two-sector arrangements exercise a central and continuing influence on strategies to expand participation in settings that combine further and higher education (Bathmaker *et al.* 2008). How and why the English system connected or separated its sectors has rarely been an explicit concern for government and its agencies. The lack of progress in securing a larger role for further education colleges as providers of higher education in their own right has much to do with the differing perspectives and competing interests that arise from sector separation. As a policy arena, the same is true for the neglect of further education in higher education institutions.

Such arrangements have made it difficult for any one body or sector to take strategic responsibility for the development and well-being of college-based higher education and university-located further education. Despite its elevation to high policy, further education colleges have still to be widely accepted as normal and necessary locations for undergraduate education. Subject to separate funding and regulatory regimes, those working in further and higher education have not seen or felt themselves engaged in a common enterprise.

Moreover, at the same time that cross-sector provision and progression has been promoted, the sector bodies have diverged in their methodologies and portfolios. The removal of the FEFC not only placed the colleges in an expanded learning and skills sector alongside school sixth forms, adult and community learning centres, and training providers. It represented a shift to a planning function and then to a demand-led system (Coffield *et al.* 2008). The creation of the LSC was also one of the few occasions when a public – brief yet instructive – justification has been made for maintaining a division between higher education and the rest of post-compulsory system:

> This is for two reasons. First, uniquely, higher education's contribution is international and national as well as regional and local. Although universities should be responsive to the needs of local employers and business, both to meet skills requirements and in the application of research, they also operate on a wider stage and require a different approach to funding. Second, one of the main aims in creating the new Council is to bring order to an area which is overly complex, and where there are critical issues to address about coherence and the quality of provision. Including higher education would undermine this by complicating significantly the Council's remit and making it so broad as to be difficult to manage.
>
> (DfEE 1999: 42)

The reluctance or refusal to give the colleges primary responsibility for a segment of sub-bachelor higher education, underpinned by direct funding, highlighted the variety, complexity and instability of their programmes and qualifications. In some cases, this provision was the result of opportunism and enterprise but with little integration into the management and planning of the college. In other places, the college might be party to a regional federation or network, with the lead higher education establishment and its partner colleges operating a well-developed and well-regarded system of cross-sector collaboration. Elsewhere, there were colleges with a track record and critical mass of providing higher education and who were candidates, following legislation in 2007, to gain the power to award the foundation degree.

There was no simple or clear pattern to the higher education offered in the learning and skills sector. Roughly a third of the activity was funded directly by the HEFCE, another third through indirect funding partnerships with higher education establishments, and another third mainly sponsored by the LSC. In a still marginal yet diverse part of the system, the social and educational background of its students, and the closeness of colleges to employers and the world of work, made these settings ever more important to policies on increasing and widening participation:

> HE in FECs [further education colleges] is already a distinctive part of the HE system. While it is dangerous to over-generalise about a diverse

system, HE students in FECs are more likely to be over 25, more likely to study part-time, and more likely to come from areas with low rates of participation in HE than students in HEIs [higher education institutions]. They are more likely to be studying foundation degrees and sub-degree programmes such as HNCs and HNDs.

(HEFCE 2006a: 9)

If current levels of growth had matched those during the peak years of expansion, then there might have been momentum and potential for a more visible, powerful and everyday presence in English higher education. Whether as a consequence of market forces or the organisational and administrative complexities of funding routes, partnerships and capital allocations, the static (or possibly declining) volume of higher education in the college sector has probably limited the tendencies to diversion.

Nevertheless, average rates of return for sub-degree qualifications are much closer, if not identical, to A-level qualifications than to bachelor degrees (Jenkins *et al*. 2007) and those taking sub-degree qualifications are increasingly likely to convert them into a bachelor degree. About half those completing the two-year HND went on to achieve a bachelor qualification (DfEE 2000b) and a similar proportion of students finishing a foundation degree moved in the same direction (HEFCE 2008a).

Overall, the location of higher education in further education colleges, together with the teaching of further education in higher education establishments, have each contributed to a democratisation of access. They are implicated as well in policies to steer future demand away from high-cost and high-status parts of the system. If these policies are not to produce or reinforce diversion, then efforts to enhance the status and attractiveness of short-cycle undergraduate study need to play into strategies to extend access and progression across the whole of the post-secondary system. For reasons explored in this chapter, such relationships and understandings do not always figure strongly in contemporary policy-making.

Access, participation and diversity questions in relation to different forms of post-compulsory further and higher education

The importance of prior educational experiences

Anna Vignoles and Claire Crawford

1 Introduction

Sir Lionel Robbins, in his review of higher education (HE) in 1963 (Robbins 1963) rightly pointed out that expansion of HE was both necessary, from an economic perspective, and just. At the time he wrote his seminal report, around one in twenty of each generation were fortunate enough to enter university. Since then, massification of higher education would appear to have been successful. The numbers entering higher education have increased dramatically in England over the last half century (Figure 3.1.1), with 43 per cent of each generation now receiving a university education. The Higher Education Initial Participation Rate (HEIPR) is calculated for individuals aged 17–30 and can be found at www.dcsf.gov.uk/rsgateway/DB/SFR/s000716/SFR10_2007v1.pdf. Much of our focus is on the initial participation rate amongst those aged 18 and 19, which in 2005/06 stood at 21.3 per cent and 9.7 per cent respectively (see Table 2 of this link). Some groups in particular have also increased their participation relative to 'traditional' students (defining traditional as male, white and middle class). As we have seen, in particular, women now outnumber men in HE and clearly in those terms there has been noticeable progress in widening participation to previously under-represented groups. Yet the underlying concerns of Robbins, and later Lord Dearing (1997), about providing access to university for less advantaged students, remain a major policy issue (DfES 2003, 2006). In this section, we set out a quantitative analysis of who is participating in HE in England, and the extent to which there has been a successful widening of participation to 'non-traditional' groups of students. Newly linked administrative data enable us to consider the entire

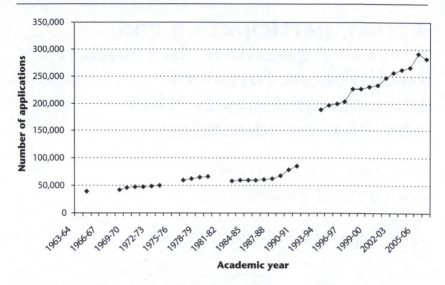

Figure 3.1.1 Long-term trend in UCAS applications amongst UK-domiciled applicants to English institutions

Source: UCAS data constructed by Gill Wyness of the Institute of Education, London. Note that there is a structural break in the data in 1992 caused by the abolition of the 'binary line' between universities and polytechnics. In this section we restrict our analysis to HE institutions, which include of course the former polytechnics.

population of state school children, including those who do not participate in HE, analysing their educational achievements from age 11 right through to potential university participation at age 18/19.

We start by considering how the likelihood of HE participation varies according to the ethnic, gender and socio-economic background of the young person. In light of findings about ethnic and gender gaps being reduced or closed, we focus particularly on the extent to which differences in university participation between advantaged and disadvantaged students are driven by their very different prior educational experiences. Specifically, we ask: are young people with similar educational trajectories and GCSE/A-level scores making similar HE participation choices regardless of their economic background? If so, then this would suggest that much of the inequality in HE participation is a result of prior educational experiences, and that making more money available for poorer students at the point of entry into HE, for example in the form of bursaries, might not be particularly effective at widening participation. Note that our definition of HE participation is restricted to participation in HE institutions only as a result of the limitations of our data, although we of course recognise the important role of further education institutions in widening access to higher education.

Controversially, we also challenge the notion that policy should focus simply on whether or not individuals participate in HE. Rather, we report on the *nature* of HE participation of different types of student, identifying which types of institution certain students are particularly likely to enrol in. This is important from an economic justice perspective as previous research has suggested that non-traditional students are concentrated in new universities (Connor *et al.* 1999) and that the economic value of a degree in the labour market varies substantially according to the type of higher education institution attended (Chevalier and Conlon 2003). The nature of HE participation may also become increasingly important as the variability in graduate earnings increases (Walker and Zhu 2009; Green and Zhu 2008) and the most recent cohorts of graduates face a decline in the average economic return to a degree (as is predicted given the recent increase in the supply of graduates). In an era of over-supply of graduates and a tendency for recent graduates to end up in non-graduate jobs (McIntosh 2005; Green and Zhu 2008; Dolton and Vignoles 2000), it will potentially become even more important that all groups of students have access to high status institutions, since degrees from these institutions are likely to provide some protection against poor graduate labour market outcomes.

To undertake this analysis we use a unique new dataset which combines large-scale, individual-level administrative data on a particular cohort of state school pupils as they progress through the education system. Unlike previous work, our analysis is based on both HE participants and non-participants, allowing robust conclusions to be drawn about the factors determining HE participation.

We proceed by giving a brief account of relevant policy frameworks that may impact on HE participation and review existing evidence. We then discuss our findings, including how they might inform us about the most successful ways in which to widen participation in HE in the future.

2 Policy framework

In terms of the widening participation policy agenda, there has been a particular focus on the under-representation of socio-economically disadvantaged pupils in HE. This is partly because the empirical evidence suggests that the gap in HE participation rates between richer and poorer students, and between higher and lower social classes, actually widened in the UK in the mid-to-late 1990s (Blanden and Machin 2004; Machin and Vignoles 2004; HEFCE 2005a; Glennerster 2001), although this trend has since reversed somewhat (Raffe *et al.* 2006). Recent evidence from HEFCE (2005) indicates that the 20 per cent most disadvantaged students are around six times less likely to participate in higher education compared to the 20 per cent most advantaged pupils. Other disparities in the HE participation rates of different types of student are also of key concern however, and we did not restrict our analysis to consideration of socio-economic background. For instance, we also consider gaps in HE participation rates by ethnicity and gender. As noted in the introduction to this volume (see also HEFCE 2005a), the rise in gender inequality has been dramatic, as higher female attainment in school continues on into higher education, and the evidence base suggests substantial differences in HE participation rates across different ethnic minority groups (Dearing 1997; Tomlinson 2001).

Concerns about who is accessing HE increased following the introduction of tuition fees in 1998. Although the fees were means tested, there were fears that the prospect of fees would create another barrier to HE participation for poorer students in particular, as argued in Callender (2003). However, whilst there is evidence that poorer students leave university with more debt and may be more debt averse in the first place (Pennell and West 2005), there is no strong empirical evidence that the introduction of fees reduced the relative HE participation rate of poorer students (UUK 2007; Dearden *et al.* 2008). Certainly, as Figure 3.1.1 suggests, the introduction of fees in 1998 was not associated with any sustained overall fall in the number of students applying to English higher education institutions.

The evidence base on the determinants of university participation is extensive. We know that an individual's probability of participating in higher education is highly related to their parents' characteristics, particularly their parents' education level and/or socio-economic status, as well as their gender and ethnicity (see, for instance, Blanden and Gregg 2004; Carneiro and Heckman 2002, 2003; Gayle *et al.* 2002; Meghir and Palme 2005; Haveman and Wolfe 1995). We also know that socio-economic, gender and ethnic gaps in education achievement emerge very early on in a child's life (see, for example, CMPO 2006 and Feinstein 2003 for the UK; Cunha and Heckman 2007 and Cunha *et al.* 2006 for the US). This raises an important policy question: do inequalities in educational achievement widen as a child passes through the education system, or does the system serve to narrow some of the socio-economic, gender and ethnic gaps in cognitive achievement that exist on entry into school? If the education system had no effect, we might be tempted to conclude that only interventions early on in a child's life were likely to be successful in raising educational achievement and hence the likelihood of going to university. In the US context, for which there is more robust evidence, it appears that barriers at the point of entry into HE, such as credit constraints (i.e. the inability to borrow), do not play a large role in determining HE participation (Cunha *et al.* 2006; Carneiro and Heckman 2002). This view is highly contested, however, with Belley and Lochner (2007) providing evidence that credit constraints may have started to play a potentially more important role in determining higher education participation in the US in recent years. In the UK context, the existing evidence is mixed on this point and has been severely constrained by limited data (see two major studies by Gayle *et al.* 2002 and Bekhradnia 2003). We do know, however, that there are well documented but highly contested education achievement inequalities in primary and secondary schools in the UK (see Sammons 1995; Strand 1999; Gorard 2000).

Of course, even if prior achievement explains much of the difference in HE participation rates of different groups, there remain potential barriers to participation at the point of entry into HE, many of which are reviewed in this book. These factors, which vary by gender, ethnicity and socio-economic background, include financial 'barriers', lack of childcare and other forms of caring responsibilities, to name but a few. Quantifying the relative importance of these factors is extremely difficult, although the evidence base as a whole was reviewed both by Dearing (1997) and more recently for HEFCE by Gorard *et al.* (2006). Although Gorard *et al.* acknowledged that these factors are important, they concluded that prior attainment was the key to explaining differences in HE participation rates, and made the case for further careful quantitative analysis of this issue. Gorard *et al.* (2006) also raised the philosophical issues surrounding the role of poor prior attainment, asking whether if prior attainment does indeed signal merit and the ability to benefit from HE, is making it easier for individuals without the necessary qualifications to enter HE the right policy response? We abstract from this philosophical debate and focus on providing empirical evidence as to whether poor prior attainment is indeed the main reason why certain types of student have lower HE participation rates.

3 Data and methods

Our work on HE participation relies on a new combination of large-scale, individual-level administrative datasets that have been recently linked by the Department for Children, Schools and Families and the Department for Innovation, Universities and Skills. We have data on a particular cohort of children, namely state school pupils who were in Year 11 (age 15/16) in 2001/02, from age 11 through to age 18. We are able to observe whether they continued into post-compulsory education in 2002/03 and 2003/04, and into higher education in 2004/05 and/or 2005/06, at age 18 or 19. This means that we can look at the academic trajectories of males and females from poorer socio-economic backgrounds and ethnic minority groups and identify if and when their relative education achievement falls away.

We use quantitative methods to undertake our modelling of the decision to participate in HE at age 18/19 (see Chowdry *et al.* 2008a for a full account). Specifically, we use multivariate regression analysis which enables us to consider the roles of socio-economic background, ethnicity and gender in determining HE participation, whilst simultaneously taking account of other factors that may influence such decisions. Of particular importance is the role of prior achievement. We include results from national assessment tests (also known as Key Stage tests or SATs) at ages

11, 14, 16 and 18. We also include as many other covariates as the administrative data provides. Specifically, we include a neighbourhood-based measure of parental education, month of birth, ethnicity, whether English is an additional language for the student, whether the student has statemented (more severe) or non-statemented (less severe) special educational needs (all recorded at age 16), and the secondary school they attended at age 16. Note that we do not observe individual parental education in any of our data-sets, so we instead make use of a local neighbourhood measure of educational attainment from the 2001 Census. This is recorded at Output Area (OA) level (approximately 150 households) and is mapped in using pupils' home postcode at age 16. We calculate the proportion of individuals in each OA whose highest educational qualification is at NQF level 3 or above, split the population into quintiles on the basis of this index and include the top four (highest educated) quintiles in our models.

As discussed above, we also want to explore the type of HE institution (HEI) attended by students from different backgrounds. We know which HE institution each student enrolled in and from this we construct from our data a simple binary indicator of institution type. This measure combines data from the 2001 Research Assessment Exercise (RAE) with information on whether the institution is a Russell Group university. Specifically we take all members of the self-defined Russell Group. We then include any other university that is not a member of the Russell Group but that has an institution average research quality score from the 2001 RAE that exceeds the lowest average RAE score of the Russell Group institutions, giving a total of 41 institutions defined as ' 'high status'. Our definition of a 'high status' university is therefore based purely on research quality. Using this definition, 35 per cent of HE participants attend a 'high status' university in their first year. Of course, we recognise that such definitions of institution status are, by their very nature, contentious and to some extent arbitrary. In particular, different academic departments within HEIs will be of differing research quality and we ignore such subject differences. Furthermore, university research quality may not necessarily determine the quality of undergraduates' HE experiences. However, obtaining a degree from a Russell Group institution and attending an HEI that scored highly in the RAE exercise currently results in higher wages (see Iftikhar et al. 2008, which confirms evidence from Chevalier and Conlon 2003 that the wage premium associated with having a degree tends to be greater from such high status institutions). Thus the type of HE being accessed by different students is an issue that is crucially important for future economic equality. Furthermore, as the heterogeneity of students and universities increases so too will the variation in graduate earnings, thus it seems sensible to consider different types of HE experience, although it is not yet clear whether in the future the wage differential between different types of universities will increase or whether the biggest differences will be across subject areas.

There are two issues to bear in mind when discussing our findings. First, our measures of family background are imperfect. Ideally, we would want rich individual-level data on students' socio-economic background. However, administrative data in the UK are currently weak on the provision of socio-economic background information for students: this makes monitoring the educational achievement of more disadvantaged students challenging, and is clearly a policy issue in itself. Whilst socio-economic data is collected for HE participants (in data held by the Higher Education Statistics Agency), this kind of information is not collected for the general population of school children, and we would urge policy-makers to make collection of such data a priority. For the purposes of the graphical analysis presented in this chapter, we therefore rely on a dichotomous measure of whether or not the pupil was entitled to free school meals (FSM) at age 16. This is recorded for all state school students, regardless of later HE participation. We recognise that this only measures quite extreme socio-economic deprivation and provides us with very little information for students further up the socio-economic distribution. However, it is an extremely useful way of monitoring HE participation amongst the very poorest students (see Chowdry et al. 2008a for other analyses where we make use of additional measures of material deprivation derived from neighbourhood level measures of socio-economic background based on census data, e.g. the index of material deprivation).

The second issue is that we are driven by our data to analyse only young HE entrants, that is, those starting university at age 18 or 19. This is a limitation given the importance of mature students in widening parti-cipation and one that reflects the absence of good quantitative information on the education trajectories of older students.

4 The socio-economic gap

As is well known, children from poor backgrounds remain far less likely to go to university than more advantaged children. This is shown in the left-hand panel of Figure 3.1.2 for females and Figure 3.1.3 for males. This socio-economic gap in HE participation has been persistent in the UK over time (Gorard et al. 2006), although in our data we can only consider the socio-economic gap in HE participation for pupils in one particular cohort, namely those potentially starting university at age 18 in 2004–05 or age 19 in 2005–06. For this cohort, the raw gap in HE participation rates between FSM and non-FSM pupils is sizeable, suggesting that non-FSM pupils are more than twice as likely to enrol in higher education as their FSM counterparts. This may, of course, be the result of a range of factors, such as gender, ethnicity and prior achievement. However, when we apply our multivariate regression models (which take into account other factors that may influence whether or not an individual enrols in university), these gaps largely disappear. In particular, once we allow for pupils' prior achievement from Key Stage 2 (sat at age 11) to Key Stage 5 (sat at age 18), it is clear that students with similar levels of achievement in secondary school are more or less equally likely to participate in higher education, regardless of their family background (shown in the right-hand panel of Figures 3.1.2 and 3.1.3). Our work therefore confirms that the reason why poorer students do not access higher education to the same extent as their more advantaged counterparts is not because of choices being made at age 18, but because disadvantaged students do so poorly in secondary school.

In our data we also have information on which secondary school each pupil attended. We found, unsurprisingly perhaps, that poorer children tend to attend lower-achieving secondary schools. While we cannot prove a causal link between the quality of secondary schooling accessed by a pupil and his or her academic achievement, different types of students seem to be accessing schools of different quality, and this is likely to be part of any explanation of the lower academic achievement of poorer children.

We also examined the nature of HE participation for advantaged and less advantaged pupils. Similar findings arise. As is evident from Figures 3.1.4 and 3.1.5, pupils who are eligible for free school meals are considerably

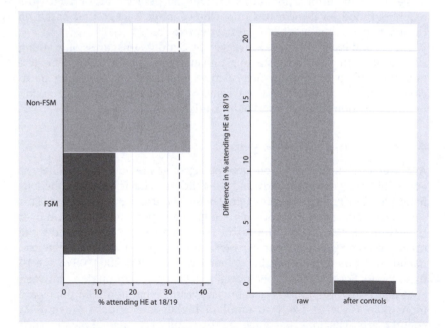

Figure 3.1.2 Raw socio-economic gap in HE participation rates at age 18/19 for females (left-hand panel) and difference after adding in controls (right-hand panel)

Note: the dashed line indicates the average HE participation rate amongst all females

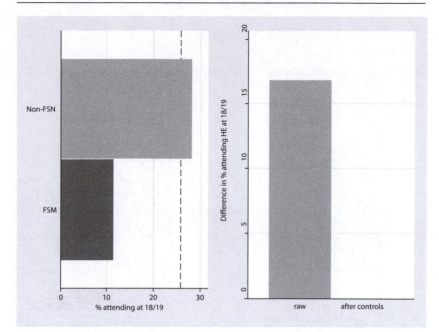

Figure 3.1.3 Raw socio-economic gap in HE participation rates at age 18/19 for males (left-hand panel) and difference after adding in controls (right-hand panel)

Note: the dashed line indicates the average HE participation rate amongst all males

less likely to enrol in a 'high status' university. Yet once we allow for pupils' other characteristics and, in particular, their primary and secondary school achievement, we find that the gap in the HE participation rates at elite institutions between richer and poorer students is much reduced though not negligible.

5 The ethnic gap

There are also large disparities in the likelihood of participating in higher education (Figures 3.1.6 and 3.1.7), and particularly in the likelihood of participating in a high status institution (Figure 3.1.8 and 3.1.9), by ethnicity. The raw ethnic gaps in HE participation for both women (Figure 3.1.6) and men (Figure 3.1.7) suggest that most ethnic minority students are significantly *more* likely to participate in higher education than their White British peers (although only students of Other White, Chinese, Mixed and Other ethnic origin are more likely to attend a high status institution). Patterns for ethnic minority men and women are quite similar. We then estimated regression models that accounted for a range of other factors that influence HE participation. Once we allow

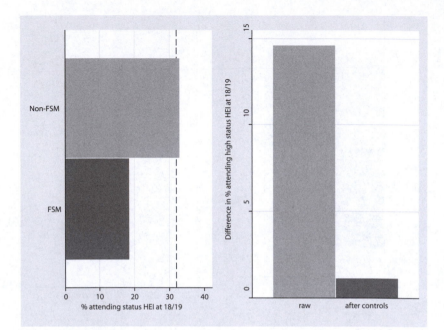

Figure 3.1.4 Raw socio-economic gap in attendance at a high status
institution amongst female HE participants and difference after
adding in controls

Note: the dashed line indicates average attendance at a high status HEI amongst
female HE participants

for prior achievement, all ethnic minority groups are more likely to go to
university than White British students; they are also at least as likely to
attend a 'high status' institution.

We also find that there is more upward mobility, in terms of academic
achievement in secondary school, for most ethnic minority groups than for
White British children, consistent with work from CMPO (2006). This
reinforces the generally positive story that emerges from our research
about the narrowing of ethnic gaps in education achievement and HE
participation.

6 The gender gap

There are sizeable differences in the average HE participation rates by
gender, as noted earlier. Figures 3.1.2 and 3.1.3 show HE participation
rates for females and males separately. It is noticeable that the raw socio-
economic gap in HE participation is greater for females than for males.

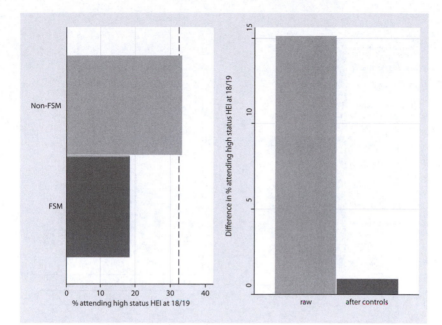

Figure 3.1.5 Raw socio-economic gap in attendance at a high status
institution amongst male HE participants and difference after
adding in controls

Note: the dashed line indicates average attendance at a high status HEI amongst male
HE participants

However, these gaps disappear for both males and females once controls
for prior achievement are added. Gender ethnic interactions are also
important. For both males and females, Indian, Chinese, Other Asian and
Mixed ethnic groups have higher than average HE participation rates.
However, some important gender differences emerge when we control for
prior achievement. For instance, Black African women have a slightly
higher than average HE participation rate, whilst Black African males have
an average HE participation rate. Once we allow for prior achievement,
Black African females are no more or less likely to participate in HE than
their White British counterparts. Black African males, by contrast, remain
significantly less likely to participate in HE than White British males even
after controlling for pupils' prior achievement.

Generally, the pattern of HE enrolment in high status institutions is
similar for males and females, which clearly represents a dramatic shift
since Robbins (1963) when the gender imbalance was stark particularly in
high status universities such as the Oxbridge institutions. However, once

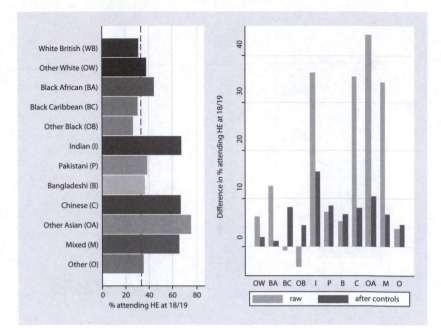

Figure 3.1.6   Raw ethnic gap in HE participation rates at age 18/19 for females (left-hand panel) and difference after adding in controls (right-hand panel)

Note: the dashed line indicates the average HE participation rate amongst all females

we interact gender with ethnicity, differences do emerge. For instance, Black African females are slightly more likely to enrol in a high status institution once we allow for prior achievement. By contrast, Black African males are not. Our evidence supports the view that progression through the education system is both gendered and varies by ethnicity. Considering interactions between gender and ethnicity is particularly important when considering HE participation.

7 Discussion

Our quantitative evidence suggests that the key concern going forward in terms of widening participation in higher education (HE) should be the gap in participation between richer and poorer students. We observe a sizeable socio-economic gap in HE participation for both men and women, and indeed the raw gap is somewhat larger for women. These gaps can, however, largely be explained by the weaker academic achievement of disadvantaged children in secondary school. The socio-economic gap that

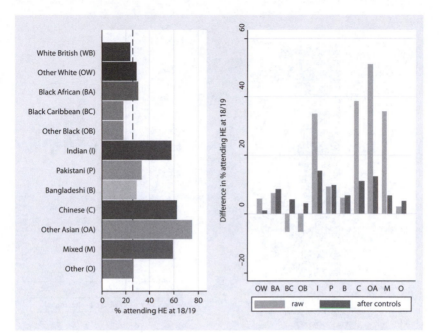

Figure 3.1.7 Raw ethnic gap in HE participation rates at age 18/19 for males (left-hand panel) and difference after adding in controls (right-hand panel)

Note: the dashed line indicates the average HE participation rate amongst all males

remains on entry into higher education, after allowing for prior attainment, is small. This implies that widening participation in higher education requires intervention well before the point of entry into HE, which raises challenging questions about the efficacy of widening participation policies aimed at 18 year olds. Socio-economic gaps in education achievement are emerging at (or before) age 11 and throughout secondary school, so intervening during post-compulsory schooling is unlikely, according to our analysis, to have a serious impact on encouraging poorer students into higher education. That is not to say that universities should not carry out outreach work to disadvantaged students who continue into post-compulsory education. But this approach will not tackle the more major problem that underlies the socio-economic gap in higher education participation, namely poor prior achievement. Effective primary and secondary school interventions designed to improve the performance of disadvantaged children are what is needed.

Of course improving standards in secondary school and raising the achievement of disadvantaged pupils has been a policy aim for many

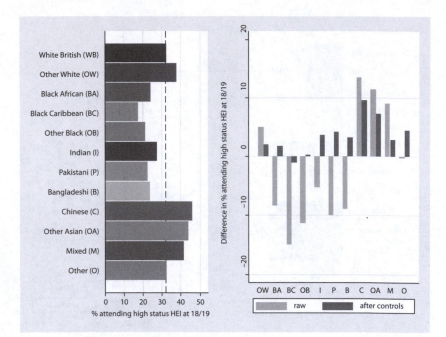

Figure 3.1.8 Raw ethnic gap in attendance at a high status institution amongst female HE participants and difference after adding in controls

Note: the dashed line indicates average attendance at a high status HEI amongst female HE participants

years. Bringing it about in practice is extremely hard. In our analysis, we find that poorer children access lower quality secondary schools (as measured by value added), so addressing school choice and access issues could perhaps play a role in addressing higher education participation gaps. We might also learn from our encouraging findings about ethnic minority students. Other evidence has shown that ethnic minority students make greater progress through secondary school than their White British peers and we show that they have (by and large) higher HE participation rates after controlling for their prior achievement. However, some caution is needed. HE participation patterns vary by gender and ethnicity and by type of institution. There are some ethnic minority groups who remain under represented in high status HE institutions relative to White British students, for example, Black African males. We therefore need to better understand whether particular policies have brought about different patterns of educational progression. Whilst we address some of these issues in this volume, such as the role of higher education in the further education sector

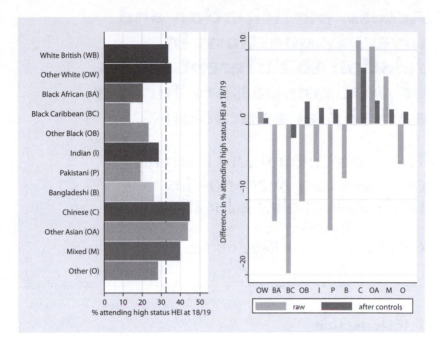

Figure 3.1.9 Raw ethnic gap in attendance at a high status institution amongst male HE participants and difference after adding in controls

Note: the dashed line indicates average attendance at a high status HEI amongst male HE participants

and indeed the importance of teaching and learning in schools and post-compulsory education, more needs to be done to fully evaluate specific widening participation policy interventions. Finally, we cannot forget that children have more to their lives than school. Our data does not contain information on children's family background, such as their parents' aspirations and their family environment, which may play a role in the achievement and aspirations of young people. Thus our evidence can only be used to highlight the fact that different groups of student make different progress in the educational system and early gaps in educational achievement appear to explain much of the large socio-economic gap in HE participation we observe at age 18/19.

Access, participation and diversity questions in relation to different forms of post-compulsory further and higher education

The socio-cultural and learning experiences of working-class students in higher education

Gill Crozier, Diane Reay and John Clayton

1 Introduction

Our research has taken place during a period of policy-driven widening participation in higher education and at a time when, in both the UK and globally, there has been concern about breaking down the exclusivity of university education (McDonough and Fann 2007). In spite of the relative success in increasing participation in higher education generally, concerns remain about the social class gap in entry to higher education (HEFCE 2005b); in 2005 UCAS reported that 24.72 per cent of those accepted at university were from the four lowest socio-economic groups and in 2004 it was 25.61 per cent (Shepherd 2007) indicating a decline. Also whilst universities are reporting success in widening participation there exists an apparent polarisation of types of university attracting working-class and minority ethnic students (Sutton Trust 2000, 2004, 2007). There is also considerable concern with student retention (HEFCE 2005) and the fact that the universities with the most success at widening participation also have the highest drop-out rates (HEFCE 2005) suggesting a causal relationship.

Whilst there has been substantial research on retention (Gorard *et al.* 2006; Yorke and Longden 2004; Tinto 1993, 1996) issues and increasingly the processes of university choice (Harvey *et al.* 2006; Gorard *et al.* 2006; Reay *et al.* 2005; Nora 2004; Moogan *et al.* 1999; Modood and Shiner 1994), there is limited research on student experiences once at university and especially working-class students, which is the focus and concern of our study. Whilst our research is not concerned with retention as such, we believe that our fine-grained analysis of the social, cultural and learning experiences of working-class students provides insights into the complexities of student life and what influences students to persevere or might cause them to give up. This is particularly important given the findings of the retention research which point to a combination of factors that are unique to the individual student (Yorke and Longden 2004) and as Harvey *et al.* (2006) say 'to focus [solely] on retention is to risk mistaking the symptom for the cause'.

The limited research that has been carried out into working-class student experiences of university (Archer *et al.* 2003; Archer and Hutchings 2000) was located in one modern university in a metropolitan context (Quinn 2004). By contrast our research takes place across three geographical areas and in four different types of higher education institution (HEI). This is important given that cultural experiences are influenced by geographical context (e.g. Massey 1996; Nayak 2003) and the institutions represent different missions and success in widening participation.

Moreover, there is a tendency in the policy discourse and literature to use terms such as 'non-traditional' (e.g. Bowl 2006) and 'diverse', often conflating mature, minority ethnic, women and working class (Gorard *et al.* 2006). Our research focuses primarily on working-class students' experiences. However, we recognise that social class and identity formations are complex. The intersection of gender, 'race', ethnicity and age with class is therefore central in order to discern and unpick the specificity of their experiences. This is, therefore, a sociological study of the students' dialogic relationship between their social positions and their cultural and learning experiences. This is not a study of the process of learning but rather of the interrelationship of the social and cultural with the learning experiences together with the structural and organisational circumstances provided by the respective institutions.

Historically, working-class people have been 'pathologised, demonised and held responsible for social problems' (Skeggs 1997: 76). Moreover, within the widening participation and retention discourses, working-class students are often constructed as problematic, potential drop-outs and a risky investment for HEIs (Leathwood and O'Connell 2003). Our research presents a very different picture of high commitment and resilience.

Archer and Hutchings' (2000) study of one modern university discussed constructions and concerns of risk, costs and benefits of university participation. Our research has explored how students manage the academic in relation to their social selves across four very different types of institution. We were concerned with how they navigate and relate to the university both academically and socially in order to develop 'academic ability' and accrue educational knowledge (cultural capital) which they can turn into success. Lave and Wenger (1991) present a socio-cultural theory of students' engagement with their learning, demonstrating the importance of the social as well as the learning contexts. However, their understanding of power relationships and structural concerns is limited (Fuller *et al.* 2005). In order to develop our understanding of student experiences and interrelated processes we preferred to employ Bourdieu's (1990a) concepts of habitus, cultural and social capital and also field and aspects of Bernstein's (1996) pedagogic device rather than Lave and Wenger's more cognitive approach.

The nature of the 'field' in our study comprises the university, the subject disciplines and the social milieu as well as the field of higher education at a national level and how these fields are engaged with by the students. Bourdieu likens the field to a competitive game for which there are rules. Not everyone has knowledge or equal knowledge of these rules whilst others have particularly advantageous knowledge and different amounts and volume of 'capital' with which to play (Bourdieu and Waquant 1992: 98). In addition they hold differing dispositions – habitus with which to employ these capitals. Hence there are power dynamics and contestation within all fields. The fields are the context of scarce resources – in terms of our study, ultimately high-level qualifications but also access to tutor time, materials, knowledge sources and so on – conducive to studying, and as part of this a source of accruing further capital (Crozier *et al.* 2008).

2 The research study: aims and objectives, and methods

The overarching aim of the project was to explore working-class students' experiences of higher education; the impact of these on their learner and socio-cultural identities; the implications for their progress; and the extent to which these experiences are gendered and 'raced'. More specifically the research sought to:

- compare and contrast the social and cultural experiences of working-class students in different types of universities/higher education institution;
- examine the impact of these experiences on their learning and academic progress primarily from their own perspectives but also if possible those of their tutors;
- discern the impact of the university experiences on the constructions and re-constructions of the students' identities and explore the processes of compliance or resistance with which students engage in order to position themselves as effective learners;
- contribute to the theoretical understanding of social class and learner identities within the higher education context.

Our focus was on undergraduate students 18 years and above from working-class backgrounds including white and minority ethnic women and men, accessing them initially in years 1 and 2 of their degree course.

We also collected data from middle-class students in order to locate the perspectives of the working-class students.

Mixed methods were employed in two stages, across four institutions comprising an elite, old university; a red brick, old university; a new university; and a college of further education, located in three different geographical areas. These different types of institutions were chosen in order to discern a cross-section of student experiences. We focused on different disciplinary areas but where possible the same subjects in all the universities (given the hierarchy that exists between subjects (Bourdieu 1988)). (See Appendix 3 for more information about the institutions, methods used and the explanation of social class.)

3 Different learning and social contexts: the four HEIs

The four very different HEIs embody different institutional missions and thus attract different types of students in terms of wealth, social class, qualifications, age and ethnicities, although gender seems to be more evenly balanced across the universities (HESA 2005). Expectations and delivery of programmes differ across the HEIs and subjects together with unequal material conditions: unit of resource, collateral, endowments, research funding; together with different histories, traditions and perceptions of worth and status locally, nationally and internationally. All of this impacts on pedagogy and students' social, cultural and learning experiences (Bastedo and Gumport 2003). In Bourdieu's (1990a) terms, these 'fields' are complexly differentiated.

Our data suggest there is 'an institutional effect' or institutional habitus (Reay et al. 2005) which acts as an intervening variable, providing a semi-autonomous means by which class processes are played out in the HE experiences of students. The HEIs in our study have institutional habituses in which their organisational culture and ethos is linked to wider socio-economic and educational cultures. Hence, as indicated below, there are greater differences between the university experiences than between the students' experience in each university or subject (see also Crozier et al. 2008), although that is not to suggest that the working-class students had the same experiences as the middle-class students.

Eastern College where students undertake vocational foundation degrees, mainly on a part-time basis, is situated in an economically disadvantaged area devoid of the usual attributes of a university town; for example, there are no bookshops or theatres. The students tend not to go to the partner university (Northern University) to avail themselves of the learning resources there and nor do they identify as university students. Tutor support varies across the subjects and is influenced by student numbers and tutor personalities.

At Northern University, most of the students live at home (70 per cent of questionnaire responses) and work in part-time employment between at least 10 and 20 hours per week (64 per cent). Whilst there is a range of university support addressing study skills, finances, health and counselling and accessible tutors, there was no structured tutorial support. Through a system of online learning whereby students were encouraged to access lecture notes and related learning materials, frequently eschewing the need to attend the university, Northern students were increasingly left to their own devices.

At Midland the type of support was similar although more module and personal tutor contact seemed to be available. Only 10 per cent of the questionnaire respondents lived at home, and 30 per cent had only limited part-time, weekend employment. The key difference between these two universities and Southern is the way the support is provided in a general way rather than specifically student targeted.

At Southern University the students have to live on campus at least in their first year and are forbidden to take paid employment during term time. Most are young and tend not to have other family commitments. Once accepted into the university, resources are targeted to ensure individual success for all. Each term students receive detailed feedback on their progress which happened variably elsewhere. They are immersed in their subject and the academic culture and the college system provides a personalised student support network.

Eastern College and Northern University essentially offer their students a resource to enable them to improve their position in the labour market, suiting the needs of local, putative, 'non-traditional' students. Southern University draws the students into what is effectively an exclusive club where they are 'bound in' as lifelong members. Many of the students we interviewed referred to the University as the (Southern) 'bubble'. In between these extremes Midland University draws on a more diverse student intake in terms of geography and ethnicity, and provides an environment in which social and cultural opportunities are promoted alongside the academic aspects of the university experience.

The implication is that the students' lives revolve around their HEI to different extents, with the degree prioritised in different ways in the light of other concerns and commitments.

4 Preparation for university

Habitus is the embodiment of history, 'internalized as a second nature . . . [it] is the active presence of the past of which it is the product' (Bourdieu 1990a: 56). Having the kind of history that matches the present conditions facilitates one's engagement with that present reality. All middle-class students to varying degrees had more preparation for university life and knew what to expect than all the working-class students in our study. Most were given advice by parents or family members with many of these having been to university themselves. In addition their schools groomed them, endowing their habitus by providing insights and relevant experiences. According to the questionnaire responses, the highest proportion of students whose family members had been to university was at Southern University (83.2 per cent) and of these 19.2 per cent had a family member who had also attended Southern University before them. This compares to 70 per cent of Midland's students, 58 per cent of Northern's and less than 50 per cent of Eastern College students. For 86 per cent of those Southern students compared with 21 per cent of Northern students, 'family member' included one or both parents. The student below gives an indication of the importance of family interventions:

> My school didn't really do a lot. They were big on getting people to uni, but just getting them there. They didn't do much once you were there, they didn't really prepare you for once you were there. But my parents have both been to uni so they sort of had an idea of what was going on, which was useful.
>
> (Male, middle class, Northern University)

Most of the middle-class students in our sample described an experience of being brought up in a culture of entitlement, nurtured and groomed for university education and future success and fulfilment. As Rebecca (middle class, Midland University, Economics and History) said:

> at school I felt that it was sort of assumed that once you passed your, if you passed your GCSEs and did well enough to carry on to A-levels, that I don't think in our school there was many other options or it wasn't encouraged, that you weren't encouraged to think of other options other than applying for university. . . . So sixth form was very much about preparing you for university and getting you into that mind and kind of saying okay now write a practice personal statement, now write your real personal statement, have you done enough experience of voluntary work to write on your personal statement? And it was all about coming to university really.

And Helen talking about her school:

> But I think it was very much geared towards sending you to university, it was all about getting good grades, good enough for you to go sort of thing.
>
> (Helen, middle class, Midland University, Economics and History)

Part of the preparation for university is the inculcation of self-confidence, the disposition to study, to relate to this academic milieu. The middle-class students we spoke to displayed substantial self-confidence compared to the majority of the working-class students. Although they talk about their anxiety on first going to university with respect to meeting new friends, they seem quickly to overcome this. They do not talk about academic anxieties in the same way as the working-class students. These are successful people, who have rarely if ever failed. If they do not get good results, they blame it on not having worked very hard. They describe themselves as 'clever' or 'bright' and have high self-expectations.

This contrasted with the working-class students at Northern and Midland who often had had a negative school experience and also attended poorly performing schools in terms of GCSE league tables (Reay *et al.* 2009) and held few expectations of sending pupils to university. In some cases these students ended up at university because of the 'second chance' opportunity of Access or post-19 FE opportunities. Even in the case of the Southern working-class students they arrived there almost serendipitously. For the middle-class students going to university was a right of passage, for the Northern and to a lesser extent the Midland working-class students several said they felt at times they could not believe they were there at all. These two Northern University History students express this clearly: Arthur had enduring anxieties about his ability and in particular initial anxieties about failing, 'My thoughts have always been, at my lowest point, it's always, I'm not capable of doing it'; Barbara felt self-doubt, 'Academically wise I keep thinking I shouldn't be here; that you know I'm not up to the level.'

5 University life: the socio-cultural experience

One of the great achievements of the English HE widening participation policy and strategies is that it has helped working-class students to overcome that sense of place that leads to self-exclusion from places that they do not feel that is rightly theirs (Bourdieu and Wacquant 1992: 72), as our research also demonstrates. However, getting the university place is not the end of the story for working-class students. On going to university, working-class students are faced with middle-class worlds with which they are or tend to be unfamiliar and need to find or devise ways of engaging or at least coping.

Given students' lack of prior knowledge, our findings show the importance of conveying not merely information about the course programme to the student but also the importance of ensuring students develop an understanding of the 'invisible' pedagogy (Bernstein 1996; Crozier and Reay 2008): the rules of 'the game' (Bourdieu 1990a) and expectations. Becoming 'bound in' is one means of achieving this. At Southern University, it is an overt process and some working-class students are overwhelmed and intimidated by it (Reay *et al.* forthcoming). At Midland University the process is more implicit and in part is perpetrated through the system of clubs and societies, together with the opportunities generated through the students' halls of residence. At Northern and Eastern neither of these 'strategies' applied. It is through the association with students, who bring a range of classed experiences and high-value capitals themselves, that pedagogical ethos and academic expectations are propagated. For those living at home (Northern and Eastern students mainly), the students continue to socialise with their home-based friends and have limited interactions at the university. Many of these working-class students are time poor; for most their degree is not central to their lives but is fitted in around their busy, and demanding schedule of employment, domestic care and family commitments.

Although the working-class students in our study do not dwell explicitly on their social anxieties, many, especially at Midland and to some extent at Northern, demonstrate a psychic response by strategically opting out and therefore avoiding the university social milieu and in some cases prefer to live at home or return home at weekends (Clayton *et al.* forthcoming). For middle-class students the opposite response to the social aspects of university seems to be the case. For most these were a key reason for going to university in the first place.

Through these examples we can see the middle-class students have learned dispositions which fit with the context of the university and are thus enabled to generate further habitus through a range of social interactions. The working-class students may also do so in different ways across the different institutions but, as we have argued, on balance they have fewer such opportunities. The more students withdraw from the field, either intentionally or not, the less access they will have to the means (habitus and cultural capital), or opportunity to acquire it, to compete for scarce resources.

6 Learner experiences and academic progress

The working-class students therefore across these different HEIs are variously 'integrated' (Tinto 1993). Their personal experiences and histories gave rise to a spectrum of learner behaviours in the HEIs which, combined with the institutional habitus, had a powerful impact on how the case study students developed as learners over the research period. At one end the College and Northern where for the students, jostling work and family commitments with doing a degree, the development of student learner identities was not central. For mature students and younger women their learner identities, stemming from previous school experiences, remain relatively fragile and unconfident. However, this self-doubt expressed about their worthiness of being at university at all, as Leathwood and O'Connell (2003) and Bartky (1990) argue, is less about personal inadequacies and more to do with systems of oppression and social relations.

Students at Southern and to a lesser degree Midland had been identified as high achievers from early on in their school careers, equipping them with confident learner identities. Enveloped in a highly competitive, learning intensive environment at Southern and captured by the social but also academic ethos at Midland, being a student becomes the individual's main source of identity. This in itself becomes generative of success. At Southern being an academically successful student becomes an all-consuming preoccupation.

The powerful influence of the institutional cultures can be seen in the students' reference to the pressure on them to excel at Southern or feelings of not being sufficiently challenged, articulated by some Northern students (93 per cent of Southern students rated intellectual challenge as either 5 (high) or 4, compared to 56 per cent Midland and 39 per cent Northern). At Northern, exceptional students stood out and had to rely on their own motivation and self-regulation (Vermunt 1998), whereas at Southern they competed for the 'exceptional' status (see also Reay *et al.* forthcoming).

The structure of the pedagogy had a strong impact on the students' ability to make sense of and navigate their way through the learning process and to acquire in Bernstein's (1996) terms the 'realisation and recognition rules'. These structures are, for example, tightly 'framed' (ibid.) at Southern, thus facilitating this acquisition, and weakly framed at Northern, thus impeding it. At Northern where students were not required to attend lectures, were permitted to hand in work late and could re-sit failed assessments several times and where relationships with tutors were informal, they also lamented being left to their own devices and desired more structured discussion of ideas (see also Crozier and Reay 2008).

At Southern with its stronger framing and intense 'pacing', seminars and tutorials are explicitly about mastery and competitiveness. The norm is to be extremely hard working to the point of not being able to switch off. Working-class students at Southern, notwithstanding their social anxieties, are enabled to succeed. At the other institutions the process is more complex and convoluted. There are tensions between the academic rigour and requirements and desire to accommodate a diversity of personal experiences and commitments as explained by the tutors we interviewed, particularly at Northern and Eastern. The research shows that unintentionally, this often has a counterproductive effect.

'Belonging and fitting-in', a central theme in widening participation discourse (e.g. Read *et al.* 2003; Archer *et al.* 2003), often attributed as a barrier to university access or access to learning, is more complex and nuanced than hitherto suggested. It is not, in our view, a unitary experience but applies to both learner and social identifications. At Northern and Eastern, the working-class students fitted in socially with some ease but as learners several of the Northern students who felt passionate about their subject, were committed and hard working, felt at odds with their peers who tended to be more laid-back learners (Reay *et al.* 2009). On the other hand, working-class students at Southern, whilst at times anxious and overwhelmed by the social aspects, are much more like fish in, rather than out of, water, academically. On going there they find, in a sense, the coming together of their academic/learner identities, surrounded by others intellectually like them in contrast to their school experiences. For Midland students there is more diversity in all respects and therefore more opportunities for the students to find their niche, and people with whom they can or want to identify.

All the students in our study succeeded academically (including, for example, four firsts and several going on to postgraduate study) displaying significant levels of commitment and resilience, at times against the odds. For all students studying is challenging, angst ridden work, but for some it is made easier than for others.

7 Surfing the boundaries: the impact of the university experiences on students' identities

As we have already indicated, to different extents the students in the different HEIs experienced competing identities which impacted on their social involvement and also academic behaviour. However, we found no evidence of the dis-identification Skeggs (1997) writes of in her study of working-class women. Rather, a strong sense of class pride amongst the case study students, especially in their own achievement at having got to university (Crozier et al. forthcoming), was asserted. But whilst there was little attempt to seek middle-class respectability (ibid.) in an overt sense, it became clear that the students' identities were challenged by others or by their perceptions of how others saw them in a negative and conflictual way.

Although at Northern the working-class students felt socially comfortable blending into the 'expressive order' (Bernstein 1975), some expressed the anxiety of potential rejection on leaving this apparent comfort zone, such as Kylie who had applied to an elite university for postgraduate study. At Southern, students experienced 'the shock of the elite', which meant they could take nothing for granted (Reay et al. forthcoming), and at Midland, both white and Asian students talked about seeking out people 'like them' rather than being forced to fit into social networks with which they did not feel comfortable. This defended behaviour did compound a certain marginalisation as Nasir gradually realised when he reflected on only knowing 'other' Asians.

While middle-class students are located in a familiar social field, working-class students experience a disjunction between their habitus and field experience and they find they are forced to engage in acts of reinvention; for them habitus is 'being restructured, transformed in its make up by the press of the objective structures' (Bourdieu 2005: 47). Although none talked about proactively changing in order to access requisite capitals to progress academically, there is evidence of the need to change an accent or ways of presenting themselves in order to be taken seriously, as one young male South Asian student at Midland put it. Classed and ethnicised masculinities frequently emerged as an issue when students referred to their experiences in the university. At Midland working-class male, white and Asian, students were often constructed by their middle-class counterparts as 'threatening' and 'unrefined'. One South Asian student mused on whether this was class or ethnically based or indeed both. Another working-class male student at Southern talked about the contrast between his 'drunken antics . . . having a laugh' with friends at home, whilst at Southern you need to 'tiptoe' around people, and 'watch what you say' for fear of offending them or in case the sentiment is misunderstood.

However, the working-class students are not merely adapting to or managing their social and cultural identities in the university, they have to do something similar in their home communities. Not only do they need to 'code switch' between different sites and social milieux but more than that there are other possibly more challenging or complex strategies required, such as turning away from old friends with whom they find they have nothing left in common – a concern expressed particularly by male students. Also Bhavesh, for example, at Midland, as a successful academic student had to deal with accusations of 'acting white' (Fordham and Ogbu 1986) from his peers at home, which confronts him with a dilemma as to who he is.

For the women students, identity conflicts most often manifested themselves in these latter respects, with the challenge to the gendered expectations of mother, daughter, sister and so on. The students' families seemingly relied heavily on them and there were often tensions between university and family competing demands. As Edwards (1993) has noted these are greedy institutions but unlike her we found that it was not only mature students who were affected.

Consequently the students move in and out of different identity constructions between university and home, marked out by class, ethnicity, masculinities and gendered expectations. Their identities are thus fragmented and often contradictory: a 'lived identity' (Grossberg 1996: 91) formation akin to 'a kind of disassembled and reassembled unity' (Haraway 1991: 74 cited in ibid.). Some embrace this change but most dip in and out and occupy the twilight space of identity, or what Bhabha (1996) calls 'the in between space (in Grossberg 1996: 91). They are hybrids but this hybridisation is not a bringing together of equal parts. It is the struggle over unequal differences that is troubling and disruptive (see Crozier et al. forthcoming for more on this).

8 Conclusions

Existing research in relation to HE student success indicates that in the UK there is an emphasis on the importance of prior educational experience (Mussellbrook and Dean 2003; Wingate and Macaro 2004), whilst in the USA there has been a greater concern with 'integration' (Tinto 1996; Pascarella and Terenzini 2005). Utilising the concept of habitus and institutional habitus (Reay *et al.* 2005) we have shown how, in related but different ways, both of these aspects are important for the development of effective learner identities. Our data reveal not only the powerful influences of prior learning experiences and dispositions but also the dynamic between these and students' academic contexts as well as university strategies to 'bind in' the students. However, there are also problems with the strategy of 'integration' with the emphasis on the student to change rather than the institution and its inherent practices; these as we and others (e.g. Bowl 2006; Leathwood and O'Connell 2003; Stewart 2008) have shown are classed, raced and gendered. In particular through this comparative study, we point to the significance of structural inequalities that exist between the universities and how these impact on the experience of the students.

The mechanisms by which such inequalities have been perpetuated in the learning situation, albeit frequently unrecognised by tutors, have been explained, in part, by utilising aspects of Bernstein's pedagogic device (1996). Strong framing (Bernstein 1996) of teaching is associated with social control and reproduction. Once the student has been accepted, Southern University, protecting its reputation, has to ensure that s/he succeeds. Tight control over the learning experience is thus a prerequisite. The strong framing provided clear sequencing of work and led to clarity of expectation – a visible pedagogy. Based on a clear and informative structure, the working-class students, whilst initially unprepared for what to expect, were enabled to develop strong confident learner identities and behaviours leading to success.

At Northern the loose framing intended as a supportive approach in many ways has been seen to compound students' lack of cultural capital and confusion. For them the experience is frequently fragmented and the lack of intensity unintentionally conspires to undermine the efforts of those who are ambitious and passionate about their subject. Students' anxieties about what they do not know and the implications of this for their progress is at times palpable. This renders them dependent learners, craving tutor contact and the desire to be told what to do. Where students start their university careers without the 'realisation rules' (Bernstein 1996), then loose framing (usually associated with creative possibilities) rather than liberating student learning would seem to have the opposite effect.

We have also shown the necessity of separating out learners from social identities, and the need to understand the varying extent to which individuals are able to move in and out of different identity positionings. So, for example, our Southern students are increasingly able to be recognised as highly successful learners rather than as working-class young men and women. In Eastern and Northern, however, class identities are more fixed and fixing.

Working-class students as we have shown can benefit from the institutional effect of a privileged university. However for all working-class students to different degrees there are psychic costs involved in the identity struggles as learners in a middle-class milieu. For some the process is more about finding themselves than changing and are thus liberatory. Although the students are confronted with their own difference and do at times adapt and reformulate their identities accordingly, this is not a passive capitulation. Whilst the process can be troubling, following Bhabha (1996) and Bakhtin (1981), we argue, it can and for most of them has been, agentic. Universities traditionally have not been places for the working class. Here we demonstrate how the working-class students navigate their way through at times inhospitable but frequently unknown waters, making or appropriating the space for themselves and hopefully 'others like them'. In these ways, as others have found (Goodwin 2006), the working-class students develop resilience in the journey towards success.

Access, participation and diversity questions in relation to different forms of post-compulsory further and higher education

Learners' transition from vocational education and training to higher education

Hubert Ertl, Geoff Hayward and Michael Hölscher

1 Introduction and context

The current debate on widening participation in relation to Vocational Education and Training (VET) needs to consider two issues. First, as we saw in the introduction, educational participation beyond the compulsory school age has increased in the UK since 1945, with a massive increase in participation in full-time provision between 1985 and 1994. The increase can partly be attributed to the increased availability of vocationally oriented qualifications aimed at 16 year olds. Definitions of what constitutes 'vocational qualifications' differ greatly in terms of what they classify as 'vocational'. The analysis here follows pragmatic considerations which are based on classifications of qualifications as used by UCAS because this is regarded as the only sensible way to interpret qualification backgrounds on the basis of access datasets compiled by UCAS.

Vocationally oriented qualifications were seen as a decisive pre-condition for widening participation in HE (see, for instance, Education and Employment Committee 2001: 33; HEFCE 2000). However, international studies have shown that this connection is not necessarily valid. For instance, the empirical study of thirteen countries by Blossfeld and Shavit comprehensively negates the thesis which assumes 'that educational expansion results in greater equality of educational opportunity' (1991: 29). The same conclusion was reached in a more recent study of fifteen countries (see Shavit *et al.* 2007). In terms of access to HE, despite the overall expansion of the sector, the incremental growth in student numbers remains greatest for middle-class students holding traditional GCE A-level qualifications (Ball 2003; Sutton Trust 2005).

The second issue is that the increase in participation in post-compulsory education suggests that the expansionist aims have been achieved in secondary education, partly by a substantial increase in participation in vocationally oriented programmes. However, a US study of educational participation concludes that: 'vocational education at the secondary level . . . does inhibit students' chances of continuing on to college and as such, it probably inhibits their chances of reaching the professions and most prestigious occupations' (Arum and Shavit 1993: 20). Investigation into the educational value of these qualifications as currency for further progression has concluded that they only offer a 'mirage of wider opportunities' (Pugsley 2004: 28). Each wave of new vocationally oriented qualifications has added to the tendency towards educational credentialism.

Within current UK policy a key lever for raising the perceived value of Vocational Qualifications (VQs) is to ensure that they provide a means for progressing into, and providing a solid basis for, study in higher education. This policy is framed around the social acceptability of VQs to HE by young people and their families based on signals from HE (Pugsley 2004). However, little is known about the transition into, and progression within, HE of those holding level 3 VQs.

This study investigated whether growing participation in VET has resulted in increasing participation of people with a vocational background in UK higher education and whether this has, in turn, contributed to widening participation in terms of women and men from socio-economic backgrounds and/or regions that had not previously participated. Existing studies (Gokulsing et al. 1996; Bynner and Roberts 1991; Ainley 1999) cannot provide an overview of the current situation, given recent qualification changes such as Curriculum 2000. Furthermore, such research could also provide important insights for those hoping to use the new diplomas to support progression into higher education; for example, what qualifications to incorporate as additional and specialist learning. The project also looked at the first-year experience of students in higher education and combined this with application and access data.

The *Degrees of Success* project aimed to investigate how people with vocational qualifications make the transition to higher education and consisted of three interlocking parts. First, based on an analysis of large-scale student datasets, we look at the transition patterns of students with VET qualifications to HE, comparing the transition success in terms of access and retention with that of other students. We then provide some explanations for the differences in transition patterns by looking at data from five institutional cases studies on expectations and perceptions of preparedness of students.

2 Transition patterns

The investigation first involved using large administrative datasets supplied by UCAS and the Higher Education Statistics Agency (HESA) for the academic years beginning 1995, 2003 and 2004. The spread of years encompassed the changes to the post-16 curriculum known as the Curriculum 2000 reforms. This involved the introduction of a reformed GCE A-level, split between AS and A2, and vocational successors to Advanced GNVQs, called initially Advanced Vocational Certificates of Education (AVCEs), subsequently applied A-levels and now just GCE A-levels. The reformed GCE A-levels and the AVCEs were unitised according to a common format which, it was hoped, would lead to an increase in mixing and matching of the two types of qualification by post-16 learners. More traditional vocational qualifications, such as NVQs and SVQs, remained available along with a host of vocationally related and other vocational qualifications, such as BTEC Nationals. Students taking these qualifications and the new VCEs (along with their Scottish counterparts) were designated as being in a vocational pathway in our analysis. Learners taking GCE A-levels or Scottish Highers and Advanced Highers were deemed to be participating in an academic pathway.

2.1 Applicants' qualification background

The first step in the analysis was to assess how application rates from the different pathways had changed over time. The UCAS datasets contain reasonably detailed (but not exhaustive) information about prior qualifications. On the basis of this information, five educational backgrounds could be differentiated (Hölscher and Hayward (2008) provides further details of the coding frame):

* general academic
* vocational
* Foundation and Access courses (FaA)
* other
* no qualifications.

Table 3.3.1 shows the changes in proportions applying for HE from the different qualification groups. There are distinct changes over time. The number of applicants holding a general academic qualification has increased by 5 per cent over the last ten years, resulting in an overwhelming majority of applicants coming through the traditional general academic route. An even larger increase can be found for applicants holding vocational qualifications. They increased their share from around 18 per cent to 25 per cent over the same time span. However, the biggest increase can be found for 'other' qualifications. UK and Overseas Degrees account for just over 20 per cent of all 'Other' qualifications in 2003 and 2004. Interestingly, the share of people coming from a Foundation/Access (FaA) background is more stable over time, despite the introduction of the new Foundation qualification during the period analysed. Around 44 per cent of these applicants have completed the newly introduced Foundation courses (not available in 1995). Foundation courses are one-year university preparation courses suitable for mature students who may not have formal qualifications, and also for students of any age without the entry qualifications for specific degree programmes, especially overseas students who have studied a non-British curriculum. The number of applicants with no reported qualification has decreased by half.

One main message from Table 3.3.1 is the overall increase in the different types of qualifications held by an individual. We provide a more comprehensive analysis of the UCAS applications dataset in Hölscher and Hayward (2008). While in 1995 only a small minority (7 per cent) held qualifications from different pathways, this number has increased to 27 per cent in 2003/04. The increase of around 12 per cent in the overall figures of applicants (see Table 3.3.1) was accompanied by an increase in the diversity of the qualifications held from different pathways. Thus, the increase in the shares of applicants holding a certain qualification does not tell the whole story. The figures for each year in Table 3.3.1 add up to more than 100 per cent because women and men can hold qualifications from more than one strand.

The different combinations of qualifications were therefore recoded into distinct qualification pathways. Out of the four qualification strands, seven 'educational pathways' an applicant could progress through to HE were created:

- only general academic ('Academic')
- only vocational qualifications ('Vocational')
- only Foundation and Access-courses ('FaA')

Table 3.3.1 Qualifications held by applicants (%)

	1995	2003	2004
General academic	70.7	75.3	75.7
Vocational	17.8	25.8	24.9
Foundation/Access	7.8	8.6	8.9
Other	5.1	13.5	14.1
No qualification	6.0	3.5	3.2
TOTAL	107.4	126.7	126.8

Source: UCAS applications data

Note: more than 100%, as applicants can hold multiple qualifications

- only other ('Other')
- academic and vocational qualifications ('Ac + Voc'),
- academic and FaA ('Ac + FaA')
- any other combination ('Other combination').

Table 3.3.2 shows the proportions progressing through these pathways, now adding up to 100 per cent.

The growing diversity of qualification types that applicants hold is again clearly visible. The first three groups decreased over time, while 'Other' and combinations of different pathways increased. Nevertheless, the 'Academic' group is still the biggest, accounting for more than half of all applicants.

The increase in vocational qualifications (Table 3.3.1) is mostly a result of an increase in their combination with academic qualifications. While the 'Vocational' group was much larger than the combined 'Ac + Voc' group in 1995, it decreased over time, and in 2003/04 the combined group is the larger group, having more than tripled its share of all applicants. However, the changes might be, at least in part, a result of changes in the coding of data by UCAS for the different years. It would appear, though, that the curriculum 2000 reforms did achieve a desired outcome: an increase in the proportion of students that hold both vocational and academic qualifications.

Hölscher and Hayward (2008) provide a more detailed analysis of the socio-demographic characteristics of learners progressing into HE through the different pathways shown in Table 3.3.2. Looking at these characteristics, it becomes obvious that vocational routes open access to HE for non-traditional students, that is, they contribute to reaching the policy targets for widening participation. Applicants with a vocational background are from lower socio-economic groups, are more often male and from a non-white ethnic background and are more often disabled, than those from the traditional general academic route.

Table 3.3.2 Qualification pathways (%)

	1995	2003	2004
Academic	63.4	50.8	51.3
Vocational	13.6	10.1	9.5
FaA	6.2	3.9	4.2
Other	3.5	5.9	6.0
Ac + Voc	4.2	14.1	13.7
Ac + FaA	1.5	3.2	3.1
Other combination	1.6	8.5	8.9
No qualification	6.0	3.5	3.2
Total	100	100	100

Source: UCAS applications data

However, their distribution over the HE sector is very uneven: they are over-represented in new institutions and other HE providers, such as FE colleges, and under-represented in the old HEIs. The possible economic and policy consequences of this are discussed in the concluding chapters of this volume.

2.2 Transition success

The figures in Tables 3.3.1 and 3.3.2 were constructed from UCAS data about applicants. The next step is to assess the success of the transition process for those with VET backgrounds into HE compared to other applicants. This assessment was made using a longitudinal dataset which enables a learner to be tracked from their point of application to the end of their first year in HE. This longitudinal dataset was constructed by matching 2002/03 UCAS data providing information about applicants with the corresponding Higher Education Statistics Agency (HESA) data for those who subsequently progress into HE in the academic year 2003/04.

While this is a potentially very large dataset it does have certain limitations; for example, the UCAS data do not contain data for those applying via direct entry, many of whom will be part-time students and older (and thus non-traditional). Furthermore, these data tell us nothing about students who did not apply to HE at all even though they may have had level 3 qualifications which would have supported their progression. However, Fuller *et al.* provide insights into this group in Chapter 5. In addition, there is much missing data. To cope with these issues the analysis was confined to those individuals from the HESA dataset who were in their first year of study, were studying full time for their first degree, who were aged under 21 years (non-mature), attending English HEIs, and were matched with the UCAS data. This gives a total of 204,567 cases. This represents the population of these individuals, that is, this is not a sample but a census, so making judgements about differences between sub-groups using inferential statistical procedures is not appropriate.

This combined dataset was then used to answer two questions. Compared to students with other educational backgrounds, how likely are applicants with a VET background to:

* be successful in reaching HE once they have made an application?
* reach the end of their first year of university study, that is, not drop out?

Figure 3.3.1 provides data on the percentage of students applying from different pathways who are successful in obtaining a place in HE and continuing into their second year. Clearly compared to traditional A-level students, those with VET qualifications have a higher risk of both not obtaining a place in HE and then of dropping out during or at the end of

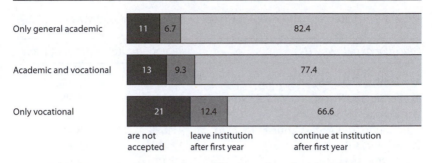

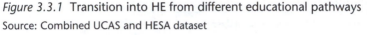

Figure 3.3.1 Transition into HE from different educational pathways

Source: Combined UCAS and HESA dataset

their first year. The efficiency of the transition process is clearly much higher for those combining academic and vocational pathways: they are nearly as successful at entering and completing their first year of HE as those with only general academic qualifications.

The reasons for the poorer application success rate for those with VET qualifications are difficult to understand. It is most likely the result of an interaction of processes operating at the level of the students (perceptions, self-limitations) and at the level of the institutions (tracking, problems with admission for non-traditional qualifications). For example, an analysis of an addition UCAS dataset on non-placed applicants, within which those holding VET qualifications are over represented, reveals that those who are not placed are likely, for example, to apply to just one or two HEIs often local to them (Wilde and Hölscher 2007). Such behaviour, while rational for those with family responsibilities, for example, nonetheless limits scope for being successful in the application process. Within HEIs there is a degree of ignorance about the possible utility of non-traditional qualifications to support progression into HE and the continual reform of the 16–19 education and training system militates against HE admission staff understanding an increasingly complex qualifications landscape (Wilde *et al.* 2006). Clearly this is an issue that requires further research.

2.3 Retention and drop-out

A particular concern here is how educational background affects retention. Table 3.3.3 provides figures for retention and drop-out rates for those progressing through different pre-HE pathways.

From this simple cross-tabulation it is evident that a VET background clearly has a negative impact on retention rates at the end of the first year of study. This could be the result of several factors. Clearly one of these is prior attainment – we can assume that those with higher prior attainment are more likely to stay on in HE. Second, the risk of dropping out could be

Table 3.3.3 Retention and drop-out rates by educational pathway

Educational pathway (N)	Retention rate	Drop-out rate
Academic (150,786)	92.9%	7.1%
Academic and Vocational (23,235)	92.1%	7.9%
Vocational (15,581)	86.4%	13.6%
Foundation and Access courses (5,716)	91.6%	8.4%
Other (8,979)	87.4%	12.6%
Total (204,567)	92.1%	7.9%

Source: Combined UCAS and HESA dataset

influenced by the institution chosen. The HEI might be highly competitive or offer bad teaching and support for VET students. Third, the chosen subject may influence the likelihood of dropping out. Some subjects may be more difficult and therefore have higher drop-out rates.

The influence of these factors could also be different for different educational backgrounds. For example, it might be the case that vocational qualifications prepare students well for some subjects (resulting in a low drop-out rate), but not for others (resulting in a higher drop-out rate). Or it might be that some institutions offer teaching styles that are adapted to the needs of students with 'non-academic' qualifications. Some HEIs might provide other forms of institutional support specifically geared to meeting the needs of VET students. To test these alternative explanations multi-level analysis was undertaken.

2.4 Multi-level analysis

A fixed effects model (see Hölscher 2008 for technical and statistical details) indicates that:

- increased tariff points (a proxy for prior attainment) significantly reduces the probability of drop-out;
- belonging to a higher socio-economic group, being black or Asian, and having a disability all significantly reduce the risk of drop-out;
- gender has no significant effect on the likelihood of dropping out;
- controlling for these socio-demographic variables VET students are significantly more likely to drop out compared to those from a traditional academic background, but there is no significant effect for those progressing through other non-traditional routes such as access courses;
- those progressing through a combined academic-vocational route are not significantly more likely to drop out compared to those progressing through the traditional academic route;

- progressing through clearing significantly increases the risk of dropping out.

It would seem then, *ceteris paribus*, that progressing to HE through a VET pathway is associated with increased risk of dropping out by the end of the first year compared to students progressing through a more traditional academic pathway. However, in a fixed effects model we assume that the effect of progressing through the VET pathway is the same in all institutions. It might be that some institutions are more responsive to VET students. We have concluded that lecturers at different HEIs have very different attitudes towards students with a VET background which determines their responsiveness to these students' particular needs. (This is further presented in Chapter 7.) To assess this requires the use of a random slopes model which allows the VET background variable to have a different influence in different HEIs. In this model, unlike the fixed effects model, the main fixed effect of the probability of dropping out for those progressing through the VET route, compared to those progressing through a more traditional academic pathway, is no longer significant.

What this means is that the influence of VET background on the propensity to dropout is significantly different for different institutions. The evidence indicates that in institutions with high drop-out rates, VET students have an increased risk of dropping out. Which institutions are these? The evidence from this analysis is equivocal. It is certainly not the case that new, other HE providers and old institutions differ significantly from each other. There is some evidence to suggest that a higher research quality rating, as proxied by the RAE 2001 scores, slightly reduces the risk of drop-out, but Quality Assurance Agency for Higher Education teaching quality scores are not correlated with the propensity to drop out.

It could be that VET students do better in institutions with a greater proportion of VET students (an observation often made for minority ethnic students). There is some weak evidence to support this view: it does appear beneficial for VET students to study at an institution with high proportion of VET students. However, we cannot establish if this effect is a result of motivation effects on the student level or a more sensitive approach of these institutions towards the needs of VET students using the administrative datasets employed in this analysis.

To conclude, the multilevel analysis suggests that institutions seem to have a greater influence on the likelihood of dropping out than subjects. Contrary to the descriptive analysis results, the multilevel analysis reveals that progressing through a VET pathway does not increase the risk of drop-out per se. Such students are more vulnerable and have an increased risk of dropping out in HEIs with higher drop-out rates overall. It seems as if VET students perform better, in terms of reduced risk of drop-out, in HEIs with a higher proportion of VET students. Possible explanations for this pattern of behaviour are not well documented in the literature and need to be sought in the case study data.

3 Transition experience

A lack of appropriate teaching and support structures at HEIs were put forward as one possible reason for the overall higher drop-out rates of VET students compared with students from an academic background. The varying degrees to which HEIs make an effort to accommodate VET students or not could also explain the significant differences in drop-out rates of these students between HEIs. However, both explanations rely on the assumption that the different qualification background of VET students results in particular needs and expectations of this student group. This assumption is now discussed in the light of our questionnaire data.

3.1 Expectations and 'preparedness' of students

We conducted two questionnaire surveys with the entire intake of students in three subject areas (business, computing and nursing) at five UK HEIs for the 2006–07 academic year. The analysis here focuses on questionnaire items in the first questionnaire related to expectations and perceptions of preparedness of students in order to develop an understanding of possible differences in what different student groups expect and need from HEIs (see Appendix 4 for details).

In the questionnaire we asked the students to express their degree of agreement with three statements concerning their preparation for their course, expectations of their course and expectations of their HEI (survey items 12a, 15b and 18b, given in the following tables). The students answered on a five-point scale ranging from 1 ('unprepared/not met') to 5 ('well-prepared/completely met'), and additionally, in items 12b, 12c, 15a and 18a, they were asked to give further details about their response.

In Table 3.3.4 one can see the mean scores (and standard deviations in brackets) for questions 12a, 15b and 18b by the qualification pathway of the students who responded to those items. Mean scores of 3 or higher indicate agreement with the statements; the higher the mean score the stronger the agreement.

Despite the differences in the means, considering the large standard deviations, it can be concluded that there are no systematic differences in the overall perception of preparedness and expectations between the students in our sample according to their educational background. The same is true if the data on preparedness is analysed in terms of subject and higher education institutions (Dunbar-Goddet and Ertl 2008).

Important differences appear, however, when the open-ended responses of students to items referring to preparedness and expectations are analysed. In these items, students were asked to explain what made them

Table 3.3.4 Mean scores (and SDs) by qualification pathway

Item	Aca-demic	Voca-tional	FaA	Ac + Voc	Over-all
12a Please indicate, on a scale of 1 to 5, how prepared you feel for your current course	3.50 (.80)	3.64 (.86)	3.42 (1.08)	3.68 (.81)	3.59 (.84)
15b Expectations of course: Please indicate, on a scale of 1 to 5, how far those expectations have been met to date	3.33 (.96)	3.31 (1.04)	3.15 (.86)	3.37 (.98)	3.35 (.99)
18b Expectations of HEI: Please indicate, on a scale of 1 to 5, how far those expectations have been met to date	3.63 (.85)	3.59 (.96)	3.32 (1.07)	3.76 (.91)	3.66 (.91)

Source: Transition to HE Questionnaire (Ertl and Dunbar-Goddet 2008)

feel prepared for their current course and what kinds of expectations they have regarding their HEI. The categorisation of open-ended answers was developed by grouping responses in emergent themes, rather than by imposing pre-conceived categories. This process resulted in a rich tapestry of patterns in student responses, which highlights the diversity of students' backgrounds and resulting assumptions about, and perceptions of, HE. Ertl and Dunbar-Goddet (2008) provide illustrative examples of the categories developed for the analysis of open-ended questionnaire items.

As can be seen in Table 3.3.5 there is a stark difference between the academic and vocational students in what they report makes them feel prepared. For the students with an academic background it is mainly academic preparatory work and for those with a vocational background time and activity organisation are the main sources of preparedness. VET students also regard the advice and guidance they receive as a main source of preparation.

The analysis of the complementary question (*Please tell us what makes you feel unprepared*) indicates that nearly all the categories of qualification backgrounds report that what makes them feel unprepared is mainly a lack of academic skills and confidence. However, this is more pronounced for students with a vocational background compared with their counterparts from an academic background (Ertl and Dunbar-Goddet 2008).

The responses to the open-ended questions regarding expectations of course and HEI were also coded according to categories emerging from

Table 3.3.5 Sources of preparedness by qualification pathway

Category	% within pathway	
	Academic	*Vocational*
Academic preparatory work	25.77	10.17
Prior qualification	24.23	16.95
Advice and guidance	19.07	22.03
Motivation and family support	11.86	11.87
Prior work experience	10.82	15.25
Time and activity organisation	8.25	23.73
Total	100	100

Source: Transition to HE Questionnaire (see Ertl and Dunbar-Goddet 2008)

the data. Table 3.3.6 provides an overview of the most important categories of expectations given by academic and vocational students regarding their HEI.

The overview shows that the category 'providing a learning environment' is the most important expectation for both groups of students. However, this is closely followed by the expectation that institutions should 'provide support and guidance' as far as vocational students are concerned – a category that is less important for academic students who are more interested in the qualification at the end of their course. Even more striking is the result that over 20 per cent of vocational students in our sample explicitly stated that they have no particular expectations of their HEI at all. Together with the high expectation of support and guidance, this seems to indicate a pronounced uncertainty of vocational students about the

Table 3.3.6 Students' expectations of institutions by qualification pathway

Category	% within pathway	
	Academic	*Vocational*
Provide a qualification	24.61	13.64
Provide a learning environment	31.94	29.55
Provide support and guidance	18.32	27.27
Provide facilities or resources	12.04	4.55
Provide a social environment	9.95	4.55
No expectations	3.14	20.45
Total	100	100

Source: Transition to HE Questionnaire (see Ertl and Dunbar-Goddet 2008)

context in which HE takes place and a strong need for assistance in developing an understanding of this context at the beginning of their HE studies.

Accounts in student interviews show the variety of teaching strategies and support mechanisms that HEIs employ to respond to the needs and expectations of students with a vocational background. For instance, students from all five institutions investigated (but not necessarily from each programme) mention support groups in which VET students come together and discuss their particular problems. However, the organisation of these groups varies from those formally organised by the teaching staff who also provide input and advice in these groups, to groups initiated by students themselves, in some cases overcoming substantial difficulties regarding finding space and time. The analysis of the interviews we conducted with teaching staff at our five case study institutions demonstrates that lecturers' awareness of the particular needs of VET students ranges from highly developed to non-existent (see discussion in Chapter 7). It can therefore be concluded that the evidence on what VET students look for in HEIs and what they find in HEIs and the discrepancy between the two can to some extent explain diverse patterns of drop-out of these students across the sector.

4 Conclusions

The analysis regarding expectations of and preparedness for higher education study presented shows notable differences between students with different educational backgrounds. The most important difference between students coming to HE from VET compared with students coming with academic qualification is the greater need of VET students for advice and guidance. This is reflected in the data on students' expectations as well as on their perceived preparedness for HE study. An in-depth analysis of the responses to the relevant open-ended questions in our questionnaire and of interviews with students shows that the kind of advice and guidance VET student have in mind is not what standardised advice services at HEIs usually provide. Instead, these students look for individualised support which takes their particular situation and needs into account. Evidence from interviews with students also suggests that for many VET students, academic advice on how to effectively integrate their vocational background and experience into their new learning environment is central to this individualised support. This kind of support can only be provided by their lecturers and academic tutors.

Access, participation and diversity questions in relation to different forms of post-compulsory further and higher education

Seamlessness or separation: negotiating further and higher education boundaries in dual sector institutions

Ann-Marie Bathmaker

1 Introduction

The growth of 'dual sector' institutions, which offer what in England would be defined as 'further' (post-school, but not necessarily higher level) as well as 'higher' education, is one aspect of increasingly differentiated systems of higher education in a number of countries. Gareth Parry's chapter in this volume (see Chapter 2) sets the scene for how researchers in a number of countries have investigated the emergence of dual-sector institutions and their role in creating a seamless system of lifelong education which overcomes the boundaries between different sectors in post-secondary education (Doughney 2000; Gallacher 2005; Garrod and Macfarlane 2007; Keating 2006). A seamless system, it is argued, might promote social justice, by improving progression into higher education by those traditionally under-represented in HE (Garrod and Macfarlane 2007).

This section focuses on how seamlessness plays out in practice, by considering students' experience of moving across boundaries between further and higher education in 'dual sector' FE/HE institutions. It draws on data from the FurtherHigher Project, which focused on the role of dual sector institutions in widening participation in England. One strand of the project considered the relationship between further and higher education in four exemplar institutions, focusing on the opportunities and practices related to internal transitions. Fieldwork for the study involved eleven learning sites across the four institutions. Eighty-two students were interviewed during 2006 and 2007, as well as lecturers involved in teaching the students. Students' experiences in two learning sites are referred to in this chapter: one which came closest to seamless internal connections between FE and HE provision and the other where there was strong separation. The focus here is on what students' experience of moving between FE and HE reveals about the possibilities for seamlessness in these two dual sector institutions.

Notions of seamlessness and duality do not go uncontested in the literature on widening participation. Young (2006) believes that seamlessness focuses on the opportunities for increasing the numbers of learners who can move easily into programmes at any level and from one type of programme to another, to the detriment of understanding the special characteristics of different forms of knowledge. I have argued elsewhere (Bathmaker 2008; Bathmaker and Thomas 2009), as does Wheelahan (2009), that duality may mean access to certain forms of (lower status) higher education only. Various researchers across different countries (Gallacher 2006; Grubb 2006) note that the latter is associated with lower level resourcing, completion rates and occupational destinations. Nevertheless, as Cristofoli and Watts (2005) in England, and Grubb (2006) in the USA observe, students would probably not have entered HE at all if their participation had not been in 'dual sector' types of provision.

2 Overcoming boundaries through seamlessness

Of the many boundaries and barriers to higher education facing students from non-traditional and diverse backgrounds which have been identified in the literature (Gorard et al. 2006), 'seamless' dual sector institutions appear to offer a distinct opportunity compared with other HE institutions to enable students to deal with boundaries related to space and place, and boundaries related to knowledge. Boundaries of space and place refer here to boundaries which turn HE into a more or less alien or familiar world. Such boundaries are therefore not just about the geographical accessibility of HE provision, but, as Patiniotis and Holdsworth (2005) discuss in their study of HE students staying or leaving home, they are about the 'ontological security' that is afforded by familiarity and confidence about space and place. Duality, with the possibility of transition from FE to HE within the same institution, suggests the possibility that HE might be rendered a less alien world.

Knowledge boundaries are here used to mean boundaries between levels and types of knowledge, particularly between theoretical and applied knowledge, or academic and vocational knowledge, and the varying relationship and balance between these different forms of knowledge at different levels of study. Here too, dual sector institutions would appear to be in a position to create connections between FE and HE study which support effective boundary-crossing. In such ways boundaries might no longer represent barriers between FE and HE. The following discussion of FE/HE boundary-crossing in two dual sector institutions in the Further-Higher project focuses on these two concerns, and contrasts one learning site which appeared to be working towards 'seamlessness', with another, where there was strong separation between FE and HE.

3 Attempting 'seamlessness': culinary education at Citygate College

The culinary education learning site represented a long-standing specialism at Citygate College (a specialist HE institution). Provision ranged from occupational National Vocational Qualifications (NVQs), through to Masters degrees. The college offered a Bachelor degree and a two-year Foundation degree in Culinary Arts. Just over 20 per cent of students on the FE NVQ3 (28 out of 137) progressed to the college's degree programmes in 2005/06, suggesting a possible seamless relationship between FE and HE.

Whereas in most sites in the FurtherHigher study there was a strong separation between FE and HE provision, in terms of both geographical location of provision and different staff teaching on programmes, culinary education at Citygate College was in marked contrast. All levels of culinary education were taught in one location in the college, because of the need for specialist kitchen facilities. This meant that tutors and students on FE and HE programmes shared rooms and resources and sometimes worked within close proximity. FE students would therefore be aware of students doing culinary education in HE. In addition, because the college was a former FE college, most of the seventeen staff teaching on the degree programmes had experience of teaching in FE and HE, and five of them continued to do so.

The FE students were therefore familiar with the environment where HE practical work took place. This was their milieu, where they were confident of their knowledge and skills. One of the students described how this confidence carried through into the degree programme, when he had to manage a group preparing main courses in the kitchen during his first year on the degree:

> I was the only FDA, ex NVQ. I'm the only one who really knew how to do the cooking like, so I had to be chucked on that section because that was the hardest section [main courses]. So the rest of them – I'm not saying they don't know what they're doing but they haven't got as much experience.
>
> (James, Culinary Education, Citygate College)

Students' confidence also appeared to be strengthened by the pride they showed in the college. The students we interviewed identified with the college in ways described by Marks (2002) as more typical of students attending 'old' universities:

> I thought the College has probably the best reputation in the country – well it does have the best reputation.
>
> (Paul, Culinary Education, Citygate College)

> They say it's the best one in the country isn't it I think. You've got to have the best haven't you?
>
> (Matt, Culinary Education, Citygate College)

The college's reputation matched their aspirations to become chefs, for, as James explained, students dreamed of running their own business:

> Well I want, like everyone else, I want my own little place but I just want to work up to somewhere, nice place, head chef or manager, something like that. And then years down the line a little place somewhere.
>
> (James, Culinary Education, Citygate College)

In the practice context the FE students saw themselves as fitting in readily to a familiar environment. In contrast, students found the difference between theoretical study on the degree and their previous experience in FE much more challenging. On the NVQ programme James explained:

> We didn't really get the theory, it's just the odd, probably one lesson a week we did theory, back then that was just to fill in so you could answer the questions at the end of the folders. . . . But now this is a lot of theory so . . . it is quite stressful.

Students were also faced with the demands of academic writing:

> We've only been here three days and we've done lots of writing – I got out of the habit of doing that in the last two years but I'll get back into it slowly.
>
> (James, Culinary Education, Citygate College)

They also had to work more independently. Matt explained that on the NVQ 'you'd always do everything in class, you never did anything at home'. Now, James commented:

> It's taught different. Last year they went through it all and helped you. This year it felt like they just gave you the papers and you had to figure it out really.

So their confidence in the practical environment did not follow through into more theoretical work. Paul explained that he was:

> Nervous, because you don't want to fail but there's always that little niggling thought at the back 'what if I fail that exam or fail the coursework' or whatever, just that little tiny voice saying 'what if?'.

HE tutors were aware of the different academic demands of the FE NVQ programme and the degree, and attempted to bridge the boundary between the NVQ and HE study in two ways. First, the college ran a Foundation degree in parallel to the Bachelor programme. The Foundation degree was closely aligned to the Bachelor degree, and it effectively amounted to a form of *streaming* for those with lower prior academic achievement. Second, the college ran a one-week Academic Bridging Programme during the summer before the start of the degree course. The sessions included work on research skills, note taking, time management, referencing, writing reports and preparing and giving presentations.

These efforts at bridging were rather curious however, for the Foundation degree was not run any differently from the Bachelor degree. Moreover, alongside the one-week academic bridging programme, the college offered a much longer five-week Practical Bridging Course for students from an academic background. One of the course tutors believed that this discrepancy was because the FE students who progressed to HE would only be those with good GCSE results and, she believed: 'they don't find it particularly taxing' (Mary, CAM first year co-ordinator), but her comment did not match the perceptions of students above.

4 Constructing separation: BTEC National Sport at East Heath College

In contrast to culinary education at Citygate College, the BTEC National in Sport at East Heath College was an example of strong internal separation between FE and HE. All the college's FE and HE provision was separated geographically, and involved completely different staff. Encouraging students to consider internal progression to HE was little different from considering moving elsewhere, as the BTEC course leader explained:

> We have the little bits of the flyers that come over, we've had someone from HE introduce themselves and we've invited the Sports Science person over and they come and talk to the second years.
>
> (Laura, course leader, East Heath College)

Moreover, the college's Foundation Degree in Sport Science was not a viable progression route from the BTEC course, despite the similarity of course title, because:

[The students] need a good science background and a lot of them aren't necessarily strong on that side of things, which is why we went to a general sort of Sports Development/Fitness [National Diploma].

Progression would only be possible if the FE students took an additional academic science qualification at level 3. While the BTEC National Diploma in Sport was selected to suit the sort of students who attended the FE part of the college, it appeared that the HE course was aimed at a different market. Perhaps not surprisingly, none of the nineteen students on the BTEC programme in 2005/06 progressed to the college's degree in Sport Science.

Instead of encouraging internal transitions, staff helped students to negotiate the boundaries between FE and HE by providing significant support in choosing destinations beyond the college. A lack of family experience in higher education (no students had parents who had experience of higher education, although two students had siblings who had entered HE) meant that students relied on tutors' help. This involved not just guiding them through procedures, but advising them whether a particular course was the right place for a person like them. Jessica explained:

I asked for advice because sometimes you had to go for recommendations and say I'm going to go for this, is it possible? She said 'Yes, it's suitable you are able to cope with it.'

(Jessica, Sport student, East Heath College)

Luke made similar comments about support from his personal tutor:

She has told me where to look and helped me look on some of the sites to find out what courses, and then once I've found them she's gone through and said 'Yes, that's the sort of thing you are looking for, that isn't, that is.'

(Luke, Sport student, East Heath College)

Clearly, the opportunity to take a vocational level 3 course at East Heath College, and the support and advice provided by tutors with students' applications to HE, represented ways in which widening participation in HE was encouraged. But these activities appeared to be untouched by the dual sector nature of the institution. Moreover the different demands of the FE and the HE Sport qualifications offered by the college turned what might have been a boundary into a barrier to internal progression within the college.

5 Conclusions: duality, seamlessness and widening participation

This section has looked at practices related to moving between FE and HE in two dual sector institutions in England. Such institutions are seen as offering additional ways of widening participation by providing progression routes for students traditionally under-represented in HE, but who could be defined as the 'traditional' students of further education (Widdowson 2005). Their contribution may take a variety of forms, and has involved a range of different initiatives in the English context (see Chapter 2). One way in which they may contribute to widening participation which is distinct from other HE providers is by offering internal pathways between FE and HE. Proponents of duality go further than this (see Duke 2005; Garrod and Macfarlane 2007) and suggest that duality could lead towards a seamless system of lifelong education.

However, the two examples offered in this section give rise for caution. Whilst there are increasing numbers of institutions operating in both the FE and HE sectors, their dual sector nature does not mean that they try to align or bring together their work across two sectors. Both spatial and knowledge boundaries, which have been the focus of this section, may be as strongly maintained in a dual sector setting as they are in separate institutions. What students' experience at Citygate College also highlights is that, as Wheelahan (2009: 36) has suggested, 'epistemological boundaries must be explicitly navigated rather than ignored, if students are to be supported in crossing them'.

In addition to these concerns, it is important to remember that dual sector institutions form part of a system of higher education which is not just differentiated but stratified (Scott 1995), and in this system they are positioned lower in the hierarchy of institutional status.

This links to a final important point in relation to duality and widening participation. This chapter has been silent on widening participation to students from under-represented and disadvantaged groups in terms of class, ethnicity, gender, disability or age. Rather, it has focused on widening participation in relation to students who do not have an academic learning background, who have low prior achievements and who study vocational and applied courses. This forms a major part of the work of FE colleges, new universities and dual sector institutions. By default rather than intention, this includes more disadvantaged students in terms of class, ethnicity and so on. The development of duality and aspirations towards seamlessness need to beware that they do not limit, as well as open up, the pathways that they make available to such students in the future.

Acknowledgements

This section is indebted to the work of members of the FurtherHigher Project fieldwork team: Diane Burns, Cate Goodlad, Liz Halford, Anne Thompson, Val Thompson and Will Thomas.

Pedagogies for social diversity and difference

Learning and teaching in two universities within the context of increasing student diversity: complexity, contradictions and challenges

Chris Hockings, Sandra Cooke and Marion Bowl

1 Introduction

Despite important developments in teaching enhancement in the UK (e.g. Higher Education Academy, Centres for Excellence in Teaching and Learning, Fund for the Development of Teaching and Learning), there has been little research into the implications of widening participation and increasing student diversity for classroom practice. Indeed, in their review of the impact of widening participation, Gorard *et al.* (2006) found little evidence that teaching methods had been adapted to meet the changes in the composition of the student population. Lectures remain a key mode of knowledge transmission (Lammers and Murphy 2002) and there remains a dependency on the teacher as authority within many of the teaching strategies used by university teachers. Set within this context, our aim was to work alongside university teachers in an old and a new university to explore the ways in which university teachers have reframed their under-standings and practices in response to greater student diversity in the class-room. Additionally we aimed to facilitate the development of strategies to improve academic engagement, to create inclusive learning environments and to inform policy and practice in university teaching.

The researchers and practitioners in the study needed to have a shared understanding of what was meant by 'academic engagement' so that we could recognise when students were engaged and disengaged in the classroom. We derived the following working definitions from a synthesis of theories and perspectives including the approaches to learning theories (Marton *et al.* 1997; Prosser and Trigwell 1999), theories of knowledge

(Apple 1986) and knowing (Belenky *et al.* 1997) and theories of individual and family habitus (Bourdieu 1977; Reay 1998). We were also influenced by the concepts of academic engagement (Ashwin and McLean 2004) and alienation (Mann 2001).

When students are academically engaged they adopt a 'deep' approach to learning (questioning, conjecturing, evaluating, making connections between ideas), and draw on their own and others' knowledge and experiences, backgrounds and identities in coming to know and understand. They often appear animated and animate others.

When students are disengaged they adopt a 'surface' approach to learning (copying notes, memorising or focusing on fragmented facts and right answers, jumping to conclusions, accepting) and keep academic subject knowledge and knowing separate from personal knowledge and knowing, background and experiences. They may also appear distant or isolated, distracted by or distracting to others (see also Mann 2008: 50–1 for comparable definitions of engagement and alienation). Our definitions and use of binary oppositions (engaged/disengaged, deep/surface) within them could be seen as over-simplifications of highly complex concepts. However we use them as heuristic devices for thinking about the issues. So, to clarify, first, deep and surface approaches to learning are not fixed 'characteristics' of learners. We recognise variation in the ways that students experience learning in relation to the many factors within the context. We are aware of the limitations of the approaches to learning theory and acknowledge its criticisms (Haggis 2003; Malcolm and Zukas 2001). We note, in particular, the criticism that the deep/surface model may 'reflect the value positions of wider class and social structures' (Haggis 2003: 97) by promoting 'deep' learning as an 'elite' goal to which certain types of students would not aspire. However, we share the views expressed by Marshall and Case (2005) and Ashwin and McLean (2004) in response to this criticism that the skills associated with deep learning (e.g. to relate personally and meaningfully to one's subject, to question, think critically) are skills entirely consistent with the goals of emancipatory higher education and 'crucial for maintaining open democratic society' (Marshall and Case 2005: 262).

Second, we do not see engagement and disengagement as an on/off state of mind. As others have commented (Bryson and Hand 2007), the same student may show different signs and degrees of disengagement over short or long periods, within a task or session, or over the period of a module or course. We also recognise that there may be multiple causes of and reasons for disengagement, as do others (e.g. Mann 2001, 2008; Read *et al.* 2003), and we do not see students who appear disengaged as inferior, deficient or problematic. Here we concur with Haggis (2006: 533) 'that many of the problems experienced by learners are at least partly being caused by the cultural values and assumptions which underpin different aspects of pedagogy and assessment'. Our aim in understanding disengagement therefore is to inform the development of learning environments that are personally meaningful and intellectually stimulating for students from different backgrounds. So whilst the definitions above may seem over-simplistic, they nevertheless summarise the more complex ideas that we shared. They also served as a reference point for identifying apparent engagement and disengagement in the classroom that could be explored through our analysis of a range of data sources and through discussions with students and teachers.

2 Methods of study

This study focused on eight university teachers and their first-year undergraduate students in two different universities (an old and a new university, alias Oldbridge and Newton respectively) in a range of subjects (biosciences, business, computing, history, nursing and social work). The first-year modules in these subjects attracted students from a wide range of backgrounds. Where possible we matched the teachers and their modules across the two HEIs by subject module to allow for comparisons of teaching in the same subject but in different institutional contexts. Our overarching question was: how do teachers academically engage all students within a culturally, socially and educationally diverse classroom? We took a broadly interpretative approach, seeking to understand the ways in which teachers' and students' identities influence academic engagement in the class-room, but we also adopted principles of action research to facilitate the improvement of academic engagement and the development of inclusive learning environments. (A full account of our methodology and research design is provided in Appendix 6.)

Within the first five weeks of the academic year 2006/7 over 290 students had completed a questionnaire seeking quantitative and qualitative data about themselves and their families, their conceptions of higher education, their chosen subject, the learning and teaching they had experienced so far, and their ways of knowing. They also described ways in which they felt the same as or different from other students in their module group. During semester one of the same year, we observed and video-recorded at least three classroom sessions per module (producing around fifty hours of video data). We invited students to talk to us who had appeared engaged or disengaged according to our criteria at some point during the lessons. In addition we held in-depth semi-structured interviews and focus group sessions with students from across the module groups to explore their family and educational backgrounds, and experiences of learning and knowing.

Following classroom observations, we held audio-recorded individual meetings with the eight teachers to explore issues arising from their sessions, particularly with regard to our research questions. Each teacher paired up with his or her subject counterpart in the partner institution to review their own as well as their partner's video-recorded sessions, and to compare approaches to teaching, the teaching environment and their respective groups of students. They met as a whole group on three occasions to consider the implications of the research findings for their practice. At the end of the second semester the teachers completed an open-ended questionnaire in which they reflected on their participation in the project. The themes that emerged from our analysis of the data generated from these activities formed the basis of the detailed coding scheme that we applied using NVivo 7. (See Appendix 6 and Hockings *et al.* 2008a for an elaboration of methodology and methods of data collection and analysis).

3 The students

3.1 Student diversity

From our analysis of data, a complex picture of student diversity emerged. This challenged the common view of students as 'traditional' or 'non-traditional'. Indeed we found few students who fitted these stereotypes and none could be described as lacking the skills and competences to succeed at university, as the deficit view of 'non-traditional' students suggests (see Bamber and Tett 2001; Leathwood and O'Connell 2003 for a critique of this view). Our study suggests that diversity extends beyond the structural divisions of class, gender and ethnicity. It encompasses different work, life and educational experiences, different entry routes to university and differences in living arrangements and family commitments (see Bowl *et al.* 2008a). Diversity also encompasses psychological and epistemological differences, including differences in students' approaches to learning, ways of knowing, and subject knowledge. Given our multi-faceted view of diversity, we did not focus on one aspect of student diversity in understanding academic engagement. Nor did we feel it helpful to indicate the gender, ethnicity or social class of students whose contributions we have used throughout this chapter. We only attach such categories where they are particularly relevant to the issues of learning and teaching and academic engagement.

Although the students were different in many ways, they shared a common desire to 'fit in'. With the notable exception of some mature students, most students identified themselves socially as 'an average student' (150 references). (We use the term 'references' throughout to indicate the number of statements or occurrences of the same type rather than the number of people who uttered them.) The number of references takes account of any repetition within one interview. They give some indication of scale where vague terms such as 'many' or 'some' are used. We must stress that we are not offering a positivist reductionist view here. Whilst the frequency of statements on a particular issue could simply reflect the kind of questions we asked, we believe this frequency may well be associated with its importance in participants' perceptions.

Common metaphors included being 'equal' and being 'in the same boat'.

When comparing themselves academically with their peers, over 250 references indicated a belief that other students were 'cleverer', 'more intelligent', 'more knowledgeable'. This influenced how some students formed relationships as this 'Access' entry student explained:

> if someone has an A-level in a subject, you would tend to draw yourself to people who didn't so you would have some common ground.

One consequence of associating solely with peers of similar backgrounds and experiences is that students may not be exposed to new and different ideas and perspectives that they might otherwise enjoy if their social circles had been wider (Crozier *et al.* 2008). This could impact on their learning. But whilst students appeared not to want to stand out as 'different', in interviews and focus groups they expressed a common desire for their teachers to recognise them as individuals and address their particular needs and interests. They valued the few who did so but, compared to their school and college experiences, they did not feel their university teachers had time (or in some cases, inclination) to get to know them.

3.2 Approaches to learning

When asked to recall how they went about learning something recently, some students (over eighty references) described strategies associated with a 'surface' approach. But whilst these included passive or reproductive strategies such as attending lectures, copying and 'revising' notes, some also indicated a growing awareness that the strategies that had proved effective at school or college were inadequate at university. Many (223 references) had begun to rely on themselves, rather than their teachers, for learning:

> I'd say I have to take more responsibility for my learning than I have done . . . with A-level you had [the standard definition]. This is this, this is this. You learned it by rote, you learned this is exactly what it is, get all these and I'll get three marks. [N]ow it is, understand it generally, but you sort of have to consolidate it by yourself, and maybe firm up, develop your definition yourself . . . I have to do more reading. . . . they give you kind of like the skeleton of everything and you have to go and flesh all that out really.

Experiential or problem-solving strategies were also common (seventy references) particularly among computing and biosciences students. Others, particularly in social work, business and computing (forty-three references in total), expressed a tendency to learn through discussion, sharing ideas and reflection. Nine of the eleven history students mentioned reading and 'further research' as their main learning activity. These strategies seemed to reflect the pedagogical traditions of the subject and the particular pedagogical practices of their teachers.

3.3 Subject knowledge and ways of knowing

Through their accounts of life before university, and their expressions of hopes for the future, students revealed why they had chosen their particular subjects. Whilst career opportunities and school success in the subject had influenced choice to some extent, several spoke of their 'love' of the subject often stemming from work, life or family experiences outside formal learning situations. Some students described how they connected their own, often tacit, knowledge (Polanyi 2002) of the subject with the explicit propositional knowledge presented in lessons. One interviewee explained:

> I really relate [diseases and illnesses] back to anything I've experienced myself whereas with lots of the mental health stuff I sort of like, 'oh yeah, I've seen some of that'.

Around eighty references indicated that students came to know by seeking connections between what they were studying and their own lives, or by relating it to other subjects or the wider world. Few of these, however, felt that the knowledge they had gained through life experience was valid, relevant or of interest to others in lectures. This compared to the many (135 references) who only valued the 'received knowledge' (Belenky *et al.* 1997) from the teacher (or the person marking their work) or textbooks and/or the internet (132 references) as the ultimate authorities in their search for knowledge and right answers. Further analysis of these data by subject suggested a pattern that reflected their teachers' ways of knowing in the discipline as discussed below. For example, social work and business students and their respective teachers tended to draw upon their 'subjective' knowledge (ibid.) and that of their peers, in coming to know. By contrast computing students described a more 'procedural' approach (ibid.), using trial and error as well as application of the tools and techniques of the subject to solve a range of computing problems. By breaking down and tackling increasingly more complicated problems, these students and their teachers believed they were building their programming knowledge.

4 The teachers

So far we have presented a sketch of the similarities and differences between students' conceptions of themselves and each other, their approaches to learning and ways of knowing. We now focus on the students' teachers. The three female and five male teachers were all relatively new members of staff, aged from 25 to 45. They came from middle- and lower middle-class backgrounds, (as determined by their parents' occupation). This reflected the predominantly white, middle-class academic staff population of both institutions.

When asked what they knew about the lives, backgrounds and interests of their students, the eight teachers admitted they knew very little. Most of what they 'knew' was based on their experience of past students and their assumptions of what students should know and be able to do. Nevertheless, they all articulated a view of student diversity that included ethnicity, class and gender, as well as differences in students' values and beliefs, subject knowledge and experience, and differences in their approaches to learning and generating knowledge. They all distanced themselves from the deficit view of 'non-traditional' student.

Student-centred learning was the pedagogical approach espoused by all eight teachers. This approach emphasises 'student responsibility and activity in learning rather than what the teachers are doing' (Cannon and Newble 2000: 16). One teacher described this as:

> introducing students to ideas and guiding them in finding their way through those ideas and thinking about how they use those ideas. I kind of resist telling them what the ideas are . . . It's about making those ideas come alive and helping others see the relevance for practice.

Within this overall approach, each teacher brought their own 'innovative', 'approachable' or 'energetic' style to the classroom as well as aspects of their own backgrounds and identities. They described how the epistemological traditions of their disciplinary subjects, and the communities of professional or vocational practice associated with them, influenced their own epistemologies and pedagogic practices (see also Clancy and Fazey 2008; Colley *et al.* 2003; Malcolm and Zukas 2007). Indeed, as shown above, the teachers' ways of knowing were also reflected in some of the students' accounts of their ways of learning and coming to know. For a full exploration of the impact of teacher identity on teaching and academic engagement in diverse student groups see Hockings *et al.* (forthcoming). The ways in which these teachers put their beliefs and theories into practice in the classroom and influenced academic engagement of their diverse student groups is explored in the remainder of this chapter.

5 How do teachers engage all students within socially, culturally and educationally diverse groups?

5.1 Creating individual and inclusive space

Our data suggest that students value teachers who recognise them as individuals and address their particular needs and interests. Because of the limited level of contact time and the pressure to 'cover the syllabus', most teachers in the study found it difficult to get to know their students. Nevertheless some did make time, at the start or end of sessions or during breaks, for informal discussions or 'warm-up' activities that encouraged all students to say something about themselves each week:

> F4: How she starts her lectures as well. When we walk in.
>
> F2: She makes you say something silly about yourself, but then, like, it makes you feel comfortable . . . everybody is in the same position.
>
> F4: It's daft things, but it is also teaching us other things about each other as well, without even making the effort...
>
> F2: She gets us doing, I don't know, tell us about your first holiday or.
>
> F1: Favourite film.
>
> F3: Music or. . .

Over the semester these teachers built their knowledge of individual students' lives and interests, to which they could make reference at times, thereby building rapport and acknowledging the students' different identities. This seemed to contribute to creating an atmosphere in which students could voice their ideas and opinions on subject-related as well as personal issues.

Participation was enhanced when teachers set the ground rules for inclusive and collaborate learning behaviour at the outset (see also Zepke and Leach 2007); for example, articulating an expectation that all students would contribute to classroom discussions, that students' contributions would be valued by others, challenged respectfully, and that personal issues raised in discussions would be kept confidential. These conditions created a safe, supportive and collaborative environment where students appeared to trust one another and engage academically, as these social work student testimonies indicate:

> And I'm usually the one to talk about things that are affecting you that maybe you haven't talked to other people much about at all, . . . there's a lot of trust in those little groups.

> But she's got us respecting each other as well. We are doing that here because she's built that up in us to kind of respect each other's views, as stupid as our comments may sound to one another, she's got us, 'no, no, no, that's a viewpoint and respect it, whether you agree or not!'

This contrasted with one of the computing teacher's accounts of competitive and individualistic behaviour within his group where the conditions of inclusive and collaborative learning behaviour had not been established:

a few of [the female students] had actually come to me and said 'look the guys in the group, they just don't want to participate in this [group work]. They don't want to maybe show that they have an idea that might be right.'

It must be said, however, that even within inclusive learning environments where teachers encouraged the sharing of beliefs, knowledge and experiences, some students still felt uncomfortable doing so. These students kept quiet for fear that what they wanted to say might be 'wrong' or irrelevant, or that they would be 'judged' by their peers. Some who felt confident in their knowledge, nevertheless preferred to withhold it in case they were seen by their peers as 'pretentious'. In subjects dominated by one sex, we heard accounts of marginalisation from a small number of students who felt the gender imbalance had curtailed their engagement in classroom discussion (see also Read *et al.* 2003). One male student in a predominantly female group commented:

if you say a comment forcefully, they say, 'ah, men!' You know, and they don't say it, but you can see it in their eyes . . . she's discounted what I've said because she thinks I'm being a misogynist.

So whilst some teachers appeared to have worked on developing inclusive practices so that everyone could exchange their views and opinions, the normalising effect of the majority coupled with the desire to 'fit in' often suppressed individuals' inclination to engage openly and at a personal level.

5.2 Developing student-centred strategies

Whilst the students wanted teaching to reflect their individual interests and identities, they did not expect teachers to tailor the lessons to accommodate each individual. Nevertheless most of the teachers in the study attempted to address the diversity of needs, motivations and interests by developing open and flexible student-centred strategies that enabled students to tailor the activities themselves. The following focus group extract illustrates how students engaged their own knowledge, experience and skills in response to such activities:

[the teacher] didn't say exactly what it was, but she gave us a chance to sort of give our own examples, so that we understood it, I thought that was really helpful. We had a deep discussion about it.

It stays inside when you talk about it. You have a natter and a chat and you think 'actually, you can link it with your own life experiences and things you have gone through'.

Creating this level of engagement among all students was not simply a matter of developing and facilitating 'active' learning. Rather it was a matter of creating activities that enable students to ground their learning in something relevant and meaningful to them as individuals. By drawing upon their existing knowledge and experiences, students not only shared aspects of themselves with which teachers could connect thereafter, they were also enabled to reflect upon, question and challenge their own ideas and those of their peers. Furthermore, when students got stuck or confused, rather than simply providing answers or telling students what to do, the teachers who engaged their students most effectively used questioning strategies that encouraged students to articulate their thinking openly so that they and their peers could reflect on and correct misunderstandings or errors, generate ideas and offer their insights. For example:

> every time you ask her anything, she doesn't give you *her* answer and she doesn't give you *her* opinions, she makes you find your own and that's what it is all about. I think it is a brilliant teaching method because *this* [points to head] has got to start ticking.

In this way teachers created the atmosphere in which getting stuck, being uncertain and making mistakes were positive states. Students were more likely to exercise their reasoning powers and growing autonomy.

However, contrary to our expectations, we observed a number of small group sessions of less than fifteen students in which students rarely spoke. An examination of teacher interventions led us to conclude that this occurred most frequently when teachers adopted a transmission approach, set individual rather than collaborative activities, called upon individuals to respond to closed questions, provided answers rather than helped students articulate their own thinking, or dismissed or failed to acknowledge individual contributions. Discussion under these conditions was particularly strained. Whilst small class sizes provide ideal physical conditions for discussion and interactive learning, teachers still have to create a supportive learning environment in which all students can participate.

5.3 Connecting with students' lives

Students felt most engaged when the subject matter and activities were relevant to their immediate lives or 'imagined' roles and identities (Bathmaker and Avis 2005). This was most evident among students on professional courses, such as nursing, where there was a strong vocational ethos. Teachers of modules on these courses were often seen as role models for students. They tended to enliven the sessions with recent and relevant professional knowledge and experience, connect with students' future identities, and encourage students to think like professionals rather than simply as students of the subject. One student commented:

there is always like 'Hey, let's relate it to a clinical scenario' and he is always doing that and we are constantly being reminded that you can be a nurse at the end of it . . . and they are treating us as 'Oh yeah, nurses, nurses!' And I like that approach. It is quite cool.

The sense of a shared vocational identity was less evident in modules and courses such as computing, where students might be specialists aspiring to become games developers or systems analysts, or generalists perhaps taking a computing module as a minor subject in combination with business or media studies modules. Whilst it was difficult under these circumstances for teachers to know of and connect with students' various aspirations, interests and subject knowledge (see for example Hockings *et al.* 2008b), we observed their attempts to do so by, for example, negotiating the topics and activities and adapting the syllabus to meet students' emerging interests, as this teacher describes:

We didn't entirely stay on the track that we were supposed to, and, but we did stay within the boundaries of what we are trying to achieve overall in the module and I guess it is always a dilemma . . . Shall we go off down this little alleyway because it is important learning or do we stick to . . . and in the end, I felt the material was there on [the Virtual Learning Environment] and they could look at it . . . [T]hey brought up this issue . . . and they'd also raised that the week before . . . This week, I thought 'no, it's come up again, its important, we'll go with it'.

5.4 Being culturally aware

Generally students said that they found it hard to stay engaged during lectures (see Dunkin 1983; Gibbs 1982; Ramsden 1992), particularly when the teacher introduced abstract concepts and terminology. This was not the case when teachers used examples and analogies, told stories and anecdotes to explain and illustrate complex ideas. Indeed we observed a series of lectures in which ninety or so nursing students appeared thoroughly engrossed and engaged as the teacher explained human disorders, causes and treatments, using anecdotes from his professional and life experience. As others have found (Zepke and Leach 2007), students respond well to real or practical examples, especially when the stories or images reflect their own backgrounds and identities positively. One student commented:

They are very good with choosing their wording . . . not offending anybody . . . and taking people's opinions from certain ethnic minority groups and from the general public. And treating them all the same . . . they would actually embrace the fact that . . . we are more diverse.

Nevertheless teachers' choices of resources and use of humour and anecdotes, whilst intended to simplify, exemplify and make more accessible, complex concepts, occasionally confused and alienated some students precisely because the subject matter was not aligned with or sensitive to the social and cultural diversity in the group. For example, one teacher used the UK national lottery as an example to explain the principles of probability to his biomedical science students, the majority of whom were of South Asian heritage. The subsequent group activity, based on this example, appeared to preclude the engagement of a number of students who, for personal, cultural and/or religious reasons, were unfamiliar with the rules of the lottery and/or opposed to gambling (see Tomalin 2007 for an exploration of cultural and religious diversity in university teaching). Moreover this example seemed irrelevant in the context of the subject. A student-centred, inclusive and subject-relevant alternative might have involved students generating examples of risk and probability in their own lives (e.g. the risk of students contracting meningitis at university), exploring the issues and evidence, and calculating the probabilities. Rather than feeling inhibited by their lack of knowledge about their students' cultures, interests and beliefs, this approach would provide teachers and students the opportunity to learn about and understand each other's lives within the context of the subject.

6 Contradictions between teachers' espoused theories and their practice

So far we have set out some of the ways in which the teachers' conceptions of students, learning, teaching and knowing influenced their classroom practice and encouraged inclusivity and academic engagement. Overall we observed consistency between the teachers' conceptions and their practice. However, there were occasions when some teachers practised in ways contrary to their espoused beliefs, which had negative consequences for academic engagement. For example, whilst the teachers saw themselves as predominantly student-centred, we observed some content-driven, teacher-focused (Prosser and Trigwell 1999) lessons where students appeared to be disengaged. And whilst the teachers distanced themselves from the deficit view of 'non-traditional' students, it nevertheless influenced some teachers' lesson preparation. Asked how he planned lessons for his diverse group, one teacher explained 'you have to do things from a very, very basic level, assuming nothing always'. This approach left some students under-challenged and bored (see Hockings et al. 2008b for a case study of disengagement within one subject area). And whilst most teachers included in their view of diversity, students' social and cultural differences, and spoke of the importance of using examples that are 'accessible to everybody in the class,' we observed a small number of incidents in which the use of anecdotes or jokes were socially or culturally misaligned.

Whilst the teachers had articulated sophisticated conceptions of student diversity, they did not always take these into account in their practice. In some instances their capacity to be 'authentic' (Cranton and Carusetta 2004) and to practise in accordance with their espoused beliefs was limited by institutional policies and pressures associated with inspection and accountability that made it 'too dangerous to take pedagogical risks' (Morley 2002: 131, see also Hockings *et al.* forthcoming). However, in some instances teachers were not aware of the contradictions between their espoused theories and their practice. Video recordings of classroom sessions provided the basis for exploration of and reflection on these issues and other classroom 'contradictions'. At the end of the year in which observations took place, one teacher wrote:

> by engaging with the observer in a dialogue about their perceptions, reviewing video and exploring the alternative method of listening to the 'student voice' . . . I have become more critical when approaching session planning by placing greater emphasis on the factors that are likely to impact on engagement with learning in a diverse student body.

It could be argued that the student population in UK universities has been diverse for many years and that what we have proposed in this study as a pedagogy for diversity is in fact 'just good teaching' and nothing new. We would argue, however, that teachers today operate in increasingly complex learning and teaching environments. The huge growth in number and diversity of students, for example, has meant that they have less contact with individuals in their classes and less opportunity to get to know and explore students' different interests and experiences than they may have done fifteen years or so ago. Teaching under these conditions is often based on assumptions about students' knowledge, backgrounds and interests that can leave some students under-challenged, overwhelmed or disenfranchised. We therefore need to develop and adapt pedagogies that provide opportunities for all teachers to engage students at an individual level, but that are also workable within today's mass higher education system. Student-centred pedagogies, as established by earlier studies (e.g. Marton *et al.* 1997; Prosser and Trigwell 1999), go some way to encouraging a deep approach to learning but in order to academically engage large numbers of students from a wide range of backgrounds, these strategies must also take account of the diversity within the classrooms and address individual needs and interests. Our study suggests that for these strategies to be effective in engaging the diverse interests of students, they must also be embedded within the context of the subject and not treated in isolation or as add-ons.

We are not suggesting that teachers tailor their lessons to suit every individual. That would be unrealistic. Nor are we implying that teachers find out about 'individual learning approaches or styles, in order to diagnose deficits, and then to offer support where deemed necessary' (Haggis 2006: 521). We are, however, suggesting that teachers focus on who they are teaching and create opportunities and conditions that enable all students to bring their individuality to the learning endeavour in personally meaningful ways. Whilst these learning opportunities may draw out factors such as gender, ethnicity or family experience, equally they might draw out differences to do with students' unique learning trajectories which defy sociological classifications and which may be of equal importance to individuals. In summary, this study suggests that pedagogies that are student-centred, inclusive of individual differences, and relevant in the context of the subject are likely to widen as well as deepen academic engagement.

Pedagogies for social diversity and difference

Keeping open the door to mathematically demanding programmes in further and higher education: a cultural model of value

Julian Williams, Laura Black, Pauline Davis, Paul Hernandez-Martinez, Graeme Hutcheson, Su Nicholson, Maria Pampaka and Geoff Wake

1 Introduction

This section draws on the mathematics education project 'Keeping open the door to mathematically demanding programmes in further and higher education (F&HE)'. It focused on teaching and learning in the early part of post-compulsory, pre-university mathematics programmes (so-called AS levels in the sixth form and FE sector) – this is when students who are mostly on a trajectory towards higher education (HE) make key decisions about whether to drop maths or not, and hence whether to keep open options for mathematically demanding subjects such as science and technology in HE.

We begin with an overview of some of the project's key findings, suggesting that the education system should measure and reward what is 'valued', rather than give value to a narrow range of performances. The notion of the 'value of mathematics education' is then developed as a thread running through our analyses of (a) students' 'mathematical identity', (b) distinct mathematics educational 'activities', (c) teachers' professional discourses, and (d) institutional cultures and voices. In each case we point to the contradictions of 'use value' versus 'exchange value' of mathematics education and how these underpin tensions in the learners' and teachers' subjectivities. Briefly, the 'exchange value' of education – in which grades and credentials serve as currency – offers learners the prospect of 'a strong CV' and hence access to resources such as a university offer, or a well-paid job. Given our public sector 'audit' culture and institutional, managerial culture of 'performativity' in which measures of attainment affect college 'funding' and departmental management, the exchange value recognised in exam grades likewise motivates the teachers and administrators involved at every level. However, the high value attached to mathematics is not only because it is used as a means of selection to scarce and valuable resources, it is also useful, for example, to science and engineering, and so has 'use value'. We attribute the experience of finding mathematics education as 'interesting' and 'fun' or 'enjoyable/challenging' as also a part of its use value, in addition to its obvious utility in application. We show that these categories of value prove important in generating insights into our empirical data: these values help us to thread our analyses at different levels – contradictions between values help us to understand tensions in learners' experiences, in teachers' behaviours and attitudes, and in institutional discourses, as well as policy concerns. A theoretical discussion of the concepts and some implications and further applications of these concepts conclude the section.

The theoretical and methodological premise of the study was that learners gather the resources from which to construct themselves as mathematicians (in some very broad sense) from their experience of mathematics education activities, for example in the classroom. We analyse practices such as 'classroom mathematics' and even 'biographical interviewing' as 'Activity', in the Cultural-Historical Activity Theory sense (CHAT; after Vygotsky, Leontiev, Bakhtin, see e.g. Cole and Engestrom 1997). Activity here implies a socio-culturally mediated, collective, object-oriented practice. The 'object' of a mathematical activity might be a mathematical text or task that a group or class is working on – and the values and norms of mathematics involved typically mediate the goals of the activity in critical ways. An exchange-focused classroom might provide 'values' of mathematics that resource the learners' and teachers' identities in exchange value terms, and vice versa, such identifications in turn shapes subjectivities and hence give values to classroom goals and motives.

In particular, we look for cultural models of 'mathematics' arising in the classroom activity to understand how learners position themselves and construct their own particular learner disposition, as subsequently told in interviews, where their biography, and hence their learner identity is narrated. The point is to view the 'effect' of classroom mathematical practice and discourse in the inter-relation of the observed classroom practice and the trajectory of interviewed students' narratives. Values are conceived of as boundary objects that connect the classroom activity with the personal, reflective narrating activity of the individual students (and teachers). For example, we often find mathematics being constructed – in and out of the classroom, in fact – as 'hard', and 'right or wrong', 'black and white', and this cultural model of mathematics becomes a resource for students narrating themselves in relation to mathematics: in the extremes as 'maths is too hard for me', versus 'I find maths is hard but challenging'. Students' identities, particularly their designated or 'leading' identities then also serve to support certain kinds of self-positioning: for some may like a challenge, and see maths as a way of distinguishing themselves.

However, the really significant boundary object we seek to reveal here in this section of the chapter is the 'value of mathematics education' that may arise in classroom activity, say, and so come to be used reflexively by the learner in their identity construction. Such values likewise mediate the work of teachers, institutions and policy. In particular, we will show how the contradictory nature of 'use' versus 'exchange' value provides analytical insight. But first, let us look at the evidence, the main findings of the survey study, those that speak to policy and public interest, as well as to learners, teachers and practitioners.

2 Main substantive findings for policy and practice

Our study included a survey of measurements of learning outcomes that allowed us to analyse 'effectiveness' from different perspectives. The learners' disposition towards further study and 'self-efficacy' were constructed to contrast with learners' grades and actual decisions to study mathematical subjects in HE. The survey methodology allowed us to formulate regression models for learning outcomes related to background variables (class, gender, etc.) as well as process variables (such as 'degree of transmissionist pedagogy' and contrasting 'use' versus 'traditional' mathematics programmes).

The methodology seized a rare opportunity to compare the traditional AS Mathematics Programme with the alternative AS 'Use of Mathematics' Programme that aimed to include more students than would traditionally be included (mostly with lower previous grades in the subject, following a wider range of other courses). It also identified an emerging policy concern with 'connectionist' teaching and constructed a self-report measure of connectionist teaching practice – essentially a 'connectionist' practice is more aligned to student-centred understanding or connection-making while 'transmissionist' teaching tends to be more teacher- and subject-centred (and performative as far as the learner is concerned). All this was complemented by studies of classroom activity and pedagogy through case studies that were ethnographic in style, and by interviews with students in the same case study institutions and matched the survey data points.

The main three findings for policy and practice were formulated as follows:

- The mathematics programme can make a difference to students continuing participation (see Table 4.2.1). Policy should give more 'value' to programmes that extend participation such as the 'Use of Mathematics' (if they want to encourage it).
- Dispositions to study further mathematics were in decline throughout the period of our study, but all things being equal the decline was less

Table 4.2.1 Percentages (by GCSE mathematics grade awarded prior to their AS) of those who have dropped out – or in brackets those who have not completed the course at the end of the year

Prog/grade	A* and A	BHigh	BInter	CHigh	CInter
AS Trad	9 (16)	18 (50)	31 (61)	26 (65)	46 (80)
UoM	12 (13)	18 (26)	9 (24)	27 (54)	18 (45)

severe for the Use of Maths students, for bilingual/EAL speakers, and for those taught in connectionist classrooms. The latter effect is mostly a result of a few of the MOST connectionist classrooms, and disappears when those classrooms are taken out of the sample. Policy may need to give more value to such 'connectionist' practices to encourage participation, especially for those with lower grades.

- Teachers and institutions tend to respond to rewards also: if policy-makers want to encourage institutions to improve students' dispositions and self-efficacy then they need to value them – similarly if students' preparedness for AS level is important, then more value should be given to higher grade GCSEs. If continuation with AS level is important, then the current practice of particularly valuing GCSE grade Cs does not make policy sense in its own terms.

The findings for policy here clearly foreground the notion of giving 'value' to practices, programmes and outcomes that policy-makers may want to encourage, and the attendant consideration of a broader ranger of measures than those currently rewarded, and signals the need to align exchange value awarded with the necessarily broad range of anticipated uses. An attractive alternative might be to suggest that policy should withdraw from the 'game' of giving value to outcomes altogether – a perhaps unrealistic offering. In considering this choice, we felt we had no alternative but to show how policy levers might impact while warning of the inevitability of unintended consequences. We will explain 'unintended consequences' as being an inevitable result of the audit process that always selects and can never equate with the full range of professional evaluation criteria relevant to the richness of practice (see Power 1997).

In the next sub-sections we report findings related to learners, learning and teaching, teachers, and institutions. Here we draw on the interview and ethnographic sides of the study, report empirical findings round the theme of values and seek explanations in a *theory* of value.

3 The learners' identity and their 'valuation' of mathematics

Empirical analysis of students' interviews about mathematics (Davis 2009) revealed (i) categories of 'values about maths' ('exchange-oriented', 'use-oriented' and 'mixed orientation') and (ii) categories of 'learning approach' ('surface' and 'not surface'), and led to hypotheses about the relations between these. These categories were empirical, yet explanatory, as they captured different ways in which students in our sample positioned themselves in relation to values and their approach to learning mathematics. For example some said they chose maths because it would look good on their CV, perhaps signalling they are 'smart', with career and financial consequences:

> No, I doubt there will be much (maths in my degree) at all. As I said I think it will show that I've got good range of abilities . . . but I guess I used to like feeling, this sounds a bit rude, but feeling like I was ahead of people, it made me feel clever and stuff. I never really found maths fun. I just always knew that it was good to learn and good to know about . . . say maths is hard to get hold of but it's worth the struggle . . . but it will get you into high paid, high ranking jobs.
>
> (David, exchange-oriented discourse, white working-class male)

David here positions himself as someone who is able and who studies mathematics solely to be able to get ahead in the future, attributing maths a high 'exchange value' that can be cashed in for a well-paid job later. On the other hand, Vladimir (below) draws on a different cultural model, which emphasises the use-value of mathematics, and so positions himself as a user of mathematics:

> Int: How do you find maths to be related to your degree? To the electronics?
>
> Vlad: It is very helpful, because the electronics is maths. If you know maths it is much easier to learn about electronics, how circuits work and make your own circuits. Usually when we present some circuits in the electronics room and you usually get sine wave and using maths you can calculate the voltages, sine-maths equations and that is really helpful. . . . Maths is essential.
>
> (Vladimir, use-orientation discourse,
> East European migrant family)

In our sample we found some students engaged with the exchange value of mathematics in extreme fashion, to the point of talking about *disliking* maths but choosing it for the sake of enhancing their CV. But for others, mathematics was said to be *essential* to their work. However, these exchange/use-value orientations are always 'mixed' or double-edged to some extent; for example, David expressed feelings of personal value and esteem gained through successes in exam performance. Similarly, although Vladimir's interview emphasised the use value of maths as essential for his current studies, there was also exchange-value implicit in his references to the grades he would need to become an electronic engineer. Other student interviews (in the 'mixed' group) balanced the importance of the exchange value of mathematics for their imagined futures, with their positioning as users of maths in the here and now, typically in their studies of other subjects such as physics.

We found that 'troubles' with exchange value usually arose when students' grade performance did not meet with their aspirations or expectations. Some of these students with strong designated professional identities (where mathematics was implicated as useful) persisted in the face of such difficulties. On the other hand, students who positioned themselves as being strongly exchange-value oriented were especially vulnerable when experiencing such difficulties – and this could lead them to adjust their aspirations, with some dropping mathematics. While students' perceptions of a high exchange value for mathematics accounted for many students' decisions to take A-level mathematics, we concluded that having a weak appreciation of the use value of mathematics could put some at risk of marginalisation or drop-out (see Davis *et al.* 2008b).

This then begs the question: how can pedagogic practices influence students' values of mathematics, that is, their relation with use/exchange-value? Interview analyses suggest that pedagogic practices and programme do influence how students perceive the use and exchange value of mathematics. Explanation of how this can happen is taken up in the next sub-section.

4 Classroom mathematical activity: transmissionist-surface or connectionist-deep

In CHAT the 'joint activity' of teacher and learners in the classroom is seen as defined by its 'object' – its motive, goals as well as the ideal-and-material object that is to be transformed into outcomes through activity. We identified two distinct, and what might be considered opposed and contradictory, ideal categories of activity in the classrooms we observed.

On the one hand, we saw activity with the motive of 'schooling' – whose conscious goal is preparing for examinations – that typically engaged students in tasks they would eventually face in terminal examinations (Leont'ev 1981). Typical lessons of this type might begin with teacher exposition of how to answer a typical question, possibly motivating students by appealing to the value of the task in an upcoming test and eventually the module examination. The teacher aligns him or herself with the students, talking of the examiners as 'they' and with the goal of making

the required exam performance as easy as possible for students (the difficulty of tasks presented gradually ramps up from easy to difficult). The students might then be expected to replicate the teachers' solution of the task with similar example problems, with the teacher helping individuals with important details in the solution process. Students in such classes particularly valued clear exposition and exemplary solutions to exam questions. Students, in such classrooms, although often quiet, would usually work in pairs helping each other as well as calling on the expertise of the teacher. Finally, the teacher might conclude a period of students practising problems by providing answers for checking, and perhaps explaining how marks might be lost or gained in the examination. The lesson is usually 'well-paced' and focused on 'right answers'. The learner is expected to practise solving questions for homework to reach a competent level of expertise and fluency in performance, bringing their individual work back for checking/marking. Ultimately this activity finds its reward in exam grades.

In such classrooms where the object of activity is focused on assessment, therefore, we observe a combination of the teacher's 'transmissionist' pedagogy, and the learners' performance-oriented, or 'surface approach' (see Marton and Booth 1997). We use the term 'transmissionist-surface' to describe teaching-learning activity in such cases, as it conjoins 'transmissionist pedagogy' and 'surface learning' approaches. The 'value' of the mathematics in this activity would seem to be emphatically 'exchange value' of mathematical performance, that is, what mathematics can earn in the test through marks and grades.

On the other hand, we observed lessons that were designed to develop and build students' conceptual understanding. Such lessons were observed to take as a starting point what the students had previously understood related to the topic at issue. New concepts – or perhaps a network of connected concepts – that the teacher sought to develop were introduced through a number of related tasks that guided the students through their learning. Students would often be expected to discuss their ideas and problems with each other in groups, and to share with the whole class, possibly having developed a poster of their work, or being brought to the board to explain their ideas. The teacher stressed 'depth of understanding' and engagement as being more important than always being right: being wrong in such classrooms was sometimes seen as an opportunity to learn and for 'multiple' methods and solutions to be explored. In some classrooms it is said to be important that learning mathematics is interesting and enjoyable, and learners may be encouraged to 'think like mathematicians'. The pace is student-centred for as long as possible.

In such activity the 'object' is the *understanding* of mathematics. We call such teaching-learning activity 'connectionist-deep', as it conjoins 'connectionist pedagogy' (pointing out connections within and between mathematics, and helping students connect with what they already know in mathematics and from other sources, especially each other) and 'deep learning' approaches, focusing on understanding, using and communicating (again, after Marton). The 'use' value of mathematics is here more visible, as mathematics is only usable in practice if it is understood, communicable and well-connected.

The object of activity is mediated by a complex of socio-cultural factors with the voice of institution being prominent: teachers did not necessarily wish to adopt the pedagogy they used, but 'performativity' (Ball 2003) often required their compliance. In attempting to understand how the different pedagogies resulted in different structuring of mathematics we conceptualised the teacher as a narrator constructing a narrative with social and mathematical strands. 'Connectionist-deep' activity requires a strong sense of teacher agency with the teacher constructing their own highly connected mathematical narrative: while such classrooms appear student-centred, there may be a strong pedagogy ensuring that students connect in a meaningful way with the teachers' key mathematical argument (Wake and Pampaka 2008). In 'transmissionist-surface' classrooms, the performance culture is reflected in the way that teachers develop their mathematical narrative: this tends to closely follow the textbook of the course, which is itself highly exam-focused. Within the restrictions this imposes, teachers may nevertheless develop strong social narratives and relationships with students that are supportive and caring as they seek to maximise attainment (see, for example, Wake *et al.* 2007).

Our binary opposition between two ideal activities is simplistic: in reality many classrooms draw on the extremes we characterise here, and teachers may quite sensibly switch between activity types according to need, and of course pressure of time and examinations. Yet it is deliberately simplistic, as it provides a powerful analytical tool showing how use and exchange value come to be 'lived' in teaching-learning activity. The contradictions in practice arise continually – even the most transmissionist teacher worries if the students do not understand the work, and may blame time pressure for causing this; even the most connectionist teacher complains about lack of time to finish the syllabus as the exams approach. Similarly the learners may ask if the time they are spending on a topic is really 'worth it' if it is not going to be tested, but will complain of being badly taught if they do not understand it.

The pedagogy instrument we constructed (Pampaka *et al.* 2008) and used to explore the teachers' self-report of their pedagogies in relation to their classes suggests that the 'transmissionist' pedagogy dominated our study sample, with only very few teachers working in highly 'connectionist' ways (though these latter classrooms were where real differences in outcomes were achieved). This finding was consistent with our own case study work too, and we now turn to the teachers' professional identities and the institutional cultures in which they work to understand why.

5 Pedagogy and the teachers' professional identity

Our comparative analysis of teachers' discourses about their teaching revealed similar conflicts between their 'value-ing' of pedagogic efficacy (see Williams *et al.* 2009). On the one hand, there is the pre-eminent need to help the students score high grades in mathematics in the inevitably approaching test or exam (the A-level years are the most intensively examined period in most students' lives, with as many as twenty to thirty exams in two years). On the other hand, there is a need to develop understanding, or even pleasure through the work. This is most keenly expressed by one teacher as an institutional imperative:

> Because I feel the pressure on, I've got twenty-five, twenty-six weeks in a year to get through three modules and this how I feel, which is what I've got to do. You know I wouldn't call that teaching, what I did today. I don't think it is anyway. There might have been one or two good things in there but mostly it is just trying to cram things in as fast as possible. And it is a nightmare but that is how it is. You know, because at the end of the day what I get judged on is results: in September, results. And if they haven't (got the grades) my head's on the block . . . the results are everything . . . I do tend to try to bring some interest and explain things if I can, but I do tend to say this is going to be on the exam, it's going to be worth X number of marks, that's why we're doing it.

A close analysis of two contrasting teachers' biographies was revealing also of the ideological underpinning of professional identity by different 'values' (see Williams *et al.* 2009). We found that the rare 'connectionist' teacher narrated her professional identity as one who (at least partially, and within limits) tends to resist conformity, while also asserting that a connectionist approach in the classroom is essential to the effective development of the learners as mathematicians – and so 'use' value oriented.

However, our study concluded that the majority of our teachers were at a very sharp end of a conflict between the use value of mathematics and its exchange value, and this was expressed in terms of the pace and priorities of the work, and the imperative of approaching assessments that 'count'. The latter was predominantly expressed as a managerial pressure from the institution ('my job's on the line') though other pressures (from parents and students) were also recognised. It is to the institution, then, that our enquiry moves next.

6 The institutional culture

The analysis of our case studies suggested a potential conflict between the institutions' 'duty of care' towards their students (i.e. the students'

educational needs in regards to their aspirations) and the need to maintain an institutional position in the market place (i.e. league tables,
funding, etc.).

One white working-class female student told us of her childhood dream
of becoming a scientist – ever since she saw the film *Free Willy* when she
was 8 years old she wanted to work with orcas. Indeed we found a pattern
among white working class, especially females whose models for HE drew
on the media (see Hernandez *et al.* 2008c). This ambition had crystallised
and become serious as she got advice in secondary school and found out
she would need a PhD in order to be able to research whales. However, she
had a 'strange' experience of mathematics at GCSE, as she took the lower
level tier mathematics a year early in Year 10 (getting her school a grade
C) and then spent Year 11 doing a GCSE statistics (another grade C). This
meant she had little or no experience in algebra (a topic only properly
covered in higher tier mathematics at the GCSE level). In interview she told
us this was making her learning at AS level very tough. When we asked a
reference group of teachers about this, they told us it was not uncommon
for schools to optimise their school league table performances with such
strategies – and putting students into GCSEs a year early was just one such
strategy currently on the increase (anecdotally, we are told the early entry
strategy is increasing as the national tests in Year 9 disappear).

The use (and even the exchange value) of the GCSE in statistics as a
preparation for A-level for this student was at best dubious, yet the
currency for the institution was significant, as 'another Grade C' to be
counted. Having the student take the more useful higher tier study of
algebra would make little difference to the institution. Here the dysfunction
in the system is clearly a result of the mismatch of the goals of the
institution and the learner – and one that policy-makers could – in principle
– correct by aligning the value to the institution with its use to its students.

A teacher who is involved in liaising between feeder schools and her
college told us that 'the main emphasis with the heads of maths at high
schools is to get as many students as possible through maths GCSE by
whatever means possible because it affects the (league) tables', and that a
grade C was the main goal. However, she recognised that it is possible to
achieve even a grade B at maths by having learned only 50 per cent of the
GCSE curriculum, making it feasible for a student with a 'good' grade to be
in fact unprepared (mainly in algebra) for study at A-level. Very soon many
students with a grade C (and also B) discover that they are not coping with
the work at AS level and may be persuaded by the college to switch to other
courses (geography or psychology are popular choices), despite their own
personal aspirations.

But, how does an institution reconcile the conflict between the interests
of the learner and its own interests? Interviews with the principals in our
case studies suggest that the rhetoric of the institution is to deny there is
any conflict. Thus, the institution rationalises its position by talk of its 'duty

of care' to students to counsel them to drop mathematics if early diagnosis suggests that, after having been given the opportunity, students show they are not likely to achieve as good a grade in mathematics compared to some other subject. The duty of the institution towards their students is therefore said to be to try to maximise their chances of getting the best possible results in terms of grades and, in this way, maximising the institution's performance (Wake 2009).

Of course the story here is complicated by the systemic deficiencies involved, that is, in institutional rewards being narrowly defined and in some cases clearly dysfunctional. Is such dysfunctionality inevitable in the audit culture? Experience across the public sector suggests it may be – consider health (A&E waiting periods), police (crime figures and the registering of offences) and even the financial sector (rewards for selling mortgages to customers who default). We turn to theory to try to tease out the roots of the problem.

7 Problems and contradictions for policy with regard to curriculum, assessment and pedagogy

We found that the Use of Mathematics programme does have the potential to widen participation in mathematically demanding subjects, and helps develop students' confidence through coursework assessment, and by learning through applications and use of technology. However, it highlights a key problem inherent in the system of performativity (Ball 2003) in which students are expected to learn and progress: that of 'qualification' potentially being detrimental to progression. Here we consider the qualifications or credentials as boundary objects between one phase of education and the next; for example, from pre-16 (GCSE) to post-16 (AS and A-level), or from AS and A levels to HE, and even HE to work. To be effective the certificate has to signify both exchange and use value; namely, it has to confer status on those that acquire it, and it also needs to prepare them for work at the next phase. However, this is from the point of view of the student; credentialism, as our case studies demonstrated, also has a role to play in the life of the institution, that of measuring its performance and consequently positioning it in the market. There are inevitably contradictions between these different purposes that, in turn, reflect the contradictory interests of distinct parties.

Perhaps this is most poignantly illustrated by the story of David, a white working-class male student in one of our case study colleges, which gives just one glimpse into the 'troubled' world of a student who readjusts his aspirations in response to his performance in assessment. His study of AS Use of Mathematics had successfully given him increasing confidence in mathematics following being 'dropped down' from AS Traditional Mathematics, so much so that he had formulated a plan to take up study of the full A-level in mathematics and work towards certification in one year.

However, following the achievement of 'only' a grade B in AS Use of Mathematics, which for many would have been understood as a success, he was persuaded to drop the study of mathematics altogether in favour of psychology. It was argued by his psychology teacher that this would help him to maximise his A-level performance. Therefore, instead of attempting to realise his ambition of studying for a physics degree, David dropped the idea of A-level mathematics, eventually decided to apply for an accountancy degree which he reconciled as providing status and future rewards as well as allowing him to study at a 'good' university. His alignment is with the culture of performativity which was strongly voiced in his particular college, although in a final interview he talked with some regret about having dropped maths and the opportunities this might have then afforded him to realise his earlier ambitions. Thus, in David, we have a case where the ambitions of an individual student are not supported by a system where performance of the individual is tied closely to that of the institution.

On either side of a transition point we also see tensions in how the nature of mathematics is differently valued: those of us who work in (mathematics) education will recognise the complaint that students are not well prepared for study in our subject by the phase through which they have just passed, be it, for example, between primary and secondary school, or school/college and university. From pre- to post-16 study, the key problem is identified as lack of algebraic fluency, whereas at transition into university in the study of mathematics a key problem may be the lack of understanding of ideas of mathematical argument and proof. We note that in mathematics in particular, as students study and strive towards certification in one phase, what is deemed important and highly valued can suddenly mean little or nothing in the next phase. For example, achieving a 'high grade' of a B or C at GCSE, certainly of importance to the institution contributing towards its performance table position, appears inadequate preparation for study at AS/A-level. (For example, Table 4.2.1 shows that only 20 per cent of students achieving a grade C at Intermediate GCSE ultimately achieved an AS grade in traditional mathematics in the expected time frame.)

In general, therefore, we note the importance of exchange value of certification for progression but raise questions over its use value for students as they move on to the next phase. These contradictions are exacerbated by the transition between two institutions that have their own interests at stake, as well as – or sometimes in contradiction to – their students'.

8 Theoretical considerations: consumption and production in learning, the contradiction within the commodity 'labour power'

Engestrom (1995) – developing a CHAT theoretical perspective – highlighted the contradiction between exchange and use value within the object of health services activity (namely the patient, or the treatment of the patient): the doctor may align with the patient and see the treatment as a 'use' value (the usefulness being in the restoring of the patient to health); while the service manager (who may also be the doctor) may see exchange value, that is, the unit of funding that comes to the service as a consequence of treatment. Our analysis includes this element in the object of the educational institution as an activity system. Hence the contradictions between the learners' and the institutions' evaluation of their learning arise when the resource accruing to the institution is misaligned with the use of the learning to the learner, or to society at large.

We can go further, though here there is only space to suggest further lines of exploration (for further details see Williams 2009). Our analysis of commodification of mathematical knowledge has here so far included the contradictions between use and exchange value:

1   within the learning activity itself, that is, within its object (that is, between mathematics for use and mathematics for exchange);
2   within the subjectivities (or identity) of the learners (as 'exchangers' or users of mathematics, and so as surface or deep learners);
3   within the subjectivities of the teachers (as transmissionists or connectionists);
4   within the institution (as servers of the learners or as corporations with their own needs);
5   within audit policy (efficiency versus breadth of assessment, i.e. between audit and evaluation).

Additionally, CHAT suggests we should hypothesise contradictions between mathematics education for use/enjoyment versus exchange/esteem within the community/family from which the learners' also draw their values: particularly we have noted how significant is the ethnic influence on learners' repertoires and HE subject choices (see Hutcheson et al. 2008; Hernandez-Martinez et al. 2008). White working-class learners are significantly more likely to consider not going to university (perhaps reflecting family discourses of 'wanting me to be happy') while ethnic minority students tend to have strong biases for high exchange-value professional aspirations (engineering and medicine for instance, see Davis et al. 2008a).

Similarly we identify potential contradictions within the instruments of activity (the curriculum, the assessment and texts must aim to develop understanding and prepare for the exams) and between pairs of all these elements of the activity system (or between systems). For example, between the (exchange for the) teacher and the (use of mathematics to the) learner; between teacher-and-learner (and their need for 'time') and the institution (and its demand for efficiency), and hence between the institution, the served community and the policy communities (efficiency versus utility); between the feeder institution and the recruiting/selecting institution (exchange versus use of the qualifications at their boundary); and between academic credentials (exchange in the audit culture) and possibly future work activity (utility in work practices).

Lave and McDermott (2002) drew an analogy between learning and 'labour' to explain such contradictions; they argued that learning, like labour, was 'enforced' and exploited, or 'estranged' by credentialism. We have argued that they are right up to a point: to the extent that if learning is motivated by and hence managed and run exclusively for its exchange value, it tends to become inhuman and superficial. By analogy with the production of surplus value by exploited labour, they point to 'learning for credentials' as the source of exploitation of learning. At this point our theory departs from theirs (see Williams 2009).

A classical political-economic analysis of learning-and-teaching activity would rather posit this activity as being both consumption and production: (i) consumption by and leisure for the learner, and (ii) production of the next generation of labour power (by teachers', as well as learners' activity). Labour power for Marx was the commodity 'bought' for a time from workers by capital: the source of all surplus value being the productive use of this labour power in unpaid time. The notion that learning, like eating and so on, is consumption (of knowledge and education) that restores the worker needs some working through. Because education is inter-generational – like parental nurturing – it is subject to all kinds of market lag and particularly state mediation. Both are significant, with tendencies to dysfunctional planning, politicisation and over-production. Nevertheless the end-product is the presentation of educated labour power to capital for exchange on the labour market and for its 'use' in the 'factory' for producing surplus value: the more intense the knowledge economy the more critical to productivity does education become.

Thus the 'use' of learning in this theorisation is (i) immediately for the leisure or consumption of the learner, and (ii) in enhancing the labour power of the learner-as-future-worker. The value of mathematics in the former case is immediately 'useful' – and is usually expressed as a matter of 'enjoyment', 'understanding' and 'interest'. The value of mathematics in the latter case is mediated by a series of exchanges which are state organised though our audit culture as exam-related performances: these exchanges are eventually realised in the use of labour in production many years later. Thus the exchange value *must* be realised eventually in the economy in one or the other kind of use value else over-production will eventually lead to a crisis – our own educational credit crunch.

In conclusion, the series of use–exchange contradictions we have discussed throughout our analyses have a political-economic basis in the inter-generational, state-mediated, reproduction of educated labour power for the knowledge economy. The audit- and performance-culture instantiates these contradictions in practices and discourses throughout the educational (and wider) activity systems, and permeates students' and teachers' lives and identities through and through.

The project set out to understand teaching and learning practices (i) in relation to the institutional and wider structures (e.g. programme, assessment regime, professional cultures etc.) and (ii) in relation to students' identity, that is, their construction of themselves as learners. Understood as an activity system, the classroom involves learners and the teacher in joint activity on mathematical tasks, and we have argued that the primary contradiction in the activity resides in the value of the mathematics projected onto the task. This is reflected in contradictions within the subjectivity of the learners (and the teachers), within the institution itself and its communities, within the instruments that mediate learning and teaching and within the interpersonal relations and division between learners and teachers themselves. While the contradictions in value may have systemic and even an economic base, they are realised (and represented in our data) as cultural and discursive conflicts and troubles.

Further work is currently underway to explore the contradictions involved in 'transition'; for example, when students leave compulsory schooling and go to college/high school, or leave college/high school and go to university. We are seeing here that the activity in the 'feeder' institution is heavily exchange-motivated by the assessment scheme that provides credentials to the learner but also gives value to the feeder institution by awarding entrance to high-value programmes or courses or selecting institutions. However, the use value of the knowledge in the recruiting or selecting institution is always in doubt, and transition problems often result from this contradiction.

We suggest that this approach and analysis will be valuable in similar contexts, and the emphasis on theory provided in this paper has been directed to this end. Mathematics provides a particularly acute case of contradictory values because of its core position in education for STEM and current STEM policy drivers, yet might one not replace 'mathematics' by any other object of learning in the analysis presented here?

Outcomes in terms of age-based participation

Diversity of experiences in higher education

Anna Vignoles and Nattavudh Powdthavee

1 Introduction

In this section of the chapter we focus on the retention of different types of student (particularly those from disadvantaged backgrounds) in higher education, using similar data and methods of analysis as described in Chapter 3, Section 1, and we also present the results of an analysis of the degree class achieved by students. Gender (Richardson and Woodley 2003; McNabb *et al.* 2002; Chapman 1996), disability (Purcell *et al.* 2005), ethnicity (Connor *et al.* 2004; Purcell *et al.* 2005; Broecke and Nicholls 2007) and social class (Johnes 1990; Smith and Naylor 2001) have all been found to be significantly associated with non-completion or degree class or both.

To put the analysis of non-completion into context, we note that England has historically had high levels of student retention in higher education (Dearing 1997; NAO 2007). Recent data suggest that 91.6 per cent of full-time students starting university in 2004/05 continued into their second year and 78.1 per cent are expected to complete their degree (NAO 2007). However, as the sector has expanded, the rate of non-completion has risen (Johnes and McNabb 2004). This motivated our research into non-completion. There have also been concerns that some types of students have lower levels of degree achievement (Dearing 1997), again motivating our interest in degree classification.

In our project we investigated whether disadvantaged entrants to higher education have a higher probability of non-continuation after the first year of a degree course, given their level of prior achievement. In other words, does disadvantage and poverty mean that even if you can get into university, you are then more likely to struggle and eventually not continue with your degree? Alternatively, it may be that poorer students are no more likely to 'drop out' than other students with similar levels of (low) prior achievement. We also investigated the class of degree achieved by different types of student, although our data on pupils' prior educational achievement were much weaker for this particular analysis and we therefore place somewhat less weight on these results.

2 Previous literature

We start by discussing what we mean by non-continuation. Tinto (1993) draws a clear distinction between voluntary withdrawal and forced withdrawal, hypothesising that the causes of these two phenomena may be different. Brunsden *et al.* (2000) provides a contrary view of the appropriateness of the Tinto model. Clearly to provide analysis that might fully inform policy, we need to identify the reason why students fail to complete their studies. Forced withdrawal is generally associated with academic failure. However, defining what we mean by *voluntary* withdrawal is more problematic: students may appear to voluntarily withdraw from their degree because they *anticipate* failing their examinations. In any case, large-scale quantitative evidence on the causes of non-continuation is extremely limited (see Johnes and McNabb 2004, for an exception) and in our data we were unfortunately not able to distinguish between different causes. We were, however, able to ascertain whether family background and student characteristics are the main determinants of non-continuation or whether poor prior academic achievement is the key factor – we do not apportion blame here as it is a normative and moral judgement and not appropriate.

Taking non-completion in a general sense to cover both academic failure and voluntary withdrawal, why are we concerned about this phenomenon? One concern is the economic costs associated with non-completion: the notion that there has been a waste of resources if a student starts but does not complete a course (Yorke 1998). Students who start but do not complete their degree studies also do worse in the labour market than their peers who did not participate in HE at all (Schuller *et al.* 2004), although of course this may simply reflect the fact that students who do not complete their degree have other characteristics that make them lower earners. Another potential concern is the impact of non-completion on the student's well-being, that is, the sense of failure that a student may feel after 'dropping out'.

At the same time, it needs to be recognised that progression through higher education may not be linear. Intermittent learning may be both inevitable and desirable in order to achieve balance with other commitments in learners' lives (McGivney 1996). Labelling (temporary) withdrawal as academic failure or wastage would seem inappropriate (Johnes and Taylor 1989). This is not merely a semantic debate. Higher education institutions face clear incentives to encourage student completion in the 'normal' time and non-completion is penalised. If non-traditional students are more likely to withdraw, this may lead to a tension between the widening participation agenda and the desire by HEIs not to incur penalties from student withdrawal (Palmer 2001).

There is robust evidence from the US that poorer students 'drop out' to a greater extent (see Corrigan 2003; Haveman and Wilson 2005). Similar patterns have been found in the UK for a subset of universities (Jones and McNabb 2004; Smith and Naylor 2001; Bennett 2003). In this section of the chapter we report the results of a large-scale quantitative analysis of non-continuation for the entire population of under-graduate students in every university in England (Powdthavee and Vignoles 2008).

We also analysed degree class achieved, which is somewhat controversial given the substantial variation in the proportion of different degree classes awarded across institutions with similar student intakes and the well-publicised problem of consistent grading (see, for example, Smith and Gorard 2007; Richardson and Woodley 2003; Chapman 1996; Silver et al. 1995; Molinero and Portilla, 1993; as well as the recent Burgess report from UUK 2007, and Yorke 2007). Degree class achievement also varies substantially by subject of degree (Smith and Naylor 2001; Johnes and McNabb 2004; Purcell et al. 2005). These caveats aside, previous research has found some pupil characteristics to be associated with average degree class achieved (Richardson and Woodley 2003; Hoskins et al. 1997), although much of this evidence is from specific groups of students/ institutions rather than across the sector as a whole (see Richardson and Woodley 2003; McNabb et al. 2002; Chapman 1996; Purcell et al. 2005; Connor et al. 2004; Broecke and Nicholls 2007; Johnes 1990; Smith and Naylor 2001).

3 Methods

This research relies on quantitative modelling methods. Specifically, for the non-continuation analysis we used linked administrative datasets, namely, the English National Pupil Database (NPD)/Pupil Level Annual School Census (PLASC) and individual student records maintained by the Higher Education Statistics Agency (HESA). These data are maintained by the Department for Children, Schools and Families. In fact we have data on all students in schools funded by the state in England, that is, more than half a million students. These data are unique in that they include information on each pupil's personal characteristics (e.g. ethnicity and indicators of their socio-economic background) and also provide a complete record of the child's educational achievement from age 11 onwards, that is, their Key Stage 2, 3, 4 and 5 results. The university records (HESA data) contain information on the degree subject, institution and other details of each student's university education for all students studying for a first degree at UK universities. With these two sources of data linked together, we have longitudinal data on a cohort of students from age 11 through to potential HE participation at age 18 in 2004–2005 and continued participation at age 19 in 2005–2006. School administrative records are fuzzy matched to higher education administrative records using a variety of variables including name, date of birth and postcode. The matching process was carried out by the Department for Children, Schools and Families.

For the analysis of non-continuation, the dependent variable is simply whether the student continued from one year to the next, that is, continued at the same university from 2004–2005 to 2005–2006. We are therefore only able to measure non-continuation after the first year of study. HESA data suggest that non-continuation is highest in the first year of study so we feel that our analyses are informative.

As was the case in the quantitative analysis in Chapter 3, the data have a number of limitations. The indicators for students' family backgrounds are problematic. We use student reported data on the socio-economic status of their parents for those who provide such information. For those who do not supply information on their parents' occupation, which includes all students who do not apply through the UCAS system, we use a combination of individual level information (e.g. whether the individual received Free School Meals in secondary school) with information on the socio-economic status of the student's neighbourhood (based on data linked in from the census on the basis of the pupil's postcode). Another limitation of the analysis of non-continuation (but not of degree class achieved) is that we are only able to consider young HE participants, that is, those participating at age 18. The drop-out behaviour of older HE participants may differ, so our results on non-continuation specifically, cannot be generalised to include older students.

For the degree class analysis we rely on Higher Education Statistics Agency data for 2003/04, which is more limited because it includes sparser measures of students' prior educational achievement. It is necessary to use the HESA dataset for the degree class analysis because it includes students completing their final year of study, whereas the other administrative dataset does not. Consequently, we put more weight on the non-completion results.

4 Results

Our results suggest that, in the UK, there is a significant gap in the non-continuation rate between advantaged and disadvantaged pupils and different ethnic groups. This is similar to other countries such as the US. Table 5.1.1 gives some key statistics on the characteristics of those who enrol in university (column 1), those who continue their studies after the first year (column 2) and those who do not continue (column 3). Students who continue their studies after the first year are much more likely to come from a higher socio-economic background (e.g. to have a parent in a professional occupation). Those who continue are far less likely to have been eligible for free school meals in secondary school. Interestingly, and consistent with other evidence (Chowdry et al. 2008b; Wilson et al. 2005), those who continue into the second year of study are

Table 5.1.1 Non-continuation rates

Variables	Enter HE at 18		
	All HE participants	*Continued to year 2*	*Dropped out year 1*
Social class: Professional occupations	0.204 (0.403)	0.208 (0.406)	0.116 (0.320)
Social class: Associate professional and technical	0.118 (0.323)	0.119 (0.324)	0.101 (0.302)
Social class: Administrative and secretarial	0.080 (0.272)	0.081 (0.273)	0.066 (0.248)
Social class: Skilled trades	0.092 (0.289)	0.091 (0.288)	0.094 (0.292)
Social class: Personal service	0.027 (0.162)	0.026 (0.161)	0.033 (0.180)
Social class: Sales and customer service	0.021 (0.145)	0.021 (0.144)	0.029 (0.168)
Social class: Process, plant and machine	0.062 (0.241)	0.062 (0.242)	0.061 (0.239)
Social class: Elementary	0.036 (0.187)	0.036 (0.187)	0.037 (0.189)
Social class: Missing	0.153 (0.360)	0.145 (0.353)	0.304 (0.460)
Male	0.432 (0.495)	0.432 (0.495)	0.429 (0.495)
Free school meal	0.049 (0.217)	0.048 (0.214)	0.074 (0.262)
Other White	0.025 (0.157)	0.025 (0.157)	0.025 (0.156)
Black African	0.012 (0.112)	0.013 (0.113)	0.009 (0.095)
Black Caribbean	0.009 (0.097)	0.009 (0.095)	0.013 (0.114)
Other Black	0.004 (0.066)	0.004 (0.066)	0.003 (0.058)
Indian	0.051 (0.221)	0.053 (0.224)	0.023 (0.151)

Table 5.1.1 (continued)

Variables	Enter HE at 18		
	All HE participants	Continued to year 2	Dropped out year 1
Pakistani	0.025 (0.156)	0.025 (0.156)	0.022 (0.147)
Bangladeshi	0.009 (0.096)	0.009 (0.097)	0.007 (0.086)
Chinese	0.008 (0.089)	0.008 (0.091)	0.001 (0.043)
Other Asian	0.005 (0.074)	0.005 (0.075)	0.002 (0.053)
Mixed ethnicity	0.010 (0.101)	0.010 (0.103)	0.005 (0.075)
Other ethnicity	0.014 (0.118)	0.014 (0.118)	0.012 (0.112)
Unknown ethnicity	0.101 (0.301)	0.102 (0.303)	0.085 (0.280)
N	121827	114586	7241

Source: National Pupil Database/Pupil Level Annual School Census and Higher Education Statistics Agency student record. See Powdthavee and Vignoles (2008) for full details.

also more likely to be of Black African, Indian or Chinese origin (although these differences are generally not large or significant in a statistical sense). Males are less likely to participate in HE but once they enrol in higher education are no more likely not to continue their studies as compared to females.

In our modelling we take account of all these characteristics and prior educational achievement simultaneously. Much of the socio-economic gap in non-continuation rates disappears once we allow for students' prior achievement. Some of the apparent difference in first year withdrawal rates between students from higher socio-economic status backgrounds and those from lower socio-economic status backgrounds is actually attributable to differences in their academic preparation for HE. However, an important socio-economic gap in non-continuation remains and its magnitude appears relatively sizeable, given that the proportion not continuing into their second year of degree studies is quite low (6%). For example, we find that once we allow for pupil's prior achievement, a pupil from a professional background is 0.6 percentage points less likely to withdraw than a student from a managerial/senior official background. Equally a pupil whose parents are in sales and customer service occupations is 1.6 percentage points more likely to not continue their studies than a student from a managerial/senior official background.

Not all previously under-represented groups in HE had higher non-continuation rates. For instance, once we allow for prior achievement, we found that ethnic minority students were not more likely to withdraw from their studies than White students. Furthermore, using slightly different data that included all ages of student (i.e. it specifically covered mature students), we found that older students had lower non-continuation rates than younger students.

On the issue of degree classification, we found that older students, who are disproportionately female, are more likely to achieve a first-class degree, although as has been said we know less about pupils' prior educational experiences in these data. Even when we considered results by gender, we found that mature students are more likely to achieve a top-class degree. We also found that students entering higher education with qualifications below level 3 achieve lower degree classifications than those entering higher education with level 3 qualifications, whether A-levels or vocational equivalent.

Previous literature has found that males were more likely to achieve a top-class degree than females. In our analysis, however, we were able to examine the role of gender controlling for a range of other factors that might influence degree classification, such as socio-economic background. In contrast to the earlier literature, we found that women are marginally more likely to achieve a first-class degree now than men. Although the use of different data and methods could potentially explain why we find this result, given the massive expansion of female participation in HE, it is more likely that women are now genuinely out-performing males in HE. Further confirmation of this key finding in recent cohorts is needed.

The data we used to analyse degree class had some admittedly very limited information on disability. Specifically, we know whether the individual has a self-declared disability and 7 per cent of our sample had a known disability. Thus the disabled category could cover a wide range of disabilities. Furthermore, students are not obliged to provide any information on whether they have a disability or not nor do they have to provide details on the nature of that disability. We therefore recognise that this measure is problematic when using it to determine whether or not disability is related to success in higher education. Our evidence indicates, consistent with previous evidence, that disabled people are significantly less likely to obtain a first-class degree, although the magnitude of the effect is small. Disabled students in our data are no more likely to not continue with their studies however, as compared to those students who are not disabled.

5 Conclusions

The English higher education system has a relatively low non-continuation rate, as compared to other countries. However, whereas HE participation rates are very similar for more and less advantaged students once you allow for their prior educational experiences (Chapter 3), this pattern was not completely mirrored in our analysis of non-continuation. We found that more disadvantaged male and female students were more likely to not complete their university studies, even after taking full account of their prior educational achievement. For example, our analysis suggested that a pupil whose parents are in sales and customer service occupations is 1.6 percentage points more likely to not continue their studies than a student from a managerial/senior official background. Given an average non-continuation rate of 6 per cent in the first year of study, this is a sizeable gap in non-continuation between higher and lower socio-economic status students.

The data we used on student mobility from HESA also suggest that the English HE system is relatively rigid, in terms of allowing/enabling students to move in and out of the system and to move across different institutions. Fewer than 3 per cent of students transfer between HE institutions. This implies that students who are not continuing with their studies are not simply transferring to other institutions. Given the limited credit transfer arrangements between institutions, this is not surprising. However, it is possible that students who do not continue with their degree may return to HE much later in life. We would not observe these returners in our data.

Our analysis of degree achievement was necessarily more limited, as our data lacked such rich measures of prior educational experience. With that caveat in mind, we found that mature students and women in particular were more likely to achieve a higher degree classification. In summary therefore, whilst we should be concerned about students from lower socio-economic status backgrounds withdrawing from their university studies, we should not fall into the trap of thinking that all previously under-represented students do poorly in HE. Indeed, if we view degree class as an indicator of success in HE, some previously under-represented groups, such as mature students, appear to have greater success in HE. After allowing for other characteristics including prior achievement, mature students achieve higher levels of degree class achievement than younger students, for example. This finding potentially relates to the findings in Chapter 5, Section 2, of the importance of motivation and purpose in mature students' decision to participate or not to participate in higher education.

Outcomes in terms of age-based participation

Educational decision-making, social networks and the new widening participation

Alison Fuller and Sue Heath

1 Introduction

There is a growing emphasis within UK education policy on encouraging adults to gain higher level qualifications through participation in higher education (DIUS 2007). However, little previous research has focused on the decision-making about education and careers of individuals who possess the qualifications normally required for enrolment on higher level courses but who have not, as yet, participated. Similarly, little is known about the values people in this category attach to formal learning or the potential relevance of HE to their lives. This chapter makes a contribution to the knowledge base in this area.

This section of the chapter is organised into four sub-sections: outlining the background to our research; identifying the conceptual lenses we have found helpful in exploring network-based decision-making; identifying four key findings from the research; whilst the conclusion draws out some implications for policy and identifies areas for future research.

2 Background to our research

In recent years, much government policy attention has been directed at trying to remedy the under-representation of young people from lower socio-economic groups in higher education (HE). At the level of individual choice, the social science literature has drawn primarily on data at school level and the immediate post-compulsory phase. Despite the growing interest in, and research on, widening participation in HE and decision-making about educational participation, the knowledge-base is uneven in a variety of ways. First, most research focuses on young people in the conventional age band for progressing to HE or in the years immediately preceding their post-18 decisions (*inter alia* Ball *et al.* 2002; Brooks 2005; Reay *et al.* 2005). There has been much less interest in widening participation in HE across the life course and particularly for adults aged 30 plus. Second, there is a tendency for research to focus on the experiences of participants in HE even when exploring non-participation. The shortcomings of using participants as proxies for non-participants have been highlighted by Gorard *et al.*, who refer to this as the problem of 'missing comparators', suggesting it arises as a consequence of 'the difficulty of identifying and then including students who choose not to participate in post-compulsory education' (2006: 146). We have sought specifically to target this group. Third, although decision-making about educational participation is often theorised as a socially embedded practice, the research itself is often based only on individual accounts rather than on the first-hand accounts of other network members. Our research provided the opportunity to start to address these limitations (a) through its focus on adults who despite having the qualifications which would allow them to enter HE had not chosen to do so, and (b) through collecting evidence from across inter- and intra-generational social networks, rather than focusing on the accounts of individuals in isolation from this broader context.

Since the start of our research in April 2006, the government has accepted the recommendation of the Leitch Review of Skills (2006) that at least 40 per cent of adults (aged 19–65) should be qualified to level 4 (HE level) by 2020, up from a current rate of 31 per cent. A further factor focusing attention on adult participation across the life course is the projected demographic decline in the number of young people. Between 2010 and 2020, there will be a reduction in the number of 18 year olds by 100,000 or 15 per cent. Patterns of participation in the existing adult workforce are, then, coming increasingly under the spotlight in the policy push to widen and increase participation in HE. Most recently, we have seen a shift from what we might call the 'old widening participation focus' in which adults, particularly those aged 30 plus, were seen as peripheral targets for widening participation, to the current policy position where they have become central to the government's competitiveness and new widening participation goals. However, relatively little is known about the attitudes to learning, qualifications and higher education of the people in their thirties and beyond who are now going to be encouraged to pursue higher level qualifications. The focus of our study, then, on adults who though they have the qualifications to enter HE have not yet done so, is timely and contributes much needed knowledge about the characteristics of this 'potentially recruitable' group.

Our research had two overarching aims:

1   To examine the extent to which HE is conceived as within the bounds of possibility for 'potentially recruitable' but 'non-participating' adults.
2   To explore how attitudes to HE and decisions about participation are distributed across, embedded within and negotiated within inter-generational 'networks of intimacy'.

For the purposes of our research we defined 'potentially recruitable' to HE in terms of whether someone has attained a level 3 qualification (equivalent to two A-level passes), as this is the level of attainment usually required for entry. We know from the Labour Force Survey that around 20 per cent of the working population (approximately 6 million people) currently have level 3 as their highest qualification. While mature applicants are not always required to have a full level 3 qualification to be accepted into HE courses, because of their prior relevant experience, using this level of attainment as an indicator of recruitability to HE enables a clear focus on a specific and very large group of people who possess the qualifications to enter HE but who, so far, have not chosen to do so.

We have been very conscious of the need to problematise the notion of 'non-participation' in our research. The apparently straightforward distinction between 'participation' and 'non-participation' becomes less clear on closer inspection and questioning: what counts as participation? Is it access to HE that is important, actual completion of a course, or attendance over a particular period of time? Similarly, it is not clear that people should be labelled 'non-participants' when they may well participate in HE at some point. In this regard, we have examples in our data of people who talk about progressing to HE 'in time' or, in the case of some women with young children, when they perceive 'the time will be right'. We think it is unhelpful, then, to conceive participation and non-participation as fixed states.

Our second overarching aim relates to our interest in exploring decision-making as a collective as well as a personal process, and the extent to which people's decision-making is reflective of the norms and values in their social networks of families and friends, or 'networks of intimacy' (Heath and Cleaver 2003). In our review of the literature, we noted that educational decision-making is often theorised as a social practice yet the research itself is often based on individual accounts. Rather than adopting this conventional approach, we have set out to explore the value of network-based research in helping us to understand decision-making.

3 Network-based decision-making and conceptual lenses

We conceived networks of intimacy as sites of varying forms of social, cultural and economic capital that provided a critical context within which individuals' thinking about HE would be embedded and co-constructed. We were interested in exploring educational decision-making across the life course and so prioritised a consideration of the impact of specific life stages on decision-making, rather than the impact of age per se, and also sought to foreground intergenerational perspectives on these issues. An emphasis on life course and generation provided a powerful tool for considering the embedded nature of educational decision-making and allowed us to unpack the influence of history, biography and structure on contemporary perspectives on HE as well as on individuals' decisions (or non-decisions) about whether to participate in HE.

Underlying our interest in networks of intimacy is the idea that the relationships and contacts they entail have 'value', which is often referred to as social capital. The nature of this value becomes apparent in the attitudes and rationales for decision-making about educational participation and careers expressed by members of the same social network, and in whether decision-making is an active or much more passive 'going with the flow' process. Several of our network case studies have revealed the existence of shared attitudes to learning, education, qualifications and careers. In one network, for example, there was a particularly strong collective view that 'we're not a clever clogs family, we're just ordinary' (Heath *et al.* 2008). The network interviews also generated evidence on the choices that were considered normal for people with their particular background, gender and life-stage – that is, 'people like us'. It seems to us that these decisions could often be better interpreted as non-choices rather than active choices in the sense that individuals were doing what was expected of them by others within their network. In this regard, we have evidence that interviewees tended to work in the same occupational and employment sectors, such as the armed services or banking, as other members of their social networks. In these cases the decision to enter the sector in which the network has tradition, experience and connections appeared to be the default option, and had a knock-on effect on further decisions about educational progression and participation. An important aspect of the focus on the social network, then, is that it sheds light on the value of different sorts of interpersonal ties and the extent to which they can provide introductions to other networks; for example, relating to employment or education. Adopting a qualitative approach to social network analysis can reveal how a collective 'habitus' is helping to shape the trajectories of members as well as the existence of sub-groups and cultures; for example, between friends or parts of the family represented in the network (Heath *et al.* forthcoming)

Figures 5.2.1 and 5.2.2 present two ways of illustrating the social relations within our networks. Figure 5.2.1 offers a way of depicting the inter-generational nature of networks and Figure 5.2.2 provides an illustration of the strength and nature of 'inter-personal ties' between network members (Granovetter 1973). Our study is relatively unusual in seeking to explore the influence exerted on decision-making by a diverse intergenerational range of personal contacts – whether parents, children, grandparents, siblings, partners, friends or workmates – and in particular in seeking to foreground the network itself as an important unit of analysis. Our approach does not preclude an analysis of individual accounts of decision-making, yet the nature of our data means that we are also able to explore *relationship*-based accounts, such as the specific interaction

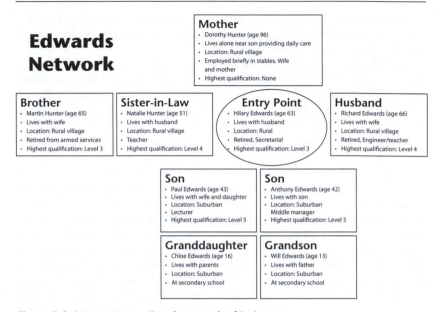

Edwards Network

Mother
- Dorothy Hunter (age 96)
- Lives alone near son providing daily care
- Location: Rural village
- Employed briefly in stables. Wife and mother
- Highest qualification: None

Brother
- Martin Hunter (age 65)
- Lives with wife
- Location: Rural village
- Retired from armed services
- Highest qualification: Level 3

Sister-in-Law
- Natalie Hunter (age 51)
- Lives with husband
- Location: Rural village
- Teacher
- Highest qualification: Level 4

Entry Point
- Hilary Edwards (age 63)
- Lives with husband
- Location: Rural
- Retired, Secretarial
- Highest qualification: Level 3

Husband
- Richard Edwards (age 66)
- Lives with wife
- Location: Rural village
- Retired, Engineer/teacher
- Highest qualification: Level 4

Son
- Paul Edwards (age 43)
- Lives with wife and daughter
- Location: Suburban
- Lecturer
- Highest qualification: Level 5

Son
- Anthony Edwards (age 42)
- Lives with son
- Location: Suburban Middle manager
- Highest qualification: Level 5

Granddaughter
- Chloe Edwards (age 16)
- Lives with parents
- Location: Suburban
- At secondary school

Grandson
- Will Edwards (age 13)
- Lives with father
- Location: Suburban
- At secondary school

Figure 5.2.1 Intergenerational network of intimacy

between parents and children – for example, or between siblings, friends or partners – alongside *network*-based accounts, which may be embedded across the network as a whole or within specific parts of the network.

There is a rich tradition of work within the sociology of education which has focused on the ways in which decision-making can be construed as a process which is embedded within social networks. Bourdieu's work on habitus and the transmission of forms of capital stands as a critical benchmark and inspiration in this respect (e.g. Bourdieu, 1976, 1986), whilst the work of Coleman (e.g. 1988) and, more recently, Putnam (2000) has also been used to explore the degree to which forms of social capital embedded within families and communities affect the ability of individuals to participate and be included within civic society, including in the sphere of education. Putnam defines social capital as 'connections among individuals – social networks and the norms of reciprocity and trustworthiness that arise from them' (2000: 19). He goes on to draw attention to the distinction between 'bonding' and 'bridging' social capital. The former refers to the values of solidarity, mutual reinforcement, support and specific forms of reciprocation associated with homogeneous groups, whilst the latter refers to more diffuse and indirect forms of linkage and reciprocation between and within groups.

Our analytical approach also includes a concern with life course. The term 'life course' is used to refer to 'a sequence of socially defined events and roles enacted by an individual over time' (Giele and Elder 1998: 22).

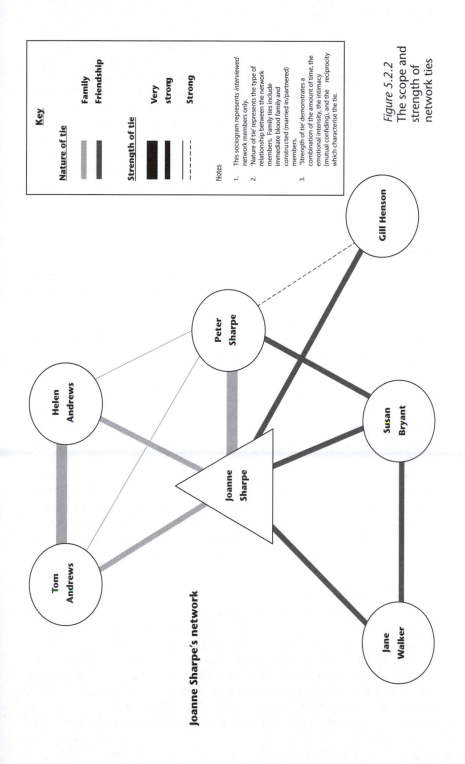

Joanne Sharpe's network

Key

Nature of tie

Family
Friendship

Strength of tie

Very
strong

Strong

Notes

1. This sociogram represents *interviewed* network members only.

2. 'Nature of tie' represents the type of relationship between the network members. Family ties include immediate blood family and constructed (married in/partnered) members.

3. 'Strength of tie' demonstrates a combination of the amount of time, the emotional intensity, the intimacy (mutual confiding), and the reciprocity which characterise the tie.

Figure 5.2.2
The scope and strength of network ties

Unlike the term 'life cycle', it does not assume that those events and roles are biologically determined or that they will necessarily proceed in a pre-defined sequence. Nonetheless, there is a powerful normative element to popular understandings of the life course, inasmuch as individuals themselves often judge certain events in their lives to have occurred at the right or the wrong time. And perceptions of 'the right and wrong time' tend to be strongly linked to an individual's generational positioning: whether in terms of their *family* generation – whether they are in the grandparent, parent or child generation, for example – or in terms of their *cohort* generation – membership of a particular cohort, such as the generation raised during the Second World War, or the 1960s generation (Miller 2000).

4 Key findings

Our empirical research involved two phases (see Appendix 7 for more details). Phase one included interviews with thirty-two key informants representing a range of national, regional and local organisations with policy and practice interests in supporting greater HE participation. Phase two consisted of interviews with sixteen entry point individuals with level 3 as their highest qualification and members of their networks of intimacy. A total of 107 people were interviewed in sixteen case study networks. We interviewed males and females across a wide age range, although most were of working age (see Appendix 7 for details of sample characteristics). The youngest respondent was 13 years old and the oldest 96 years (both these individuals actually came from one network in which we interviewed four generations of the same family). The overall sample, including entry point individuals and other network members, has generated a relatively large number of adults, forty-four in total, who have the qualifications to enter HE but who, so far, have not chosen to do so. Most of these individuals had left full-time education before the age of 18 and many of them had acquired their level 3 awards after the age of 21. Ninety per cent of them had obtained vocational rather than academic qualifications at level 3 and most were in skilled and supervisory level employment.

4.1 Sources of advice

The first finding we want to highlight is grounded in the data from our first phase interviews with key widening participation stakeholders, but has also been strongly corroborated by the accounts of our network participants. It is striking that no single agency has the widening of participation in HE across the life course as its core mission. Three quarters of the thirty-two widening participation stakeholders we spoke to in 2006 worked specifically with under-19 year olds, whilst those working with older groups were largely concerned with increasing adult basic skills to level 2

(Fuller and Paton 2008), which equates to five GCSE's at A* to C or their vocational equivalents, or were more concerned with raising skill levels in particular employment contexts. At the time of this fieldwork, no single agency had responsibility for providing impartial advice and guidance on education and employment decisions to adults across the life course, and specifically in relation to opportunities for higher level study. Following the government's acceptance of the analysis of workforce skills presented in the Leitch Review, it announced its intention to develop the Adult Advancement and Careers Service (AACS). The new service is due to be rolled out in 2010 and 2011 (/www.iagreview.org.uk/home_aacs.asp for details) so, as yet, it is too early to see what sort of advice and guidance will be offered to adults seeking higher level skills and qualifications. Neither, in our stakeholder research, have we found any evidence of universities directly reaching out to the sort of people who have participated in our research, despite their 'potentially recruitable' status (Fuller and Paton 2008). As a consequence, the adults in our sample were mostly reliant on 'hot knowledge' (Ball and Vincent 1998) – the advice and influence of members of their informal networks – which often proved to be extremely useful, but could equally be partial, inaccurate, or outdated.

There seems, then, to be a largely untapped need for professional information, advice and guidance for adults across the life course, which would have the potential to open up opportunities beyond those already represented within an individual's social network. Workplace provision is likely to be particularly appealing to employees, given its ready accessibility, whilst community-based provision could also be of great value. One of our research participants – for example, Rosie, a 35 year old woman not in paid employment at the time of our study – received valuable careers advice through guidance sessions provided at her children's school, and subsequently gained qualifications and further guidance through a local 'family learning centre', supported by free child care provision. Our network approach suggests that if advice services such as these are genuinely valued, then their reputations will be established by word of mouth reports between colleagues, friends and family members. In Rosie's case, the family learning centre had become the hub of activities not only for her but also for several of her friends.

4.2 Relevance of HE

A second key finding relates to the potential appeal of HE to adult members of the population already in possession of level 3 qualifications. Our 'potentially recruitable' individuals are largely located in networks which are characterised by relative economic and employment stability, and most see little if any need to disturb their current employment and domestic circumstances through pursuing level 4 qualifications. The research was completed before the 'economic downturn' in the UK took hold. The growing economic uncertainty may alter people's beliefs about the relevance of HE, and not necessarily in the direction of increased participation given popular perceptions of the diminishing returns of a degree-level education. We know from analysis of the Labour Force Survey that those whose highest qualification is at level 3 are marginally more likely to be in employment than the population as a whole. When compared with the level 2 population, they are also more likely to be in skilled trades (if male) and in personal service occupations (if female) and less likely to be in unskilled and elementary occupations. This then is a population of 'ordinary' people whose participation or otherwise in HE has not until recently been considered a 'public issue', yet who will increasingly become the focus of government attention in pursuit of the Leitch Review target.

It follows that policy-makers need to demonstrate to the potentially recruitable group that there may indeed be potential benefits to be gained from participating in HE. This was by no means readily apparent to our research participants. To a large degree their perceptions were linked to the opportunity structures which had shaped their own school to work transitions. For many of the older members of our level 3 sample, the acquisition of these qualifications provided the career opportunities and trajectories that, in the contemporary labour market, were increasingly perceived only to be available to younger people with level 4 qualifications (Fuller and Heath 2008). One of our respondents, David, now in his early fifties, had entered the Civil Service straight from school at 16, and through subsequently obtaining a BTEC National qualification had gradually worked his way up to a management position. Such opportunities for internal progression, he argued, were no longer available in his workplace, with the current emphasis being on the recruitment of graduates from outside the organisation. David was aware that he would require a level 4 qualification for further promotion but also that additional qualifications would not guarantee promotion.

People such as David will need to be firmly convinced, then, that there are tangible benefits to be gained from the acquisition of level 4 qualifications, including increased job security, promotion, higher salary and new career opportunities, but this still might not provide sufficient incentive to participate. Indeed, David went on to say that he had now achieved everything he wanted to achieve in career terms and wished to focus his energies on his family and other non-work interests: 'doing HE now would take so much time . . . I'd rather spend the time doing something I enjoy, rather than something that would be seen as a chore!' Many of our respondents made very similar comments, often linked to a perception that they were now 'too old' to consider HE – a perception shared by respondents across the life course, not just those in clear view of retirement. In the current context, then (and since our research was completed), of rapidly rising unemployment and economic uncertainty, promotion of the non-economic benefits of participation may need to come more to the fore in the policy discourse than in the past when the positive economic returns to a university degree featured most strongly in appeals to increase and diversify the HE population

Other participants noted that their motivations for pursuing level 3 studies had rarely been primarily informed by a desire to progress to level 4. Lorraine, for example, a woman in her late forties who had acquired a BTEC National as an adult, had returned to study in order to prove to herself that she was capable of academic success, something which had eluded her during her compulsory schooling, and in order to establish her independence in a failing relationship. Others, such as Helen, a 21 year old training manager with two A-levels, were also keen to emphasise that there was more to life than the gaining of additional qualifications: 'I would much rather have a mediocre job and a small wage and be happy and comfortable in my life . . . you don't have to go to university to do well in life, there are other routes to success.'

On the other hand, participation trends show that there has been a strong rise in take up of HE by mature students (aged 21 or over on entry) and older mature students (aged over 30 on entry) (Fuller 2007). There are slightly more male mature entrants to full-time first degree courses than female (Archer *et al.* 2003). The older group, in particular, are highly likely to follow part-time courses, finding ways of combining a return to study with other domestic or employment commitments (Davies 1999; Brennan *et al.* 1999). In addition to their age, older students also diversify the student population in other ways. Mature undergraduates are more likely than their younger peers: to come from lower socio-economic backgrounds; to have left school earlier; to have fewer academic qualifications on entry; and to study part-time (Hogarth *et al.* 1997; Fuller 2001; Watson 2006). So, whilst our potentially recruitable sample expressed rational and understandable reasons in the contexts of their lives for not acquiring higher level qualifications, this should be seen alongside evidence which indicates that qualifications are growing in importance for a variety of social and economic reasons for other adults, including some members of our network sample who had achieved level four qualifications in mid-life (Fuller 2007; Fuller and Heath 2008).

4.3 The multi-directionality of network influence

A third key finding challenges conventional accounts that conceive social capital as being (only) transmitted down the generations from parent to child. Coleman (1988), for example, suggests that parental social capital flows to their offspring as a resource which is shared between siblings: the more children there are the less social capital is available to each (Gillies and Lucey 2006). However, other conceptions of social capital which identify the possibility for networks and families to develop 'bridging' (Putnam 2000) and 'linking' (Woolcock 1998) social capital suggest that new resources can be added to and disseminated within social groups. The possibility that social capital can be introduced as well as being depleted across parent–child generations opens up the potential for influence on decision-making to flow upwards and across the generations as well as downwards. Evidence for this multi-directionality was found in our network research.

In particular, influence was exerted within a network by those with prior experience of HE. Higher education was an increasingly common experience or expectation amongst the younger network members involved in our research, reflecting the expansion of the sector in recent years. These young people – mostly the children or nephews and nieces of our 'potentially recruitable' sample – were often the first members of their immediate families to participate. The HE experiences of these 'participation pioneers' appear to be critical in shaping the perceptions of other, especially older, network members, and not always in positive directions.

Many network members who had no first-hand experience of higher education expressed ambivalence about its value. They were proud of the achievements of their relatives and friends, but simultaneously expressed concerns about what they perceived to be the poor 'returns' from their participation in HE, and their difficulties in achieving graduate-level employment. For example, Cathy, a young woman in her mid-twenties, had graduated quite recently. She was the daughter of one of our entry point individuals and the first member of the family to participate in HE. Cathy had been unable to secure graduate level employment after she left university. The absence of any clear benefit to Cathy in labour market terms had left members of her family across the generations rather sceptical about the value of HE and its expansion, as comments from three generations of the family revealed:

> a lot if it is a waste of time and money. You get these youngsters going on courses and they finish it and they still can't get a job.
>
> (Cathy's grandmother)

> I just think there's too many people going along that road for the amount of work there is . . . I have probably said to the boys [her teenage sons] that I think a degree leaves you with a very large debt and not necessarily what you want to do in life, but I haven't suggested to them that they couldn't do it if they wanted to.
>
> (Cathy's aunt)

In speaking about Cathy's participation, her brother Paul noted that 'she'd probably have the same job without the degree, I think'. Even though participation pioneers such as Cathy had for the most part thoroughly enjoyed their time at university, it appeared that their experiences were often judged by other members of their networks in quite instrumental terms (Heath *et al.* 2008). This was not always the case, however. Another of our entry point individuals, Linda Dixon, was pleased when her daughter went to university and was not particularly troubled that Natasha, now in her mid-twenties, was not using her degree in her work. Linda believed that the experience of HE was worthwhile even if it had not clearly led to career advantage or benefits:

> And she hasn't used it [her degree]. I don't think it really matters . . . cause I think you learn so much from the whole experience don't you? . . . Just doing, you know educating to that level . . . and I don't think it matters . . . Learning about life and just what you have to do you know and building your self-confidence . . . And she might go back and use it at sometime anyway.

The example of individuals within networks who have experienced HE as mature learners exerted a generally positive influence on the attitudes of other members. Seven of the twenty-eight network members in our sample have achieved their level 4 qualifications in mid-life or later life (aged at least 34). There is some evidence that if the network contains at least one person – often a friend – who has experienced or is experiencing HE as a mature student, their example helps to open up possibilities for alternative educational, career or lifestyle trajectories within the network. Interestingly, the networks in our study in which HE appears to be more favourably viewed tend to be those which are more friendship-based, rather than those networks which are more exclusively oriented towards family members. This highlights the importance of access to alternative social networks and the links and resources they contain. It also suggests that potential university recruits might be more likely to respond to exhortations to participate if it is clear that they are indeed part of the target audience for expansion and if they can imagine following similar routes to people like themselves who have already gone into HE. One of our entry point individuals, Joanna, a woman in her mid-thirties working in a human resources role in the NHS, noted the positive example of older learners in her own workplace: 'I meet amazing people in my job now and I think wow. I mean we've got nurses qualifying all the time and they're in their fifties and things' (Fuller *et al.* forthcoming). In this particular network, three of the members (including Joanna's husband and two of her friends) had attained their higher level qualifications in mid-life. This meant that the network itself had a growing reservoir of social capital which could be drawn on by members as a resource in their decision-making about participation.

These findings illustrate, then, both the nuanced nature of network influence and its multidirectionality. Influences on decision-making can operate between and within generations, both in upward and sideways directions, and not solely from older to younger generations.

4.4 Perceived value of learning

The final finding we want to highlight in this chapter relates to the generally positive attitudes amongst our sample towards formal and informal learning. This is despite the fact that few spoke in particularly positive terms about their experiences of compulsory schooling. Stories of bullying, unsupported and undiagnosed learning disabilities, feelings of being invisible to teachers, and the negative impact on their schooling of illness and family bereavements, were widespread. Nonetheless, the potentially recruitable members of our sample have extensive experience of both informal and formal learning as adults, and are overwhelmingly positive about these experiences.

In relation to informal learning, there was a very high incidence of self-directed and non-certificated forms of learning in pursuit of personal interests. Our sample includes both aspiring and highly accomplished artists and writers, leaders and members of various voluntary organisations, keen sportsmen and women, and individuals engaged in a whole host of other hobbies and leisure activities, all involving elements of informal learning for its own sake, including for many participation in non-certificated classes. Involvement in non-certificated forms of learning was particular strong in some networks, indicating a collective disposition or learning identity. For example, two members of the Upton network, which included three generations of the family, have written books in their spare time and all members are involved in community and voluntary work including through their engagement in the Scouts, Sea Cadets, the Church, and through pursuing Duke of Edinburgh Awards. Employment is seen as a means to provide material stability and a 'good job' is one which supports a comfortable standard of living and leaves time to engage in hobbies and develop interests out of work.

In contrast, support for more formal educational opportunities appears to be strongly associated with the perceived worth and utility of specific courses and qualifications. Whilst seeing the value of lifelong learning in general terms, interviewees needed to be convinced that participation in formal courses and qualifications, particularly at higher levels, would yield tangible and easily articulated returns. Interestingly, respondents rarely invoked a discourse of 'barriers' in relation to their potential participation, but focused instead on the perceived relevance of formal learning to their personal and working lives, and the likelihood that they would acquire new skills and knowledge, not simply accreditation for what they already knew (Fuller et al. 2008). Neither was participation in formal learning widely viewed amongst our sample members in terms of a straightforward progression through the various levels of the qualifications framework; many wanted to pursue awards at similar or lower levels to their current highest qualification, a finding which has relevance to current debates concerning government funding for equal or lower qualifications.

We also have evidence to suggest that workplace opportunities exert a particularly powerful pull on participation decisions, and that there is an appetite for high-quality work-related provision, including in-house provision. Several participants had been able to pursue structured and certificated training opportunities in their own workplaces and stated that they would not have chosen to pursue these if this had involved attendance at local colleges instead. For example, Adrian, a man in his early forties working in the ship building industry, said that this would have been too much like returning to school, which had been a very mixed experience for him. In Adrian's case, given his reticence about external provision, it seemed unlikely that he would further his training beyond the courses available at work. In contrast, John, a full-time union representative in his early fifties, had had his interest in further learning awakened by in-house provision, and at the time of the second interview was considering pursuing a level 4 qualification through a local college and with some employer support. Examples such as these suggest that increasing the availability of work-related, higher level opportunities with direct employer support in funding and/or time is likely to encourage employee take up, given the level of latent demand that our research is uncovering.

5 Conclusions

In conclusion, we suggest that a qualitative social network approach (Heath *et al.* forthcoming) to educational decision-making has much to offer those working in the area of widening participation, whether as practitioners or as policy-makers, in particular in highlighting the potential limitations of approaches which exclusively target individuals rather than social networks. For instance, our findings suggest that it would be very helpful to know more about the way in which formal and less formal types of participation are valued across different social networks, as well as about the extent to which the policy concept of progression expressed in terms of qualification levels maps on to personal and collective concepts and understandings. Institutions that can provide 'linking social capital' including colleges, universities, employers, family learning centres, Learn Direct, and the new government-sponsored adult careers initiative need to develop impartial adult information, advice and guidance (IAG) services and ensure that these are readily available to those currently not participating at level 4.

Our research indicates that policy-makers face a challenge in convincing many of those already qualified to level 3 to pursue higher level awards, even if they express an interest in so doing (Pollard *et al.* 2008). At the time of writing, the deteriorating economic and employment conditions in the UK and elsewhere create an even greater test for widening participation policy. Given intense concerns about both the availability of credit and the ability of borrowers to repay loans, groups who have traditionally sought and achieved alternative routes to material and employment success may well become even harder to persuade that HE will deliver the economic returns necessary to reimburse their financial outlay. Those adults in mid-life or nearing retirement also have to take into account the more limited period of employment they will have in the 'graduate jobs' to recoup their investment, compared with younger age groups. On the other hand, the evidence from those participating in HE as mature learners (see also Chapter 5, Section 1 this volume) confirms their positive experiences of HE and the gateway it has provided to careers; for example, in nursing, surveying and teaching. As the competition for 'good jobs' increases during the economic difficulties, HE level qualifications particularly in regulated sectors which require specific qualifications for entry may grow in appeal to younger and older adults. In this scenario, the need for researchers to monitor who participates in HE, to do what and with what outcomes becomes an ever more important task in pursuit of equity and social justice goals.

In relation to the government's target for 40 per cent of the workforce to acquire level 4 qualifications by 2020, there are two particular areas that require attention. First, many in the target group have vocational awards at level 3 rather than A-levels, and they often do not perceive these as having the currency required to study at undergraduate level (see also Chapter 3, Section 3, this volume). Second, increasing take-up at level 4 will depend on the availability of easily accessible and affordable pro-grammes, which allow flexible and part-time modes of delivery. For the potentially recruitable adults represented in our sample, quality of provision and currency of the resulting qualification are important. They are attracted to meaningful education, training and career development but do not automatically associate this with gaining higher level qualifications. Gaining credentials for the sake of having credentials does not appeal to this group.

Finally, the research reported in this section of the chapter suggests that the network approach to researching education and career decision-making could provide the sort of nuanced messages to policy-makers that would help them intervene more effectively. Our evidence indicates that the work of practitioners seeking to widen participation in HE would benefit from a deeper understanding of the embedded nature of education decision-making, the variety of pulls and the consequent limitations of approaches which exclusively target individuals (rather than social networks) and younger generations. Without such an approach it is hard to see how a comprehensive understanding can be reached of the historically depen-dent, relational, personal and collective aspects of decision-making about education across the life course.

Part III

What are the overall implications for both policy and research?

In this concluding part of the book we consider how to make higher education meaningful in people's diverse lives both socially and economically. In Chapter 6 we draw together our overall findings and address the implications for policy and for research. We also provide further evidence about the implications of policies on fair access and widening participation in terms of their continuing contribution to people's economic lives and differential involvement in the labour market, whether or not a graduate and professional market. In Chapter 7 we turn our attention to the question of how to improve learning by widening participation in higher education. Here we concentrate on the broader issue of teaching and learning across the life course. We address the question of how to develop fair and equitable pedagogies for social diversity, and for engaging diverse learners across the life course.

What are the overall findings and implications for evidence-based policies on fair access and widening participation?

Miriam David with contributions from Geoff Hayward and Hubert Ertl

1 Introduction

Using our conceptual framework that we identified in the introduction, in this concluding part of the book we identify evidence-based ideas about how to extend and increase equitable or fair access to, and participation within, higher education through an array of strategies around learning and teaching. In Chapter 6 we develop the theoretical framings on social and political approaches that our research teams used and referred to in Part 2 to draw together the themes and threads that we have considered there. We discuss these various perspectives on our collective findings and then the implications for particular approaches for policies, practices and pedagogies for individuals and institutions.

In Chapter 7, we make major suggestions, therefore, about how to improve learning within higher education and across the life course on a fair and equitable basis. We also revisit the meanings of equity and fairness in access to and participation within higher education by considering their diverse and different meanings within emergent policies and practices in the contexts of changing economic and educational systems. In particular in this last chapter we will consider how to improve learning through making institutional practices more equitable, and improving pedagogies to ensure fair and equitable learning across the life course. In so doing, we are attune to the dynamic and constantly changing global and national contexts for transforming educational opportunities with respect to a digital and knowledge age in the twenty-first century. We will also offer brief commentary therefore on the changing global and digital contexts for educational and social science research on these questions.

One of the main problems about researching policies and practices about diversity, equity and fair access or participation within higher education is that this is a dynamic and constantly changing field of research and policy.

Whilst our seven projects have been alive and attentive to the constantly changing policy and practice processes and have captured evidence about these changes, they have also had to consider the complex and detailed in-depth evidence about institutions and individuals at particular moments in history. We will therefore return to consider the dynamic implications of the findings about institutional and individual changes within these constantly changing and global contexts.

In addition, all the teams were aware of the problems inherent in data collection, whatever the methodology in relation to this particular policy issue. In particular, *two gaps* have been identified which have a bearing on the robustness and quality of the data used on which to base our evidence. First, Hayward's team has commented that 'looking at widening participation issues in detail requires appropriate data which should, in principle, be available from the large-scale administrative datasets collected by University Central Admissions Service (UCAS) and Higher Education Statistics Agency (HESA) in Britain. However, at the moment, the collection, presentation and access policy for these major administrative datasets may follow political goals (for example, "parity of esteem of vocational and academic level 3 qualifications") rather than an open research agenda. This is not very helpful. Instead, better cooperation between the agencies collecting data and the research community is required. Better access to full anonymised datasets and the inclusion of some categories and variables that are particularly relevant to research should be introduced. In particular, more easily accessible data on part-time and direct entry students and their educational background is needed. *By combining different datasets our projects are contributing to progress in this direction. Only on this basis is research-informed policy possible.'*

Second, Fuller's team argues strongly, as we will show below, that 'our research has shown that there is currently *no agency with responsibility for increasing and widening participation in HE across the life course.* Inevitably, this means that the processes are fragmented and uncoordinated, leading to systematic discrepancies in policy development. The Labour Force Survey indicates that there are currently around 6 million adults (20 per cent of the workforce) with level 3 as their highest formal qualification, providing a large pool of people, the majority over 30 years old, who are "potentially recruitable" to HE.' As we shall see this has major implications for policy recommendations.

2 Our overarching findings and their implications

Our overarching finding across all the seven projects is that there remain *systemic and systematic forms of inequality for individuals and institutions across subjects and levels of education.* This is not only in higher education but also from school, family, college and other forms of learning, including work. This is despite widespread commitments to equity and diversity as defining fair access or widening participation in higher education and forms of lifelong and/or vocational learning. We have also found, however, that a *greater diversity of students is now participating in some form of post-compulsory or higher education*. This includes students or adults across a wider age spectrum than a traditional age cohort and from a diversity of families, socio-economic backgrounds and ethnicities as well as gender. These issues continue to pose challenges for English systems of higher education and extend beyond current policy concerns with the concept of equitable or fair access in expanding systems of higher education. These complexities map onto similar concerns across the UK, and more globally. We will return to raise questions about the implications of them for opportunities, outcomes and the various obstacles to their achievement given our research evidence and dynamic research approaches.

Whilst there has been massive expansion and indeed transformation of educational opportunities in England in the last decade, and especially in the twenty-first century, equitable or fair access to and participation within higher education is not achieved at *the point of entry* or transition to higher education, as we have seen. The question of the target population for policies and practices on fair access and widening participation, disadvantaged or under-represented groups as individuals or as part of a wider institutional focus, as we have already revealed, remains complexly linked to government, institutional or individual practices, identities and perspectives. There are systematic forms of difference across institutions and individuals which are reinforced through policies and policy changes and these may also be linked to definitions and types of institution. Here we draw together the complex and constantly changing definitions about both the conceptualisation and the contextualisation of the diversity of individuals and institutions within wider contexts of economic global-isation. Since the policy and practice contexts, as well as the economy, are in a constant state of flux, inevitably how to represent under-represented or disadvantaged groups and/or individuals (from poverty and poor or disadvantaged family circumstances to social class, gender and ethnicity) has key implications for policies, practices and pedagogies for the future.

To summarise the findings from our seven projects, we have grouped them into three theoretical and methodological approaches, namely those in relation to *policy*, and national or government policies on widening participation or fair access strategies; second, to *practices* and especially institutional or school, college and university practices in relation to a diversity of students as they pass through and to their achievements or outcomes; and third, findings in relation to teaching and learning or what we call here *pedagogies* for social diversity. Clearly, however, this kind of summary does not do full justice to the criss-crossing and interlocking nature of the themes and findings across the seven projects. We present first a summary of these findings followed by a summary and commentary on the key implications in the tables that follow. This approach here is based upon the summaries of findings and implications presented by the projects in their Research Briefings numbers 38–44 (June 2008) rather than the discursive texts presented in Part 2, although our analytical approach is based upon how the project teams have presented their findings and the implications in Part 2 of this book. Thus the numbered findings, and their associated implications, and their inclusion in the following three sections, are based upon the fact that the teams have presented twenty-seven findings overall (Crozier – five; Fuller – four; Hayward – four; Hockings – three; Parry – five; Vignoles – three; Williams – three). We have grouped them into nine policy; eleven practice and seven pedagogies. They play out slightly differently in terms of implications with twelve for policy, eleven for practice and only four specifically for pedagogical improvements.

As we noted in the introduction, four of our projects, using a range of theoretical and methodological frameworks, worked especially on themes relating to national policies and the impact of their findings for government action and changing strategic interventions. Thus Fuller, Hayward, Parry and Vignoles presented findings in this arena (nine policy findings overall). Again using a range of theoretical and methodological frameworks, the projects whose findings relate to institutional practices and especially actions in relation to colleges and universities with a concern for student progress and outcomes are Crozier, Hayward, Hockings, Williams, with some contributions from Parry's team (eleven practice findings overall). Finally the key findings in relation to pedagogies and pedagogical improvement for social diversity include Williams, Hockings, Hayward and Crozier with theoretical and methodological innovatory implications (seven pedagogical findings overall).

2.1 Findings on policies about fair access and widening participation in HE

First, as regards official emergent policies on fair access and widening participation, with changing policy foci we find that: 'No single [government] agency has the widening of participation in HE across the life course as its core mission' (F1). This lack poses major problems for the systematic coordination of policies on widening participation and fair access to HE especially in extending provision for adults. Indeed, our project (led by Fuller) on those adults with relevant and appropriate (level 3) qualifications found that 'there is an appetite for high quality, work-related and employer-supported provision, and for recognised qualifications that offer recipients tangible returns' (F4). In other words, whilst the English policy focus may have changed, those individuals who are now defined as part of the potential target population, especially as mature students, are not being facilitated to enter HE.

Second, the specific policies on fair access and widening participation remain overly complex and structurally unequal. As Parry and his team argue policy development for dual-sector (further and higher) education is uneven and unstable, and is led by the sector bodies for higher education (P2). In other words, the traditional HE policy focus on the universities remains dominant. Perhaps more importantly, given the shifting policy goals that we have just mentioned, there has been no systematic attempt to transform power relations between the two sectors involved in HE provision. 'Separate funding and quality regimes for further and higher education have evolved despite the lack of a developed rationale for a two-sector system' (P1).

It is little wonder therefore that we find that the 'target population' for the policies on fair access and widening participation, even for those of the relevant age group of 18 to 30 year olds, are not being satisfactorily accommodated in HE, and especially not in the old universities. There is, as we have shown, a diversity of definitions of those who are not included or who are 'under-represented groups'. As we have seen in Part 2, we have looked at several different ways of classifying such individuals from these groups.

Starting with a broad and policy-relevant definition of poverty or socio-economic disadvantage, and using receipt of Free School Meals (FSM) as the key criterion, from our large quantitative analysis (led by Vignoles) we find that 'state school children from *"poor backgrounds"* remain far less likely to go to university than more advantaged children' (V1). However, amongst the group of advantaged there now is a tendency towards more female rather than male students entering university. Perhaps more surprisingly, many ethnic minority groups of students are generally more likely to go to university than White British students. Certainly once we allow for differences in prior achievement, ethnic minority students are as likely, or more likely, to participate in higher education than White students (V3).

Hayward's team has also shown that 'the primary target groups for widening participation are over-represented in HE applicants with a VET background' (GH1). This team goes on to find that if the socio-economically disadvantaged students have a combination of vocational and academic qualifications this will significantly increase the probability of access to HE compared to VET qualifications alone (GH2). In terms of these students disadvantaged by socio-economic circumstance, or defined as 'working class' as Crozier's team used the term, then we find that 'the working class students . . . demonstrated great resilience and commitment to their studies, often in the face of adverse structural discrimination and oppression' (C3).

2.2 Findings on (institutional) practices about fair access and widening participation in HE

As regards institutional practices, another key finding across all our projects is about *prior experiences* of learning in formal school or college contexts.

The strongest finding in this respect comes from Crozier's team who argue that 'students' learner identities are influenced by previous experiences of school, their current university experience and their social circumstances' (C4).

Vignoles' team argues strongly that 'poorer and richer students who achieve similarly in secondary school have similar HE participation rates. We need to improve the achievement of poorer children in secondary school to widen their participation in HE (V2).

Similarly Fuller's team finds that: 'HE experiences within social networks critically shape the perceptions of "potentially recruitable" adults across and within generations' (AF3). In many cases then 'the "potentially recruitable" in [our] research are living comfortable, stable lives and usually see little need to participate in HE' (F2).

It is not only prior experiences within educational institutions that shape students' experiences, but it is also the *institutions* themselves, as we have begun to elaborate. On the one hand, it can be found in the colleges that prepare for participation in HE such that Williams' team also finds systemic and structural barriers to learning, namely 'A culture of "performativity" in colleges reinforces teaching to the test that can be damaging to learners' (W3). On the other hand, it may be the HE institutions themselves that reinforce systemic and structural inequalities.

Hockings' team also argues that 'university systems designed to assure quality and maximise the economic efficiency of teaching constrain teachers' capacity to create inclusive pedagogies' (CH3). Crozier's team again also argues that 'structural inequalities between institutions can enhance or undermine students' learner identities and their dispositions towards learning at university' (C1).

Hayward's team finds that these institutional practices operate in a particularly discriminatory way: 'VET students are overrepresented in less selective institutions' (GH3). Parry's team's evidence is also very illuminating about institutional foci and boundaries: 'The primary attachment of an institution is to a sector, and relationships with another sector differ in kind and intensity' (P3). 'Decisions to combine further and higher education are only partially informed by widening participation strategies' (P4). And most significantly 'the interfaces between further and higher education are configured in different ways and do not necessarily enhance internal progression' (P5).

2.3 Findings on pedagogies for fair access and widening participation in HE

Finally, turning to our findings on pedagogies for fairness and widening participation, Hockings' team is clear that 'the dominant notion of traditional and non-traditional students creates over-simplistic understandings which limit the development of inclusive, engaging teaching' (CH2).

Moreover, as Hayward's team shows 'many HE lecturers have limited awareness of the diverse qualification backgrounds of their students and their possible impact' (GH4).

Williams' team finds that addressing diversity through a consideration of appropriate educational 'programmes can make significant differences to drop-out rates and to the value of mathematics for students' (W1). They also show that '"connectionist" teaching practices can make a significant difference to students' dispositions and understanding, especially for students with lower GCSE grades' (W2).

Hockings' team also finds that: 'students value teaching that recognizes their individual academic and social identities and that addresses their particular learning needs' (CH1). Similarly Crozier's specific focus on working-class students demonstrates that their 'experiences are frequently disjunctive and marked by tension and competing demands' (C2). Finally this team finds that these different educational experiences have the effect of 'the students deconstruct[ing] and reconstruct[ing] their social and class identities creating hybrid identities' (C5).

We have listed these findings in Table 6.1.

We now consider the implications of these overall findings for policies, practices and pedagogies for fair access and widening participation. These implications have also been addressed as both bullet points and more discursively in each of the Research Briefings. There is, however, not a clear one-to-one alignment between the findings and the implications as they may impact upon policies, and policy strategies or development, practices for both institutions and individuals within and across levels of education, and pedagogical improvements for social diversity. There are twelve implications for policy, eleven for institutional practices, especially on educational developments or for educational developers, and four for pedagogical improvements, including again for educational developers.

2.4 Implications of the findings on policies about fair access and widening participation in HE

First, given the systematic and structural inequalities within systems and sectors of education at present, a major implication is that clear and explicit consideration needs to be given to transforming policy systems. Thus, our first implication is that 'further and higher education need to be regarded as parts of a common enterprise, with mechanisms to recognise and support this' (P1). Linked to this, we would argue that 'policy-makers need to address the unequal funding streams and the drift back towards a [binary] division between the different universities' (C1).

Many of these points have been elaborated discursively. Thus Parry's team argues that 'instead of separate and overlapping zones of further and higher education, contemporary conditions favour an open system of colleges and universities. The planned extension of the compulsory phase,

Table 6.1 Summary of the findings (tabulated from the seven Research Briefings)

Policy	Practice (institutional)	Pedagogy
No single agency has the widening of participation in HE across the life course as its core mission. (F1)	Poorer and richer students who achieve similarly in secondary school have similar HE participation rates. We need to improve the achievement of poorer children in secondary school to widen their participation in HE. (V2)	The dominant notion of traditional and non-traditional students creates oversimplistic understandings which limit the development of inclusive, engaging teaching. (CH2)
There is an appetite for high-quality, work-related and employer-supported provision, and for recognised qualifications that offer recipients tangible returns. (F4)	Students' learner identities are influenced by previous experiences of school, their current university experience and their social circumstances. (C4)	Many HE lecturers have limited awareness of the diverse qualification backgrounds of their students and their possible impacts. (GH4)
Policy development for dual-sector education is uneven and unstable, and is led by the sector bodies for higher education. (P2)	HE experiences within social networks critically shape the perceptions of 'potentially recruitable' adults across and within generations. (F3)	Programmes can make significant differences to drop out rates and to the value of mathematics for students. (W1)
Separate funding and quality regimes for further and higher education have evolved despite the lack of a developed rationale for a two-sector system. (P1)	Structural inequalities between institutions can enhance or undermine students' learner identities and their dispositions towards learning at university. (C1)	'Connectionist' teaching practices can make a significant difference to students' dispositions and understanding, especially for students with lower GCSE grades. (W2)

State school children from poor backgrounds remain far less likely to go to university than more advantaged children. (V1)	VET students are overrepresented in less selective institutions. (GH3)	Students value teaching that recognises their individual academic and social identities and that addresses their particular learning needs. (CH1)
Ethnic minority students are generally more likely to go to university than White British students once account is taken of their prior achievement. (V3)	The 'potentially recruitable' in (our) research are living comfortable, stable lives and usually see little need to participate in HE. (F2)	Experiences are frequently disjunctive and marked by tension and competing demands. (C2)
The primary target groups for widening participation are over-represented in HE applicants with a VET background. (GH1)	The working-class students in our study demonstrated great resilience and commitment to their studies, often in the face of adverse structural discrimination and oppression. (C3)	The students deconstruct and reconstruct their social and class identities creating hybrid identities. (C5)
Combinations of vocational and academic qualifications significantly increase the probability of access to HE compared to VET qualifications. (GH2)	A culture of 'performativity' in colleges reinforces teaching to the test that can be damaging to learners. (W3)	
The working-class students . . . demonstrated great resilience and commitment to their studies, often in the face of adverse structural discrimination and oppression. (C3)	University systems designed to assure quality and maximise the economic efficiency of teaching constrain teachers' capacity to create inclusive pedagogies. (CH3)	

continued

Table 6.1 Continued

Policy	Practice (institutional)	Pedagogy
	The primary attachment of an institution is to a sector, and relationships with another sector differ in kind and intensity. (P3)	
	Decisions to combine further and higher education are only partially informed by widening participation strategies. (P4)	
	The interfaces between further and higher education are configured in different ways and do not necessarily enhance internal progression. (P5)	

together with an expansion of higher education for adults in the workforce, will reshape the landscape of tertiary education. If the concept of further education is exposed as redundant, it should be abandoned.'

Parry's team also argues that 'more could be done to ensure a strategic approach to the coordination and integration of further and higher education. Equity agendas and skills priorities are not easily aligned, yet widening participation strategies require that progression and transfer be given as much attention as access and admission. They list possible strategic actions, namely:

- a common system of colleges and universities marked by diversity and a broad division of labour;
- a central authority with strategic responsibility for higher education and the education and training of adults;
- a more independent role for colleges at the undergraduate levels of education based on direct funding and awarding powers;
- a single qualifications and credit framework spanning secondary and post-secondary education to promote access, progression and transfer;
- a re-balancing of funding and student support to underpin part-time education and training practice in university teaching.

Crozier's team also stresses funding and elaborates these points. It asserts that policy-makers need to address the unequal funding streams that exist between old and new universities as well as between further and higher education.

Second, we have a group of implications around how to achieve equity or 'fair access' and widening participation on a more coordinated basis for individuals. This means that 'equity and skills agendas are not easily aligned, but require strong and strategic coordination' (P4). In addition, 'increasing the share of those from a VET background within the student body would contribute to wider access to HE' (GH1). Moreover, the ways in which equity or parity is defined in policy arenas becomes crucial to achieving this, namely 'parity of esteem between vocational and academic qualifications remains a myth. This has potentially serious implications for the introduction of Diplomas' (GH3).

Indeed the development of new approaches to learning and teaching 'skills' through Diplomas as well as changing A-levels will require attention. Thus, 'there is untapped need for professional information, advice and guidance for adults across the life course' (F1), or, in other words, there will need to be more policy focus on how to define the target groups for participation in HE, of whatever variety. Here Fuller's team goes on: 'from the policy perspective, it would be helpful to know more about two things: the relationship between adults' perceptions of more and less formal types of participation; and the extent to which the policy concept of progression expressed in terms of qualification levels maps on to adults' personal and collective concepts and values.' They go on to state that 'increasing take-up at level 4 will depend on the availability of accessible and affordable programmes which allow flexible and part-time modes of delivery. For the potentially recruitable adults represented in our sample, the quality of provision and the currency of the resulting qualification are important. They are attracted to meaningful education, training and career development but do not automatically associate this with gaining higher-level qualifications.'

Given the current policy commitments, Vignoles' team presents us with the following key implications, within the current system of higher stratified and structured universities, distinguishing between old (with research intensive involvement) and rather newer, more teaching intensive universities. Her team argues that 'policy attention needs to continue to focus on narrowing the socio-economic gap in both HE participation and the type of HE participation experienced' (V1). However, there needs to be some more clarity about how to define and affect improvements for components of the target group. 'The educational achievement of ethnic minority students has improved and policy attention needs to shift to the type of HE accessed by these students' (V3). They also emphasise that 'policy interventions need to encourage high achieving ethnic minority students to apply to research intensive universities and ensure that such institutions are proactive in welcoming such applications'.

If we give consideration to the implications of the dual or stratified system, policy attention also needs to consider that 'an expansion of work-focused higher education will place new demands on the access and transfer functions of dual sector institutions' (P5). Similarly Crozier's team has argued that 'students need more financial support so that they do not have to take paid employment whilst studying' (C2). This kind of a problem tends to affect those students in dual sector institutions rather than older universities. Moreover, as Fuller's team has noted, there is a need for more flexible provisions of HE and forms of employment, stating that: 'if more employers were to make this sort of provision available, the latent employee demand that our research is uncovering could be released' (F4).

Finally, there is a major educational and overarching policy implication, which leads into discussions about practices and pedagogies. This implication is stated most clearly by Williams' team, namely 'policy should reduce the pressure to teach to the test by giving value to learning outcomes of deep understanding and dispositions' (W3). This approach of 'deep understanding and dispositions' had been traditional in more academic rather than vocational forms of education until recently. Williams' team elaborated this as follows: if policy-makers want to encourage students to be well disposed to further study of science, technology, engineering and mathematics (STEM) within a performance management environment, then the development of practical usable measures of disposition and affect are important to consider. The principle should be to try to measure what we value rather than to value what we can easily measure. The team goes on to argue that the same is true of teaching practices and it is to this that we now turn.

2.5 Implications of the findings on (institutional) practices about fair access and widening participation in HE

Given our comprehensive and eclectic definitions of institutions involved in equity or fair access and widening participation, a major implication is how the differently placed and structured institutions are valued. Parry's team argues that 'further education colleges have still to be widely accepted as normal and necessary locations for higher education' (P2). It also argues that because of the complexity of educational and other missions 'dual-sector organisations do not have a specific mission, and a dual-sector identity is less evident than in some other systems' (P3). Similarly Hayward's team argues that 'processes which support combining academic and vocational qualifications need to be strengthened and developed' (GH2).

Turning to notions of the various missions of the university sector within HE, Crozier's team argues that 'universities need to be mindful of the diversity of needs, cultures and ways of being amongst their students, maintain high expectations of their students, and enable them to maximise as broadening an experience as possible' (C5). Hockings' team makes a very similar point, and links it to educational developers: 'university leaders need to ensure that systems do not limit the learning of students from diverse cultural, social and educational backgrounds' (CH3). Her team then makes the following strong recommendation that 'academic developers should help create a more sophisticated understanding of diversity that reflects students' range of social, cultural and educational backgrounds' (CH2).

Fuller's team also asserts that adults need to be encouraged to see the possibilities and social as well as economic benefits of HE. 'The potential benefits of HE need to be made more apparent to this group' (F2) and, on the other hand, institutions need to have a comprehensive outlook on their target groups such that, as Crozier's team asserts, 'working-class students should not be seen as high risk and problematic' (C3).

It is not only institutions of higher education, including both universities and some further education, for which these are important implications. Several of the teams focus on earlier levels of education, in an attempt to study the role of *'prior educational experiences'*. Thus Vignoles' team argues that 'we need to improve the achievement of poorer children in secondary school to widen their participation in HE' (V3). Vignoles' team strongly emphasises how 'widening participation in higher education requires intervention well before the point of entry into higher education to increase the attainment of children from poorer backgrounds at earlier ages'. The team also argues that 'policy solutions therefore need to address the significant gap in academic achievement between poor and rich students that is evident at the start of secondary schooling and that then widens to the end of compulsory schooling. If the performance of poor students improves between age 11 and age 16 (Key Stage 4) they are as likely to go to university as students who performed well.

Crozier's team is even more adventurous in proposing that 'more work needs to be done in primary schools to enable children to understand how to realise their aspirations' (C4). They also advise that secondary schools need to provide more information and advice about how young people can realise their aspirations.

Finally in this group of implications, Fuller's team argues that it is not just educational experiences but educational identities that are vital to widening participation. Thus a key implication is that for many adults and potential participants 'identification with entrants to HE who are "people like me" in terms of education, social and employment background influences decision-making across and within generations' (AF3).

2.6 Implications of the findings on pedagogies for fair access and widening participation in HE

Having raised the issue of how academic or education developers might transform pedagogies or teaching and learning for social diversity, we turn to the implications for pedagogies. Thus, Williams' team is absolutely explicit about what kinds of pedagogical improvements are required, namely arguing that 'if we value inclusion, and outcomes such as under-standing and disposition, more connectionist teaching should be encour-aged' (W2). Similarly Hockings' team asserts that 'university teachers need to develop inclusive pedagogic practices and curricula that take account of the diverse interests and needs of students in each class' (CH1). Her team argues that 'this requires more than a simple technical response. Teachers need the opportunity to reflect upon their own identities as learners and teachers, to consider issues of cultural, social and educational diversity and difference among students, and to be aware of their impact on the learning and teaching environment.'

Hockings' team also argues imaginatively that these would lead to improvement and 'enrichment'. Increased student diversity offers a rich classroom resource of knowledge and experience that can enhance students' understanding and increase academic engagement. But university systems designed to assure 'quality' and maximise the economic efficiency of teaching resources reduce teachers' scope to make the most of this potential learning resource, and constrain their capacity to create inclusive pedagogies. This has implications for university leaders concerned with resource planning, quality enhancement, and learning and teaching. They need to invite challenge to the status quo, and value teachers' lived experiences. They should try to prevent systems and policies from limiting the learning and teaching of students from diverse backgrounds.

Hayward's team also argues that 'more appropriate approaches to teaching and learning in HE require better understanding of students' VET backgrounds' (GH4). They go on to say that 'our findings also suggest that students' educational backgrounds should be considered more carefully in the design of teaching and learning in HE. This might involve developing mechanisms for the transfer of application data from admissions units to HE lecturers, support for lecturers in finding out about the aims, content and structures of vocational qualifications, and increased collaboration between VET and HE institutions.' The team also argues that it is important to strengthen lecturers' ability to respond to the diverse educational background of students in a meaningful way. This can contribute to a pedagogically driven conceptualisation of teaching and learning in HE.

Williams' team is also very clear and explicit about the appropriate strategic pedagogies, asserting that 'programmes should be designed to engage students in meaningful uses of mathematics, e.g. via modelling coursework' (W1). The team elaborates this as 'the structure of the whole programme, including assessment, materials and technologies, is important to what is learnt. It needs to be designed and continuously monitored with great care for the full range of valued learning outcomes. Currently there is no sense of a design behind curriculum development nationally.' It also goes on to say that 'widening the participation of young people in mathematically demanding courses means recognising the diversity of learners' "repertoires" of aspiration. Dialogue with learners must address these distinct constituencies and must be multi-voiced.'

2.7 Implications for further research

Taken together, these seven unique projects demonstrate that recent English government policies on widening participation have indeed led to increasing opportunities for learners from diverse families and disadvantaged socio-economic backgrounds. However, these policies have not led to fair or equal access to equal types of higher education that may lead to equal benefits in the graduate or professional labour markets. We could, however, see the improvement in higher education participation for women, over a long time frame, and more recently for ethnic minority groups as part of an improving process. Nevertheless, the overall lack of equity has implications for evidence-informed policies and for future research on policies and practices. Turning first to evidence-informed policy developments and a research strategy linked to official policies and practices, we would argue for more research that is policy relevant. Our detailed findings are related to HEFCE's Strategic Plan for 2006–2011, revised in May 2008 and can help develop further research.

Table 6.2 Summary of the implications (also tabulated from the seven Research Briefings)

Policy	Practice (institutional and individual)	Pedagogy
Further and higher education need to be regarded as parts of a common enterprise, with mechanisms to recognise and support this. (P1)	Further education colleges have still to be widely accepted as normal and necessary locations for higher education. (P2)	Programmes should be designed to engage students in meaningful uses of mathematics, e.g. via modelling coursework. (W1)
Equity and skills agendas are not easily aligned, but require strong and strategic coordination. (P4)	Dual-sector organisations do not have a specific mission, and a dual-sector identity is less evident than in some other systems. (P3)	If we value inclusion, and outcomes such as understanding and disposition, more connectionist teaching should be encouraged. (W2)
An expansion of work-focused higher education will place new demands on the access and transfer functions of dual sector institutions. (P5)	Universities need to be mindful of the diversity of needs, cultures and ways of being amongst their students, maintain high expectations of their students, and enable them to maximise as broadening an experience as possible. (C5)	University teachers need to develop inclusive pedagogic practices and curricula that take account of the diverse interests and needs of students in each class. (CH1)
Policy-makers need to address the unequal funding streams and the drift back towards a binary division between the different universities. (C1)	More work needs to be done in primary schools to enable children to understand how to realise their aspirations. (C4)	More appropriate approaches to teaching and learning in HE require better understanding of students' VET backgrounds. (GH4)

Students need more financial support so that they do not have to take paid employment whilst studying. (C2)

Policy attention needs to continue to focus on narrowing the socio-economic gap in HE participation. (V1)

Policy should reduce the pressure to teach to the test by giving value to learning outcomes of deep understanding, and dispositions. (W3)

The educational achievement of ethnic minority students has improved and policy attention needs to shift to the type of HE accessed by these students. (V3)

Increasing the share of those from a VET background within the student body would contribute to wider access to HE. (GH1)

Working-class students should not be seen as high risk and problematic. (C3)

We need to improve the achievement of poorer children in secondary school to widen their participation in HE. (V3)

Academic developers should help create a more sophisticated understanding of diversity that reflects students' range of social, cultural and educational backgrounds. (CH2)

University leaders need to ensure that systems do not limit the learning of students from diverse cultural, social and educational backgrounds. (CH3)

Processes which support combining academic and vocational qualifications need to be strengthened and developed. (GH2)

continued

Table 6.2 Continued

Policy	Practice (institutional and individual)	Pedagogy
Parity of esteem between vocational and academic qualifications remains a myth. This has potentially serious implications for the introduction of Diplomas. (GH3)	The potential benefits of HE need to be made more apparent to this group. (F2)	
There is untapped need for professional information, advice and guidance for adults across the life course. (F1)	Identification with entrants to HE who are 'people like me' in terms of education, social and employment background influences decision-making across and within generations. (F3)	
If more employers were to make this sort of provision available, the latent employee demand that our research is uncovering could be released. (F4)		

Our key findings centre on the definitions of equity or fair access in terms of the backgrounds of students as being poor, disadvantaged, or working class, and to a limited extent on ethnicity, or from Black and minority ethnic groups (BME). Policy interventions should either encourage high-achieving ethnic minority students to apply to research-intensive old universities, or alter the differential funding of universities so that universities are not defined solely by their research ratings in an ever more complex system of metrics. We have also provided some evidence of a key issue in relation to the age of students, and especially about when they are adults. Insofar as we have provided evidence about gender access to higher education we confirm that it is no longer seen as an issue for women, but centres more on young men with vocational qualifications. However, there is an issue about gender in relation to adult students and their forms of participation which we will refer to below.

As we have seen, prior experiences in school are very important for disadvantaged and working-class students' continuing participation in levels of education. Our evidence suggests that intervention to improve participation rates needs to occur well before the traditional point of entry into higher education at 18 or 19 years old if the attainment of children from poorer, disadvantaged or working-class backgrounds is to be improved. Key Stage 4 in state schools emerges as one appropriate point, although earlier interventions and polices may also be critical. Similarly, there is a continuing question of providing higher education across the life course, and we have also found that even if students have qualified to enter higher education either in the cohort at school, or later, they may still not find higher education sufficiently beneficial or attractive. The current policy of withdrawing funding for students with equivalent or lower qualifications damages lifelong learning.

A focus is needed on subject mixes and choices before university entry, especially with mathematics education and with Vocational Education and Training. Different types of mathematics and vocational education may lead to almost diametrically opposed types of access to higher education. Our evidence shows that students' identities, with respect to mathematics, depend upon the quality of the teaching they have received and their prior experiences of learning within compulsory education. There is also a question of the range of subjects studied at different types of university. Universities which are regarded as academically prestigious provide more science, technology, engineering and mathematics (STEM) than other institutions, so that applicants to them need more mathematics education.

Policies and practices developed to promote and provide the opportunity to participate successfully in higher education need to be more sensitive to the diversity of students and to the different structures of institutions and subject offerings. Post-compulsory educational offerings are diverse. They are structured according to prior socio-cultural contexts and learning experiences and socio-economic contexts and backgrounds. The question of student retention versus drop-out can be seen in a new way if we appreciate that diverse students acquire some qualifications that provide them with useful skills and knowledge for lifelong learning. University teachers need to develop pedagogies that engage socially, culturally and educationally diverse students more effectively, in both traditional and new subjects. We return to this question of developing pedagogies and pedagogical improvements in Chapter 7.

First we turn to the continuing several unaddressed questions about the benefits of higher education or the rates of return for an increasingly large cohort of graduates, and women especially, and in relation to graduate and professional labour markets. We present below an extended critique of the policy debates about widening participation in relation to graduate benefits in the labour market or what have been called rates of return or wage premia. These questions below are addressed in a critique of the arguments about rates of return by Geoff Hayward and Hubert Ertl based upon their work in the VET project. We will then move into a broader discussion, in Chapter 7, about how to address the question of definitions of diversity and equity for *institutional practices* for individual students, based on current policy and media debates, before turning to the question of how to develop and extend appropriate forms of teaching and learning, or forms of pedagogical improvement. Finally we address briefly the international context for improving learning by widening participation in higher education.

3 The widening participation in HE UK policy agenda: questioning the unquestionable?

Geoff Hayward and Hubert Ertl in seeking to develop an analysis of the policy debate in England about equity and access to higher education, from the perspective of their own research on Vocational Education and Training (VET), have argued that the research issues are complex because of the differing theoretical and policy perspectives on the questions. Taking a political economy theoretical perspective they draw on a more public policy discourse to situate their arguments. In particular, they argue that *little attempt has been made to examine the redistributive claims made about accessing higher education by young people through this route.* Linked to this debate about higher education participation, (VET) policy has as one of its aims increasing access to higher education via this route, but there is little research that speaks to either the effectiveness or the efficiency of this policy. For an individual, achieving access to higher education can clearly be an important good. However, from a system and policy perspective the redistributive potential of such access lies not just in participating in HE but also about where and how an individual participates: which higher education institutions (HEIs) are accessed and which subject areas? What are the returns, private and social to such participation? Could larger returns be generated by participating in alternative provision, such as apprenticeship?

3.1 An evolving policy discourse about types of equitable or fair access

It is possible to distinguish three strands of policy concerned with access to higher education: increased access, widened access and fair access. Increased access means a sheer increase in the number of students, whether in absolute terms or as a percentage of the age group. However, substantial research has demonstrated that increased access does not automatically result in a more even distribution of participation across society: rather middle-class students seemed to have benefited more from the increase in student numbers during the 1990s.

Widening access policy focused on increasing access of students from formerly under-represented backgrounds into higher education overall. However, access to higher education can still be biased because of 'constrained' choice of institutions and subjects (in terms of prior educational experiences or socio-economic backgrounds). This has an impact on the redistributive force of this strand of policy especially in an increasingly stratified system. Fair access policies are therefore intended to produce a more equal distribution of students from under-represented backgrounds over different institutions and subjects.

3.2 Widening participation and redistribution

Widening participation initiatives are intended both to reduce the institutional barriers to access – for example, through tighter coupling of VET provision to HE – and to stimulate demand among groups of under-represented learners. The general conclusion from previous research about the success of these various initiatives is mixed. At an aggregate level there have certainly been increases in participation by some formerly under-represented groups, such as women and certain minority ethnic groups. However, the long-term difference in participation between socio-economic groups remains stubbornly resistant to change. Thus in 2004/05 participation for the top three socio-economic classes stood at 43 per cent compared to 19.1 per cent for the bottom four socio-economic groups (Kelly and Cook 2007). This is based on the use of the full-time Young Participation by Socio-Economic Class (FYPSEC) figures. Changes in the way participation has been measured makes longer-term comparisons problematic. The figures here show a slight decline in participation rates as measured by the Age Participation Index (API) for the top three socio-economic groups (48% in 2000) but little change for the bottom three socio-economic groups (19% in 2000). This suggests that the narrowing of the participation rate between upper and lower socio-economic groups is a result in decline in participation by the former rather than an increase among the latter. However, such figures have to be interpreted with a degree of caution as, even though the FYPSEC is more robust than the API by social class, weaknesses remain as a result of the use of the socio-economic classification variable.

The reasons for this weak impact of access initiatives on social class inequalities in participation, for example, remain poorly understood. It could be that the initiatives have inappropriate theories of action that misinterpret, for instance, the policy targets (both individuals and institutions) or that the policy instruments (that is, the funding and regulatory mechanisms that drive education and training systems – five types of policy instrument can be distinguished: mandates, inducements, capacity-building, system-changing and hortatory (McDonnell and Grubb 1991)) being employed – primarily inducements, limited capacity building and exhortation emphasising the individual returns to investing in higher education – produce incentives that are too weak to produce the desired outcomes. Another reason is, according to Anna Vignoles, that the 'decisions' made when age 11 about educational achievement influence HE participation. A child in a challenging school who is under achieving is essentially setting him or herself up to not have the option to participate in HE regardless of the incentives for him or her to do so.

Of particular concern for this section is the extent to which the increased emphasis on accessing higher education via the VET route has produced a distribution of VET students across HEIs and subjects that can be interpreted as being efficient, both individually and socially. Such a notion of efficiency stems from an interpretation of widening access policy primarily in terms of redistribution in a policy environment where redistribution via the tax and benefit system is deemed politically difficult. Such an interpretation goes to the heart of the UK New Labour government's economic vision for expansion of the post-compulsory education and training system:

New Labour was, in part, about releasing us from an old fashioned view of the labour market. . . . In a sense, a whole economy has passed away. The central economic idea of New Labour – that economic efficiency and social justice ran together – was based on this fact. . . . Human capital was becoming the key determinant of corporate and country success. Education that for so long had been a social cause became an economic imperative. . . . The challenge today is to make the employee powerful, not in conflict with the employer but in terms of their marketability in the modern workforce. It is to reclaim flexibility for them, to make it about their empowerment, their ability to fulfil their aspirations. . . .

What all this means is not that the role of government, of the collective, of the services of the State is redundant; but changed. The rule now is not to interfere with the necessary flexibility an employer requires to operate successfully in a highly fluid changing economic market. It is to equip the employee to survive, prosper and develop in such a market, to give them the flexibility to be able to choose a wide range of jobs and to fit family and work/life together.

(Blair 2007)

Such a policy vision is predicated on a belief that:

1   The development of more diverse educational opportunities beyond the age of 16 will increase the participation rate of learners beyond compulsory schooling. In turn, the expansion of participation post-16 was regarded as a decisive pre-condition for increasing and widening participation in higher education.
2   Increasing educational participation and attainment, by whatever means, will produce both individual and social returns and economic benefits.

Within this vision widening participation should not, however, be seen as a good in its own right. It is only good if it achieves utilitarian redistributive outcomes. Certainly, educational participation beyond the compulsory school age has increased in the UK constantly since 1945, with a massive increase in participation in full-time provision between 1985 and 1994 (Hayward 2005; Hayward et al. 2004, 2005). This increase can partly be attributed to the increased availability of vocationally oriented qualifications aimed at 16 year olds. Subsequently, the Curriculum 2000 initiative increased the flexibility that was given to students to combine different types of qualification, which has had an impact on the proportion applying to HE with a mixture of vocational and academic qualifications (Hölscher et al. 2008).

UK and international research has shown, however, that these connections made in policy discourse are not necessarily realised in practice. In the UK investigations into the educational value of some vocationally oriented qualifications, in terms of their currency for further progression, have concluded that they de facto only offer a 'mirage of wider opportunities' (Pugsley 2004: 28). Instead, each wave of new vocationally oriented qualifications has contributed to the overall tendency towards educational credentialism. In terms of access to HE, despite the overall expansion of the sector, the incremental growth in student numbers remained greatest for those in the middle class holding traditional GCE A-level qualifications (Ball 2003; cf. also Sutton Trust 2005).

Within current UK policy, a key lever for raising the perceived value of vocational qualifications (VQs) is to ensure that they provide a means for progressing into, and providing a solid basis for study in, HE; this strategy has been very influential in the conception and development of the new

Diploma qualifications which will be introduced from 2008 onwards. Typically educational policy strategies are framed in terms of the acceptability of VQs to HE with the social perception of VQs by young people and their families being based, in part, on the signals that emanate from the HE sector (Pugsley 2004). However, there is a need to go beyond this to question the very basis for encouraging young people from a VET background to participate in HE: that such an investment will inevitably generate positive economic returns relative to other forms of educational investment, such as apprenticeship. This is not to question the undoubted personal value of HE for many VET students, and it is important to recognise that a HE qualification is now a necessary licence to practise in many para-professional fields, such as nursing (though this raises further questions about the colonisation of the para-professional world by HE). Rather it represents an initial attempt to gauge whether a prime rationale for widening participation – redistribution – will necessarily be met for students of concern to the *Degrees of Success* project (see Chapter 3).

3.3 Beyond the discourse of averages or a graduate premium

A key policy tool to persuade more young people to participate in higher education has been based on a policy discourse of average rates of return. Typical values for the average return to individuals can be traced back to Dearing's (1997) 'Inquiry' into higher education. The view promulgated at the time was that participating in higher education was an excellent personal investment that would generate an estimate annual private rate of return of between 11 per cent and 14 per cent. The available evidence suggests that returns to degrees increased throughout the 1990s and in the early part of this century: getting a degree certainly seemed to pay, on average. However, studies after 2002 have hinted at a declining wage premium to graduates (Purcell *et al.* 2005). Such a decline is associated with a marked increase in the proportion of graduates in the labour market, especially women (Green and Zhu 2008). This needs to be seen in connection with a growing recognition of the heterogeneity of the graduate labour market, with Elias and Purcell (2004) identifying 'new' and 'niche' graduate jobs outside the traditional professional and managerial jobs traditionally filled by graduates (see also O'Leary and Sloane 2007).

Green and Zhu (2008) demonstrate growing dispersion in the returns to graduate education between 1994–6 and 2004–6 using quartile regression. In particular they note declining returns to male at or below the tenth percentile started at around the end of the 1990s, while for women the decline occurred throughout the time period studied. Returns for men at the median rose until the end of the 1990s and then remained fairly constant. For women the returns at the median remained relatively constant throughout the period. Returns at the ninetieth percentile increased slightly for women but sharply for men. Thus, over time there has been an increase in the dispersion of returns to holding a degree such that '[w]hile the benefits of graduate education at the top end of the residual wage distribution have increased a little, at the bottom end they have sharply decreased' (Green and Zhu 2008: 3). This increase in the dispersion of returns is overlooked by focusing just on the Ordinary Least Square (OLS) regression-based measures employed in traditional rates of return analyses.

The stable OLS returns appear to support the proposition that on average the demand for graduates relative to GCSE-level school leavers kept pace with the relative supply, and is typically used to support the proposition that extra supplies of graduates are being adequately utilised (Green and Zhu 2008: 8).

By contrast Green and Zhu's explanation for the growing dispersion in graduate wages is that an increasing proportion of graduates are over-qualified for the jobs that are available. A knock-on effect of this would be to reduce returns at the lower end of the wage distribution, as such graduates fail to obtain jobs appropriate to their skill level.

Distinguishing between real over-qualification (a state where over-qualification is associated with under-utilisation of skills) and formal over-qualification (the individual is over-qualified but experiences full skill utilisation), Green and Zhu's analysis of Employee Skill Survey data indicates that real over-qualification is less prevalent for those graduating from Oxford or Cambridge, whilst the rate of over-qualification is similar for those graduating with no significant difference between those from old universities and other types of higher education institutions (HEIs). However, formal over-qualification is more prevalent in those graduating from new universities and is especially high for art and design graduates, but low for graduates in professional vocational subjects such as medicine and law. While real over-qualification affects only a small and relatively stable number of graduates (less than 10%), formal over-qualification has risen sharply over the last decade, and now represents just under one-quarter of graduates. The analysis suggests that those from new institutions, that is, those most likely to be attended by VET entrants, are likely to be over-represented in this category.

3.4 Conclusions

The findings about increasing over-qualification among graduates matter because there is pay penalty associated with being over-qualified. Further, the evidence indicates that this has increased sharply over time. What are the implications for widening participation, especially the encouragement of those following a VET route to progress to HE? In making such a judgement it is necessary to remember that from a public policy perspective it is the social returns to higher education, rather than the private returns, that should primarily determine policy judgements. Estimating social returns to higher education are notoriously difficult (Keep and Mayhew 2004). A possible externality that may enhance social returns is that it may enhance technological progress. If so, then an excess of skills, especially in the sorts of technical areas that many VET entrants enter (IT, engineering), may induce skills-based technological change (Acemoglu 1998). However, the evidence for this is flimsy (Krueger and Lindahl 2001; Keep and Mayhew 2004).

In addition, there is a need to factor in the non-pecuniary benefits of participating in higher education – social and cultural outcomes, personal satisfaction and so on. Given the uncertainties around these estimates it would be foolhardy to conclude that further expansion of higher education should be halted on the basis of a purely economic analysis.

Nonetheless, at a very minimum people making increasingly complex decisions need to be provided with genuine information about the returns to participation in higher education rather than just average rates of return. As Green and Zhu conclude:

> Choosing courses with low pecuniary returns is potentially rational and can suit the life-style choices of many. A problem arises only if young people are led to expect higher pecuniary returns than they subsequently will experience. . . . Information on returns is costly for young people to acquire (and especially beneficial when returns are changing), yet relatively inexpensive for the state to disseminate. There is a case for improved state provision of such information as a public good.
>
> (2008: 30)

We concur with such a sentiment. However, we believe that there is a need to go further. If it is increasingly the responsibility of the individual to chart their own course and choose educational investments that maximise personal returns, such information needs to allow broad comparison between the returns to participation in different pathways. In particular, those progressing to HE via a VET pathway need to consider whether participation via apprenticeship, where returns can be considerable, might be preferable to participation in HE. Obtaining such information on which to base decisions is difficult for the individual so it needs to be provided by the state. However, doing so would be politically challenging as it would lead to an acknowledgement that higher education may not pay for all individuals under all circumstances.

4 Reconceptualising equity and diversity for fair access and widening participation for individuals defined as disadvantaged

How precisely then can equitable or fair access and widening participation for the contested groups of individuals that we have identified be achieved?

Is it a question of equalising opportunities within higher education, or through earlier forms of formal education or informal learning, as has been suggested? Could we equalise amongst various disadvantaged or so-called under-represented groups, given the accounts we have heard of their diverse prior educational experiences, to ensure more equal access at the point of transition to or returning to higher education? Would institutional changes make a difference to these processes? And perhaps most importantly what kinds of pedagogies are most appropriate for making learning more inclusive and thus equitable or fair? Can these be achieved within and across all subjects, including academic, mathematics and vocational or technological subjects?

Public policy debate has often centred on whether concerns for equity or diversity as fair 'access' and participation are diluting a commitment to academic excellence, however that is defined. Transitions into universities or higher education are challenging for many groups. There is still a strong policy and practice presupposition, as we have seen, that the academic path is the 'royal road' into higher education against which all other pathways are compared. Our research on diversity and social, ethnic and gender identities, in relation to following different pathways and the subsequent opportunities they may enable, has indeed illuminated this continuing argument. As we have seen, transitions into higher education may be especially challenging for particular groups such as those from backgrounds that have traditionally seldom participated in higher education, disabled, Black and minority ethnic or even some international students, as well as for individuals and groups who have followed routes other than the 'royal (academic) road' into universities or other kinds of higher education such as with further education.

It remains taken for granted that students in England, amongst the countries making up the UK, as in Australia and North America must pass through rigorous admission procedures before enrolling at HE institutions. These may vary between types of HEI and within or across subjects in the UK. However, many HE systems have completely different ways of admitting students: some countries have no admission procedures at all. For example, in some European countries, it is not the university (the receiving institution), but the school (the delivering institution) that decides on access to higher education. Certificates of selective secondary schools often grant a kind of 'entitlement' to enrol at universities. Access and admissions policies at Asian HE institutions also have their own unique qualities. To challenge the preconceptions and embedded normative assumptions, how different education systems organise the transition from school to HE needs to problematised. In an age of globalisation, a comprehensive international comparative analysis of access and admission is essential in understanding the different ways in which access and related admission policies and procedures could be conceptualised and enacted. Thus, defining diversity and disadvantage, socio-economic disadvantage or poverty, and family backgrounds, together with ethnicity or race and gender, requires attention to the wider circumstances of individuals than merely their participation within continuing forms of education, and particularly into higher education. In that respect, league tables of higher educational institutions in terms of both teaching and research quality mask the details of the complexity of the issues and how they interact with broad and continuing systems of power relations. These are now the subject of public policy and media debate both nationally and internationally in ways unthinkable a generation or decades ago, when questions of social class participation in higher education were differently specified as we have seen.

Overall, our findings do indicate that whilst there has been major public and policy concern with widening and increasing participation in English higher education, this concern has tended to focus on highly contentious aspects of defining disadvantaged or under-represented groups of individuals. For example, at the time of writing (February 2009) the media (e.g. *The Guardian* 3 February 2009) have been paying attention to the structuring of higher educational opportunities by social class. This is part of the ongoing public policy debates about how to increase or achieve forms of social mobility. Nevertheless, the question of how to define, for operational research purposes, the question of individual or group mobility through education and into employment remains a very complex question. It is not simply a question of ensuring that more individuals from disadvantaged or under-represented groups go onto forms of higher education, including universities. As we have just noted, it may also have to do with what happens after higher education in terms of employment and economic opportunities.

Evidence from other recent studies commissioned by HEFCE would also add to these findings (e.g. Raphael Reed *et al.* 2007). Similarly there is emerging evidence about ethnic minority students moving into higher education (Hussain and Bagguley 2007). The findings, however, emphasise the diversity of student participation in a diverse higher education system, and address the question of participation across the life course. They also raise doubts about the international league table approach to higher learning, and its relevance to people across their lives. A strong knowledge base for improving the learning for diverse students from disadvantaged socio-economic family, ethnic/racial and gender backgrounds across the life course has been provided here. The findings also address the question of the appropriate national and international policy contexts for post-compulsory education to ensure a more equitable system across a diversity of subjects and higher education institutions in the twenty-first century, a point to which we return in the final chapter.

As an example, the interesting but contentious articles by Jessica Shepherd heralded in *The Guardian* (3 February 2009: 12) with the title 'White, middle class families dominate top university places' and bylines

'Richest 2% more likely to be at leading institutions and Tories and Lib Dems point to social mobility failure', only serve to provide headlines that reinforce rather than help to transform league table and social status messages. Whilst the headlines and the bylines also demonstrate some public transformations in how these traditional social science questions have now entered the public policy and media agendas, they also erase and sideline appropriate consideration of social class analysis and in relation to social mobility.

More importantly, they elide notions of ethnicity and the now fragmented form of middle classness. They also completely obscure how gender is implicated and has been transformed in the changing forms of higher education in relation to economic and knowledge developments. What has been perhaps one of the most important transformations over the last 20 years or so have been the intersections or inter-relationships between social class, ethnicity and gender, producing new and subtle relations within higher education. Interestingly, and as an aside, the articles and the evidence are often produced by women as reporters and commentators on the changes. These have also altered forms of participation and access as we have seen through our research evidence.

The headlines serve to reinforce the very issues that policy-makers have been at pains to dispel in the kinds of research that they have commissioned, most notably those reported on within this book. In particular, the evidence base for these articles is from a 'market research analyst firm Caci. Seventeen universities across Britain agreed to give the company 1,000 random postcodes of *fulltime undergraduates in their first year* [my emphasis]. The 17,000 anonymous postcodes are of the homes from which the students applied to the universities. Caci put each postcode into its demographic classification service, Acorn, to find out which rung of the ladder of affluence each of the students belonged' (ibid.: 12, column 2). Whilst trying to understand social class analysis of educational access and participation through the use of postcodes has become *de rigeur* nowadays, focusing only on first-year students who are full-time completely misses the wider transformations of higher education and forms of participation across the life course which is a theme that we have demonstrated. Our evidence shows the age, class, ethnicity and gender patterns of participation in changing forms of higher education and across the life course.

Another byline to the main article is 'This makes a mockery of the commitment to social mobility' (ibid.: 12, column 5). Whilst we might concur with the sentiment, our research has deconstructed and developed more subtle arguments but we cannot but agree that the overall impression of policy development and change is encapsulated in these headlines. The main article is followed up with detailed articles in *The Guardian Education* (3 February 2009) entitled 'Universities don't like common people, do they?' with the byline 'Exclusive figures reveal the poorest have little chance of a place' (pp. 1–2) and 'A tale of 2 cities: Bristol v Bolton: opposite ends of the prosperity ladder' (p. 3). They draw on a cursory study by 'market analyst firm Caci' using statistical work on postcodes to show that there are systemic differences between the social classes in which universities they tend to attend:

> The University of Bristol is populated by the middle classes (who are posher than John Lewis as are many others attending Russell Group universities) whilst very new universities like Bolton tend to have students from far less affluent backgrounds, including students from ethnic minority backgrounds.

> (ibid.: 2)

Another quotation given is 'For a lot of Asian parents, the closer the university is to home, the better', Azmeena Hussein, a female Asian student, is reported to have said.

Similarly these issues have become the regular topic of debate and report in the weekly magazine now known as *The Higher Education* (*THE*). However, given a more diverse audience than the assumed readership of *The Guardian* newspaper as being largely middle-class intellectuals rather than more academic and interested in the more detailed and nuanced forms of higher education, the debate is more wide-ranging. We may therefore contrast their debates the same week (namely 5 February 2009) about how 'HE in FE' holds its own in National Student Survey (p. 11). Here they do address changing forms of higher education and consider:

> students studying higher education courses in further education colleges . . . are more satisfied with some aspects of their experience than their university counterparts.

They also raise the question about their longer-term prospects and that of their age and the payment of fees as an issue relevant to participation.

5 Conclusions on evidence-informed principles for policy

We hope that our research evidence can contribute to a clearer and firmer understanding of how complex questions of social mobility are. They clearly link with how policies and practices, whilst concerned with individual mobility, do not necessarily achieve systemic changes. In fact, our evidence shows how both policies and institutional practices reinforce and systematise power differentials between types of higher educational institutions and the groups of individuals participating within them or being prepared to participate through school or college. The wider question of the dynamic and constant changes in the economic systems producing social class relations that interact with changing educational systems, knowledge and digitalisation, and institutions, makes these research questions not easily susceptible to public policy debate. Having addressed the policy implications of our evidence-informed findings on widening participation in HE, we turn now in Chapter 7 to discuss the ways of improving learning by transforming institutional and individual practices, and more importantly pedagogical improvements for social diversity. We shall conclude with reference to the wider global contexts for improving learning across the life course.

How do we improve learning by widening participation in higher education?

Institutional practices and pedagogies for social diversity

Miriam David with contributions from Gill Crozier and colleagues, Geoff Hayward and Hubert Ertl, Julian Williams and colleagues, and Chris Hockings

1 Introduction

In this the last chapter we focus on how to improve learning by widening participation in higher education. Specifically here we concentrate on transforming *institutional practices* and on developing appropriate and *sustainable pedagogies for social diversity* and learning across the life course. We focus mainly on examples from higher education but our overarching conclusion is for the institutional practices and pedagogies to be developed in schools and colleges too. Vignoles and her team argue for school transformations most strongly.

We offer four contributions from the project teams to develop the arguments and approaches. First, Williams and his team expand upon the study presented in Chapter 4 and focus on pedagogies in pre-university learning; then Crozier and her team discuss the implications of diverse institutional approaches for learning and learner identities. Third, Hayward and Ertl offer us evidence about the problems of addressing social diversity from the perspective of teachers in higher education. Finally Hockings and her team develop a strong argument for pedagogies for social diversity. We then draw these themes together to argue for the centrality of educational opportunities across the life course to ensure that they are aligned to men and women's changing socio-economic and family circumstances. We suggest an array of inclusive and personal pedagogies that might engage students of the future in educational courses and new or innovative subjects, going beyond the conventional and known subjects of the twentieth century. We try to imagine futures for higher education that go beyond the conventional boundaries of possibilities. Thus we address the current policy concerns about social mobility and how to change circumstances for underrepresented groups in an entirely new light, and yet in keeping with the intricate and detailed evidence produced from these seven unique projects on widening participation in English higher education.

2 Pedagogy in university preparation

Expanding on the project's findings about pedagogy in Chapter 4, Williams and his team argue that their research plan involved studying the contrasting teaching and learning of students in 'traditional' AS level mathematics and an 'innovative' AS level Use of Mathematics designed to help widen participation in various ways, including by providing more opportunities for classroom communication and problem solving (Williams *et al.* 2009; Pampaka *et al.* 2008). The team goes on:

Clearly we saw differences in pedagogies and learner experiences afforded by the latter programme, which encouraged modelling and applications, use of new technology by learners as well as teachers and coursework assessment. However, we also saw some quite traditional teaching on the innovative programme, and found some quite innovative teaching on the traditional programme. Many AS and A-level mathematics teachers describe their teaching as 'good, traditional' or even 'old-fashioned'. We have observed many lessons that support this: the teacher remains in firm control of the subject matter, which is clearly presented and explained, with model example problems worked through to demonstrate mathematical procedures and techniques which the students then practise when they do examples, either in class with the close attention of the teacher at hand, or for homework and handing in. This work reveals what the students have 'taken' from the lesson: we call this 'transmission' and it fits well with the discourse and technology of 'delivery'. The teacher may ask pertinent, usually closed questions to ensure learners are following their exemplary work, and may provide a model, metacognitive commentary of what they are doing and why. Many well-prepared, successful students have learnt their mathematics this way, so why change? Less well-prepared students tend to require more help than this, so transmissionist teaching may become more interactive and learners may not be expected to 'take in' such large chunks of mathematics without themselves actively practising and doing some of the mathematics themselves:

You know my sort of methods, it's nothing, it's old-fashioned methods. There's a bit of input from me at the front and then I try and get them working, practising questions . . . I teach it the way I was taught really, which was teaching them the tricks. Because with me, a lot of the understanding didn't come for maybe years and years.

(John, A-level mathematics teacher
with twenty years' experience)

However, this approach has its drawbacks: tricks without understanding seem effective in the short term to get started, to get some problems solved. But then:

> Well, it does . . . lead them up the garden path . . . and unless it's set up exactly as the question was that I showed them, they can't do it, and that's because they haven't got the deep understanding . . . because we've not given them the time to really learn how to, you know, when the question's slightly different, they can't cope with it.
>
> (John, post-lesson observation interview)

In the end, as our statistics show, many of the less well-prepared students (with GCSE grade C, and even B) do not fare well and are increasingly not allowed entry to traditional AS mathematics classes. However, in complete contrast, we saw some teaching that was closely aligned with the DFES 'Standards Unit' approach to AS mathematics in an open access context where many students had only the weaker GCSE grades. In such cases much of the lesson would be spent in group work, focused on development of concepts and understanding, group discussion and reporting to the class was common, sometimes using posters to present results of investigative work or findings. The case study college where we saw much of this pedagogy was in a poor white working-class, somewhat isolated, 'low participation neighbourhood' where – it was said – many students had low aspirations and needed help with study and communication skills. Many of the students came with relatively low mathematics GCSE grades but (in contrast with most colleges) their 'open' policy offered them a place on the AS course.

Close observation and analysis of Sally's lessons (and interviews with Sally and her students over the course of the year) showed that she took great care over issues of social inclusion, ensuring that students got to know and communicate with each other and, eventually, were comfortable with reporting or contributing ideas to the class. However, vital elements in making the developing mathematics coherent also included (i) making connections with the students' previous intuitive, everyday and mathe-matical knowledge (e.g. using formative and diagnostic assessment), and (ii) ensuring a connected, logical narrative of mathematical ideas. In Sally's classroom students were commonly challenged to solve problems, and 'think like a mathematician'. In short, with a view to the literature, we described this as 'connectionist' pedagogy, which focuses more on building under-standing through making connections between mathematics and other knowledge, as well as within mathematics (Askew *et al.* 1997; Swan 2006). Both Sally and her students supported our categorisation of this indirectly:

> Because there are a lot of maths, you get things wrong, don't you? But I want them to realise that's how mathematicians work . . . because I want them to realise that, yeah, they are mathematicians.
>
> (Sally, pre-lesson interview)

And not untypically, one of the students said: 'not only [do] you think for yourself but . . . you can ask other people why they got that and it's not just black and white, like you get to a different way to work it out . . . maths it's like really good I didn't think I'd enjoy it at all' (Katrina, Year 12, Sally's AS class).

In line with the principle of valuing and measuring what is important we therefore decided to try to build a measure of 'transmissionism' or 'connectionism' drawing on previous work by Swan (2006) who had investigated 'Transmission, Discovery and Connectionist' categories of 'pedagogic orientation' in the context of sixth form/FE college mathematics teaching. Our analysis of Swan's self-report pedagogic 'practice scale' (Swan 2006) gave us a good fit to a one-dimensional scale as shown in Figure 7.1. In this figure we show the distribution of the more than 100 cases of teacher self-report, and the named teachers who self-reported on the classes we saw them teach in our case studies.

Notice that John and Sally are at the extremes of the measure, and that while our nine case study teachers are spread out across the range, the bulk of the teachers lie somewhat higher than the middle of this scale, towards

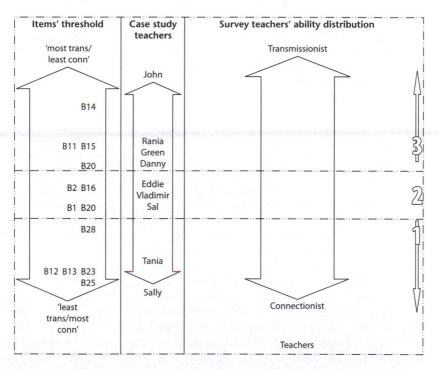

Figure 7.1 The self-reported practice scale, showing the distribution of our teachers and the eight teachers in our case studies (from Pampaka *et al.* 2008)

the 'transmissionist' end. (For fuller accounts of this work, and the details of the validation of the scale following Rasch methodology see Pampaka *et al.* 2008).

This measurement instrument allowed us then to compare teachers on the different programmes (no significant difference), and to explore regression models of the effect of pedagogy on learning outcomes (see Hutcheson *et al.* 2008). We did in fact find significant, positive effects of 'connectionist pedagogy' on learners' disposition to study more mathematics. Interestingly, this effect disappeared when two or three of the most connectionist teachers' classes were withdrawn from analysis. Thus, if increasing connectionist practices is to make an educationally significant impact on learning, it is probably in those classrooms where the teaching can be most strongly connectionist (always remembering the caveat that this is self-reported, espoused beliefs about their pedagogy).

One of the methodological difficulties here is a concern for cause and effect: we have good reason to believe from the case study work that the particular college and community context had a powerful effect on Sally's and John's pedagogy respectively (see earlier in Chapter 4, and Wake 2009). Also account needs to be taken of these teachers' professional and personal biographies (see Williams 2008). Thus, treating self-reported pedagogy as an independent variable in a regression model is a problematic simplification of what is in reality a complex context. Nevertheless the combination of statistics and our case studies suggest that connectionist practices can support the less well-prepared learners in open access contexts, and encourage such learners to study mathematics more in the future.

Hence we are confident in offering 'connectionism' as a pedagogy that contrasts with 'transmissisonism' as a cultural model of teaching practice that offers more opportunities for learners to engage deeply with mathematics, even if as some suggest it demands more time and is less exam-focused. We know (i) that most of our teachers were not at either of the extremes, and (ii) that most practice tends to be exam-focused especially as assessments approach. 'Getting connectionist', however, might come to command some priority if it comes to be seen as essential to understanding and hence making mathematics count.

We also have seen that, independent of teachers' self-reported pedagogy, the curriculum and assessment such as that of Uses of Mathematics, can offer learners more opportunities for discussion, comprehension and communication about mathematics. First glimpses of pedagogy in our current study of university mathematics suggests that – even though lectures are normally highly transmissionist, learners often forge other opportunities for engagement in learning that can help foster understanding, even informally if formal tuition does not encourage it. Abducting from pre-university contexts (where mathematics learning is largely organised and led in the classroom) to university contexts therefore should be conducted with due care. Perhaps we have to look more closely at the whole constellation of learning activities of HE students to discover the key to how students there develop understanding and get connected to mathematics.

3 Perceptions and expectations of university

Crozier and her colleagues add to their presentation in Chapter 3, and write that 'we know from other research (e.g. David *et al.* 1994) the importance of the parents' education in terms of future success for the children and equally the significance of Bourdieu's habitus (1990a) in terms of ensuring adequate preparation and the appropriate disposition for future actions and encounters. None of our case study working-class students had parents who went to university and although most knew someone who was at or had been to university they had limited knowledge of what to expect on arrival or what to do when they got there. They certainly had not experienced the kind of histories that embodied the relevant habitus to act according to the corresponding field (Bourdieu 2000), that is, the university. Much has been written about the various challenges facing working-class students particularly in relation to financial and domestic concerns. Whilst these issues facing the students in our study often leading them to adopt a strategic attitude to their studies, the process of navigation through and engagement with the university, their subject and the nature of study is more complex. Not only are their financial resources limited, so too is their route map through HE. They start out with little or limited knowledge of what to expect or what is expected of them and little understanding of the structure and overall requirements of their course. They also have limited understanding of what might be at their disposal either to further their studies or to enhance their social enjoyment. As Jamie, a Southern Law student, explained:

> when I first arrived I was completely unprepared for what [Southern] University would hold for me and it took me a while to settle in, a while to get to grips with what was wanted from me and a while to start producing and while I was still confident throughout that period I was on shaky ground compared to a lot of the other students who knew what it was all about. Now I feel like I'm a lot more cemented but it's taken a while. There's other people who have come here and are completely prepared, know what's expected of them and are used to the sort of life.

For some of the students at Northern University not only did they lack preparation for university but also their previous experience of learning had in many cases been negative and undermining and the residual impact of this seemed to remain with them. For the mature students their time away from academic study compounded their lack of self-confidence. As Arthur said:

> from a work environment to an academic one has just been a right culture shock. . . . it's difficult when you haven't, when you haven't studied for sort of, well I left school at 16, 15, nearly 16, so there was a 25 year gap of study and it was, you know the simple things . . . like reading a book . . . to glean knowledge from, is difficult. . . . I had no previous academic background, so I've had to learn as I've went along. Even sort of writing an essay, I've had to learn how to write an essay while I've been doing my degree so it's been sort of doubly difficult.

Similarly for the younger students self-doubt and lack of confidence was an enduring concern. Sarah, for example, explained the residual impact of her school experience:

> My own self doubt really, unfortunately my experience of school always taught me that I was a late learner, I never caught on particularly quickly . . . So I was always brought up with the attitude 'oh [Sarah] will never amount anything' and actually my head of sixth form tried to prevent me from doing Law.
>
> (cited in Reay et al. 2009)

As part of his theory of the pedagogic device Bernstein (2000) discussed the concepts of regulative discourse (the rules of social order) and instructional discourse (the rules of discursive order). As we argued earlier, the means by which the 'social order' in the university is maintained, are through, in part, acculturating the students. As we saw at Southern University this was an intensive, encompassing experience, by which the students developed a strong identification as university students. At Northern University and Eastern College where students most often lived at home, socialised with 'home-based' friends and divided their time between paid employment and their studies, the acculturation of the students appeared weak (Crozier et al. 2008).

3.1 Learning transitions and pedagogical issues

Given their previous educational experiences and variable learning resources and skills most of the Northern students were starting from quite vulnerable positions. As Arthur said, academic life is a culture shock. In an attempt to accommodate this and also recognising the demands of part-time employment and childcare on students, lectures at Northern University were not compulsory and few demands were made on students to read around their subject. However, small group tutorials (or supervisions) were also rare and students with little educational capital were thus often thrown back on themselves to make sense of the requirements and expectations.

Sarah, a law student, explained:

> Nothing really prepares you for going from a [school] teaching environment where you are spoon fed to coming to a lecture and you are responsible for taking notes; you don't have to show up if you don't want to; you're responsible for handing in the work. It took me a little while to adjust to that.

One of the many challenges was becoming self-disciplined, and self-regulating. As Vignoles and her team have also argued, subject contexts also differed with, for example, history being less structured than engineering which also included workshop/lab-based activities.

Other students also talked about the difficulty of managing their time and maintaining a disciplined approach to their studies:

> that's something I really need to focus on next year is time management, especially going from four to six modules. . . . I can see myself forcing myself to come into uni more . . . Whereas during the new year I was at home a lot, because you're ten minutes down the road and it's so easy just to go . . . I've got more understanding of what I'm doing, because there's nothing else to do here. You can go on the computer but you get bored of that in about five or ten minutes, so then you go back to your work. You're not distracted by TV, you're not distracted by Big Brother, you're not distracted by nothing, it's just there, you have to do it, don't you.
>
> (Lisa, law student)

Anxiety about their academic capability and the worthiness of their very presence at the university undoubtedly impacts on the students' motivation and ability to engage with the process of learning (Charlesworth et al. 2004). Although the case study students were keen and ambitious to gain their degree, some of them were also quite laissez-faire in their attitudes to work. Adam, a first-year Northern history student, for example, said he spent 30 per cent of his time per week on his studies and the rest of the time socialising. For Barbara a mature student with four children, a husband and a number of health and related issues to cope with, she found that she often could only spend ten hours on her studies, in addition to attending nine hours of lectures or seminars. For many, studying was thus about 'getting through' rather than an immersion in the excitement of learning.

However, at Southern the learning ethos and corresponding demands were very different. First, the ethos is highly competitive, something the students know from the outset given the levels of competition to get there in the first place. Similarly the peer group comprises high achievers; most have had intensive private or selective school or private tutor and very privileged educational experiences prior to coming to the university. The majority come from homes where university education is the norm and many continue to have the continued support of their schools or former teachers. This places the students in a very confident position but also creates high levels of expectation which they have to live up to. As Owen (English student) explained, on coming to the university he realised how competitive and combative the studying was going to be but, as we see here, he is aware of how motivating this is, driving him on:

> O: There is a lot of competition. . . . One thing I noticed . . . is you quickly find out what people are like from supervisions, pretty quickly in fact. You know, for example, I got a pair of girls in my supervision with me, and one girl . . . Well, when I make a point, she goes 'Oh, I see what you're seeing, yeah. But, like, if it was looked at from this view, and you take it from here, then I think it's this, this actually not X, it's Y.' So she always picks me up on stuff.
>
> I: So they always challenge you on what you say?
>
> O: Yeah, yeah, and that's brilliant. And then there's another girl who's like, 'No, think about it, come on, think about it . . . you need blah blah' and it's just a bit too, trying to get one over on you.
>
> I: Combative?
>
> O: Yeah, definitely and a bit superior. And you quickly find out what people are like.
>
> (cited in Crozier and Reay 2008)

However, for our Southern case study students, even experience of earlier academic success and a positive learner identity did not protect them from anxieties about their ability and the notions of their 'clever' and very self-confident peers.

3.2 Summary

Nearly all the students across the four institutions experienced challenge, difficulty and crises of confidence, particularly in the first year although for some it endured until they had finished. However, difficulties in adjusting are relative depending on prior experiences, learner identities and the conditions of learning. As we have discussed elsewhere (Reay *et al.* 2009), Southern students were more advantaged in range of ways in these respects than the students elsewhere in our study.

At Northern University, although tutors were available and contactable, students felt left increasingly to their own devices, either to seek out these forms of support on their own volition or to work together with their peer group. Among the women students there was some evidence of such group working and support but there were disparaging observations by the case study students of the disinterest and a certain anti-intellectualism amongst their fellow students. Some students expressed disappointment and frustration with their fellow students and thought they might have had a more enriching experience elsewhere.

In contrast, at Southern University, seminars and tutorials were explicitly about mastery and the competitiveness that underpins it. The strongest theme in relation to learning across all the Southern interviews was one of constant work and the intensity of the learning experience. Based on a clear and informative structure, the working-class students, who as we saw were very unprepared for what to expect at this university, were enabled to develop strong confident learner identities and behaviours leading to success.

Having considered the question of how learners learn how to learn in different pedagogical contexts, we now consider the perspectives of the teachers. This is from the study of academic versus vocational education and training (VET) but can be applied more broadly across the projects.

4 Perceptions and practices of HE lecturers about VET students

Ertl and Hayward report on the analysis of a series of interviews with higher education lecturers adding to their earlier presentations. The interviews were one element of the investigation of the learning experience of students who make the transition from vocational education and training (VET) to higher education (HE). Now they discuss the rationale of the interviews, report on the analysis of the data and develop some findings (Dunbar-Goddet and Ertl 2008). They attempt to establish whether perceptions and practices of lecturers can provide possible explanations of diverse patterns of drop-out across different higher education institutions (HEIs); these patterns emerged from the analysis of combined UCAS-HESA data discussed earlier (see Ertl and Dunbar-Goddet 2008; Hölscher and Hayward 2008).

4.1 Interviews and categories

The project conducted case studies of programmes in three subject areas (nursing, computing, business) at five HEIs. In each programme, one or two lecturers teaching on the course were interviewed individually or in pairs, using a semi-structured approach, giving a total sample of twenty-five lecturers. In these interviews, lecturers were asked about the following aspects of their teaching:

• awareness of differences in students' educational experiences prior to the start of the course;

- responsiveness to students' prior experience and the factors that constrain and support their capacity to respond;
- perception of different learning patterns and responses to differences;
- assessment of the potential achievement of students with vocationally
  oriented qualifications as opposed to students with academically
  oriented qualifications.

In the initial analysis and coding of the interviews it became clear that
lecturers could be grouped into three distinct groups. Lecturers in each
group shared similar attitudes towards VET students. While lecturers in
group A are clearly aware of and acknowledge the particular skills and
needs of VET students, lecturers in group B and C are less aware of students
with a VET background. The differences between lecturers in these two
groups lie in the reasons provided for not being aware of VET students and
in the responses towards these students. Lecturers in group A are more
likely to have practices in place to respond to the particular needs of VET
students than the other two groups of lecturers.

4.2 Group A: awareness and acknowledgement of VET students

Typically, these lecturers have a generally positive attitude towards VET
students, because they regard relevant work experience and knowledge
about vocational aspects as an asset:

> Business related experience could help them better understand.
>
> (Business7)

(Lecturers in each of the three subject groups were numbered from 1. The
identifiers (Subject and number) are given here to allow the reader to
attribute quotes across and within the three subjects.)

> [Vocational qualifications] prepare them sufficiently in terms of
> entering the profession.
>
> (Nursing8)

Some of the interviewees see an advantage not only for the VET students,
but also for the whole course: 'If you have other people coming in then it
becomes more multi-dimensional as a course' (Nursing11). A nursing
lecturer argues that the experiences VET students bring to the course make
it easier to 'develop more rounded nurses' (Nursing6). These lecturers argue
that other students also benefit from VET students because they are able to
provide support and share their (life and work) experiences to help others:

> Because of the wider access, we get students from different areas,
> different states of life or different qualifications. And that is a good mix

and works well actually . . . That is where the mixture works well, in terms of support.

(Nursing8)

Group A lecturers are highly aware of the particular skills and problems VET students bring to the course. As specific skills and advantages of VET students, lecturers identify a positive attitude among students towards the course, with students described as 'motivated', 'dedicated', 'supportive' and 'more mature'. They also mention advantages in theoretical and academic knowledge, pointing out that such VET students often have a good 'theoretical foundation', the 'ability to see the relevance of the theory and practice' and can produce 'elaborated and structured course-work' and that the students have advantages in practice from their previous work. Most Group A lecturers think that students with vocational qualifications have a more realistic idea than students with A-levels of the work needed to succeed on the course and to achieve their professional aims.

Group A lecturers perceive that a specific problem VET students often have is preparation for academic work and the appreciation of the importance of underlying theoretical concepts. These lecturers mention difficulties with certain aspects of academic work such as the use of 'appropriate language', 'essay writing', 'exams' and 'other assessments'. Also, VET students seem to be more likely to be 'lacking confidence' and therefore 'need a lot of support'. Some are faced with severe time problems because of other commitments such as family and financial/work obligations. Typically this has to do with the fact that many of them are older and study in the context of different life circumstances than most students coming to HE with an academic background.

During the interviews, Group A lecturers described their responses to the skills, problems and expectations of VET students in some detail. They frequently outlined the adjustments they make to their teaching approaches. For instance, they mentioned their attempts to 'create a learning environment that encourages sharing personal experiences' and their constant search for 'alternative teaching methods' which could support the learning of VET students. Most of the interviewees mention 'drawing on VET students' experiences' but give no further details. Responses that concern the teaching style and the design of the learning environment are aimed equally at the problems and the skills of VET students. Only one lecturer described attempts to address the lack of confidence of VET students:

[I] spend a lot of time building up confidence as far as I possibly can. A lot of it has to do with trying to create a sense of enthusiasm and . . . more certainty of what they [VET students] are doing.

(Business2)

4.3 Group B: VET students are no particular focus

Group B lecturers argue that the course is aimed at students with a variety of backgrounds and therefore they see no reason to look at them and respond specifically to the needs of students with a VET background. These lecturers also indicate that they have no procedures in place to record prior qualifications and are therefore not very aware of students' background:

> Again [work experience] is not a requirement, you don't have to have done this or that before they come in. . . .Some will bring it [their work experience] up but it is not something that is formally reported.
>
> (Computing5)

Nevertheless, Group B lecturers are able to list some skills and problems of VET students but in significantly less detail than Group A. For them, the awareness of particular skills and problems is a by-product of interaction with these students in class; they usually do not look for this information proactively by asking students about their experiences, unlike lecturers in Group A.

In terms of specific skills and attitudes of VET students, Group B lecturers notice a generally positive attitude towards the course and a good degree of 'dedication', 'independence' and 'motivation'. VET students also have advantages with regard to 'previous knowledge about the specific terminology'. Two of the interviewees acknowledge practical skills that lead to better results in practically oriented courses.

The Group B lecturers all perceive other commitments as potentially causing time problems for VET students. They also point out students' difficulties with academic work, in particular with exams and essay writing. One of them also noticed an attitude that is 'too focused on learning instead of understanding'. Integration into a classroom environment is regarded as problematic for some students when coming from work.

Group B lecturers consciously decide not to adapt their teaching for VET students. They try to integrate the experiences of VET students that occasionally come up in class to a certain extent in their teaching, but the fact that some students have work experience is not perceived as an advantage:

> Don't expect . . . if you haven't had [work experience] you're better or worse off than somebody else. I try to make the most of [the different experiences] but then also on the same time making clear it is not required.
>
> (Computing4)

Lecturers' responses in terms of their teaching and supervision of VET students are very limited in this group. One lecturer pointed out that large student groups make it impossible to respond to VET students in particular. Another lecturer encourages sharing work experiences in class even though he sees no clear advantage in having work experience. Another lecturer relates theory to practice in his lectures to help VET students' under-standing. Another lecturer uses the experiences only in the informal initial phase of the course because:

> in my experience the ones who claim to have covered [the topics] in an HNC quite often aren't very good at it; you are actually surprised that they have covered it.

> (Computing5)

Only one Group B lecturer was involved in admissions processes, whereas all but one of Group A lecturers were. This explains some of the differences in awareness concerning the situation and requirements of VET students between the two groups of lecturers. However, as Group B is the smallest group identified here (three lecturers), it is difficult to generate a more specific picture of characteristics.

4.4 Group C: starting with a 'clean slate'

The Group C lecturers have a very limited awareness of their students' background; they take the view that the students are starting from scratch at the beginning of the programme and so do not take the backgrounds of their students into account. They attempt to deal with every student in the same way, regardless of the students' prior experiences (which they mostly do not recognise). Consequently, the lecturers have difficulties describing specific skills and problems of specific student groups, and make no modi-fications to reflect any such issues in their teaching and supervision.

Within this group, two different attitudes are evident: most of the lecturers argue that all students have met the same entry requirements and therefore no particular measures for different groups of students need to be taken, while for two lecturers the point of starting with a 'clean slate' is reached after an induction week which is specifically aimed at VET students and aims to 'bring them in line' with other students.

There are various different kinds of reasons provided by Group C lecturers for their approach towards VET students, some of which have to do with the kinds of contextualised knowledge students acquire in VET through work experience. The following quotations indicate that this kind of knowledge is not regarded by lecturers as appropriate or helpful for HE study:

> Most of the concepts that we teach, even if [VET students] have seen them before, they can be in a new context, be a bit different. Sometimes they may perceive that they are familiar with it but they haven't really got it in the way that we teach it, at the level.

> (Computing1)

> We tend to do things that are a little bit different from things that they would have done.
>
> (Computing6)

> I don't think work [experience] helps with mathematics.
>
> (Computing2)

Although Group C lecturers perceive themselves as unaware of VET students, they are still able to list some specific skills: nearly all of them notice a good attitude, for example, a 'self-critical', 'motivated', 'independent' or 'more persistent' behaviour. One lecturer perceives VET students as having an advantage in class because of their ability to work in small groups and understand the relevance of theory to practice. One mentions the ability to work methodically and another practical knowledge and advantages in applied learning. Only one Group C lecturer is not able to identify any skills specifically in VET students. When asked about students' expectations, these lecturers mention 'realistic' or 'different' expectations as being characteristic for VET students.

Problems for VET students are identified with notetaking, autonomous learning strategies and exams. Disadvantages in terms of students' lack of knowledge of relevant theories are mentioned. VET students are perceived to be more worried about failure than traditional students and are, in general, thought to be lacking confidence. Furthermore, they are likely to have other commitments, such as families, that can create pressures and take up a lot of their time.

Of the six Group C lecturers, three did not respond pedagogically to VET students. Of those who did, one was flexible with time arrangements and the remaining two mentioned the induction week for VET students. Therefore none of the lecturers draws on the experiences and skills of VET students or reacts to any of their perceived problems other than time management.

4.5 Summary

The categorisation of lecturers in terms of their awareness of VET students as a specific group of the student cohort demonstrates variations in how VET students are perceived by university lecturers and teachers. These differences in perception contribute to the kinds of learning experience these students have in HE (Ertl and Dunbar-Goddet, 2008).

The distribution of lecturers across the three subjects in this study indicates strong discipline-specific cultures: ten of eleven nursing lecturers were categorised in group A, while only one of seven computing lecturers was.

It also emerged from the interviews that most lecturers find it difficult to assess the appropriateness of VET qualifications for HE study. This may have to do with the sheer number of different VET qualifications available and difficulties in finding concise and clear descriptions of the structure, content and assessment models of many VET qualifications. The continuous change in the qualification framework and the constant introduction of new qualifications aggravates this problem.

The interviews also show that the organisational set-up of admissions procedures has an important impact on the level of awareness of lecturers in terms of the educational background of their students. Broadly speaking, lecturers who are closely involved in recruiting and selecting students demonstrate a higher level of awareness of the particular strengths and weaknesses of particular student groups. While appropriate and effective admissions procedures will necessarily vary between institutions and programmes, the impact of admissions practices on the awareness and perceptions of lecturers with regard to different student groups needs at least to be acknowledged.

It can be concluded from our data that there seems to be a gap between what lecturers know about VET students and the way they respond to their particular needs. Even most lecturers with high levels of awareness of VET students and a generally positive attitude towards these students' backgrounds (Group A lecturers) find it difficult to make the vocational experience of these students an integral part of their teaching.

In Chapter 3 we demonstrated that the generally high drop-out rate of VET students follows highly diversified patterns, with the institution students study at having an important influence on the likelihood of drop-out. We also demonstrated that what students with a VET background look for in, and how they perceive their preparation for, their HE studies is markedly different compared with students who enter HE from the academic pathway. The variety of practices displayed by our HE lecturers demonstrates differences in how the particular needs of VET students are acknowledged. The resulting variance in student experience across different institutions and programmes might explain some of diversified patterns of drop-out of this particular student group observed in the national datasets.

We turn now to consider another approach to student diversity and the question of how to develop pedagogies for such an array of students. Hockings' team argues for an eclectic mix of teachers, drawing on the three different approaches identified by Hayward and his colleagues.

5 Pedagogies for social diversity

In Chapter 4, Hockings and her colleagues challenged the common constructions of students as 'traditional' and 'non-traditional' and presented instead a multi-faceted view of student diversity extending beyond the structural relations or divisions of class, gender and ethnicity, often now called theories of inter-sectionality (Mirza 2008). Now they present a more overarching view of how student diversity encompasses differences in work, life and educational experiences as well as differences in students' approaches to learning, ways of knowing and subject knowledge:

Our (this) more complex view of diversity has implications for institutional policy and practice in terms of the development of pedagogy and teacher development. Set within the UK context of mass higher education, increases in student diversity, intensification of academic work and neo-liberal pressures to increase accountability and performativity (Archer 2008; Beck 2002; Clegg 2008; Harris 2005) we draw out some of the institutional issues influencing the development of pedagogies for student diversity arising from our study in two universities.

5.1 Implications for developing pedagogy

Whilst students come from many different backgrounds, they share the common desire to fit in at university. But when it comes to classroom learning, they value teachers who recognise their individual academic and social identities and who address their particular needs. Our findings suggest that students are likely to feel alienated and withdrawn when the teaching and curriculum overlook their individual identities and differences. This has implications for university teachers who have little opportunity to get to know their students particularly within the context of large class sizes, increased marking and administration, and increased performance targets. Nevertheless our study showed how some teachers can and do create inclusive learning environments and encourage academic engagement of their diverse groups of students under these conditions. The following points summarise the ways in which teachers do this (see Chapter 4 for more detail):

- *Creating individual and inclusive learning environments*
  By making time to get to know students as individuals and by setting ground rules for, and modelling, collaborative learning behaviour.
- *Using student-centred strategies*
  By creating open, flexible, student-centred activities in which students can apply their own (and others') knowledge and experience.
- *Connecting with students' lives*
  By selecting and negotiating topics and activities relevant to students' lives, backgrounds and (imagined) identities.
- *Being aware of and taking account of cultural differences within the group*
  By using resources, materials, humour, examples and anecdotes that are sensitive to the social and cultural diversity of the group (Hockings 2009).

Our findings suggest that *teachers* who adopt strategies such as those summarised above provide scope for students to personalise their learning.

These strategies provide opportunities for all students to negotiate what they learn, how they learn and they create the conditions to enable students to bring their individual background, experience and identities to the learning endeavour in personally meaningful ways.

Teachers in this study distanced themselves from the view that students from 'non-traditional' backgrounds lack the cultural capital, prior knowledge and study skills to excel at university, and that their job, as teacher, is to remedy these 'deficits'. However, there was some evidence of teaching based on this assumption that disengaged some students (see Hockings *et al.* 2008b). To enable teachers to work in ways which acknowledge their students' strengths, experiences and abilities, teachers need the opportunity to consider issues of cultural, social and educational diversity and difference among students, and to be aware of their impact on the learning and teaching environment. This may require that they reflect on and reconceptualise their notions of student diversity. They may also need to consider how they might redesign curricula and pedagogy to allow for greater student involvement. To facilitate this, teachers need institutional policies which allow them adequate time and space for reflection and for pedagogical development.

5.2 Implications for teacher development

Over recent years in the UK there has been significant investment through bodies such as Higher Education Academy (HEA) and initiatives, such as the Centres for Excellence in Teaching and Learning (CETLs) and the Fund for the Development of Teaching and Learning, to enable university teachers to work towards enhancing learning and teaching in higher education. The Professional Standards Framework for Teaching and Supporting Learning in Higher Education (www.heacademy.ac.uk/ our work/policy/framework) advocates diversity and equality of opportunity as being integral to academic development programmes in universities.

However, teachers in our study suggested that the issue of student diversity and how teachers might develop their practice to embrace it was incidental within the teacher development programmes they attended. Whilst one cannot generalize from the views of the small number of teachers involved in this study, it is worth noting that similar concerns have been raised by others (see for example Nicholl and Harrison 2003; Cranton and Carusetta 2004). In particular it is suggested that academic development programmes tend to focus on the development of technical teaching skills but 'gloss over', issues such as student diversity and different forms of teacher identity.

Our research supports other studies which have suggested that academic developers need to create a climate in which teachers can debate their ideas and beliefs about students, and challenge practices and discourses that inhibit the creation of inclusive learning environments. This may mean they 'reposition' students within academic development programmes to enable dialogue between teachers and students that would help teachers 'truly see' their students (Cook-Sather and Youens 2007).

5.3 Two key messages for deepening academic engagement

Overall, our research offers two key messages for developing teaching practice to widen and deepen academic engagement. First, the need for student-centred pedagogy that engages meaningfully with student diversity (Hockings 2009). Second, the need for academic development programmes explicitly to encourage the 'acknowledgement of diversity and promotion of equality of opportunity' (Professional Standards Framework, www.he academy.ac.uk/ourwork/policy/framework) amongst university teachers. However, institutional systems that are set up to ensure increased numbers in higher education whilst decreasing the resources available for teaching constrain teachers' capacities to create inclusive learning environments. Further research is needed therefore to review and change institutional systems that limit the academic engagement of all students. Raising awareness of these issues among policy-makers, teachers and academic developers is vital.

6 Conclusions about changing global and local contexts for equity and diversity in learning and learning outcomes in higher education

As we have seen, whilst the global expansion of post-compulsory educational opportunities has been accompanied by policies to widen access and increase participation, with differences within and between nation states, the overall successes are contested. There remain diverse systems and routes that (young) people take into employment or formal education after compulsory schooling with origins in differentially structured and inequitable opportunities for education, training or employment. For example, Shavit, Arum and Gamoran, American sociologists, have undertaken international case studies, focused on notions of social stratification and mobility, using concepts of equity and diversity: 'The key question about educational expansion is whether it reduces inequality by providing more opportunities for persons from disadvantaged strata, or magnifies inequality by expanding opportunities disproportionately for those who are already privileged' (2007: 1). They compared and contrasted fifteen different countries and classified them as diversified systems of Israel, Japan, Korea, Sweden, Taiwan and the US; binary systems of Great Britain [sic], France, Germany, The Netherlands, Russia, Switzerland; unitary and other systems of Australia, The Czech Republic and Italy (ibid.: 1–35). Their focus was the 'global north' and excluded other countries of the Americas, whereas Rhoads and Torres (2006) do consider the influence of globalisation on universities in Latin America. They also excluded Africa, China, and India. Nevertheless Shavit *et al.* conclude that 'persistent inequality' (2007: 29) remains across all the fifteen countries studied.

Their case studies were conducted during the 1990s, since when global policy transformations have developed further. Indeed, they draw attention to a significant omission from their analysis of the question of gender, arguing that: our data show an average widening of the gender gap in higher education favouring women, and indicate that the gap expanded fastest in systems where attendance rates expanded most (2007: 25–7). Indeed, it is evident that there has been a significant 'closing of the gender gap' (Arnot *et al.* 1999) not only in higher education enrolments but also in participation across higher education in the UK (HEFCE 2005a). However, where gender has been acknowledged – for example, in official or Government funded-studies – the question of what might be considered the reverse 'gender gap' is addressed. Furthermore the notion of closing or 'reducing gaps' has become commonplace in official government circles. Nowadays the focus is upon reducing socio-economic (and linked gender or ethnicity) achievement gaps, as we have seen.

The evidence provided in this book, however, goes beyond the question of how to 'reduce achievement gaps' through policy measures for equity and fair access to or participation in higher education. Given our research evidence across the themes of *policies, practices and pedagogies*, we have also raised broader questions about *opportunities, outcomes* and the various *obstacles* to their achievement. The projects taken together demonstrate how equity and diversity are currently played out in the processes and practices of post-compulsory and higher education. The processes lead to different and frequently inequitable pathways for diverse and nowadays a majority of female students into highly stratified systems of higher education (defined in terms of international league tables).

Nevertheless, the pedagogies and practices of higher education themselves can lead to meaningful educational engagements across the life course. The diverse practices and critical or connectionist pedagogies within various institutional forms of higher education and within different subjects, ranging from the social sciences to those requiring mathematics or forms of vocational education, also may sustain or reverse patterns of differentiation. The learning outcomes through and across the life course illustrate that higher education can be meaningful in people's lives, authentic, practical and relevant, and as social as well as work or economic experiences.

However, we would argue in conclusion that national and international policy frameworks need to be adjusted to take account of our research evidence about both prior and current educational experiences (and the need to adjust schooling as well as post-compulsory education), the relevance of policy at institutional and individual as well as systemic levels. Pedagogies and practices which are meaningful to participants (as students and teachers) whether men or women and the inequalities in systemic, systematic and gendered provisions across the life course nationally and internationally also need attention. Across all the studies it is clear that women as well as men from a diversity of socio-economic and ethnic backgrounds are taking an increasingly active role as students within higher education. As teachers, the focus on developing creative and inclusive pedagogies predominates. Although gender is often implicit rather than explicit, and intersected with diversity, and other social, cultural perspectives and processes, policies and practices have included gender scholarship at some institutions. This also includes in new practices and pedagogies.

In particular, given that the expansion of global HE plays out differently for disadvantaged individuals, institutions and systems, what are the appropriate *institutional practices*, relationships and boundaries between different subjects and the links – formal and informal – between academic knowledge and workplace and other sources of knowledge? Moreover, given diverse routes and pathways into inequitable opportunities for education, training or employment, what are the appropriate transitions between contexts and how do we re-contextualise experience, skills and knowledge? Given, too, the interaction of learning and identities for adults through the life course, how do we help overcome the significant hurdles of diverse lived experiences outside education to make links about learning in and outside formal educational settings?

We have suggested new ideas for *pedagogies* and educational futures for the twenty-first century: to develop pedagogies that are more inclusive given the increased diversity in the HE population, with increasing numbers of students entering the system without an expectation of having a traditional academic engagement with their studies, and a consideration of pedagogical approaches in which learners teach each other and explore why deep-level learning results often seems to point to an interesting possible educational future for the twenty-first century.

However, given the rapidly changing contexts of higher education, national government and institutional forms, there is a continuing challenge both within and between contexts about whether academic labour markets are fit for purpose in the twenty-first century with the possible disjunction between the range of tasks and activities that will be required of university or college staff in future and the way academic labour markets operate in most countries. In other words, in the changing nature of knowledge and learning within and across diverse forms of higher education, there is the challenge for academic and educational developers of the integration of different kinds of knowledge, whether as informal or formal learning.

7 A vision for the global academy

Finally a vision for fair access, equity and diversity in participation in the global academy would surely incorporate the uses of critical and connectionist pedagogies, including developing inclusive and yet personal pedagogies to ensure that people's lives across the life course were enhanced and improved. This would not only entail the production of knowledge for policy but collaborative approaches for the twenty-first century, including incorporating a diversity of teachers in the processes of ensuring that the inclusive and flexible curricula have a strong impact upon learning outcomes and success. If we value inclusion, teachers, practitioners and policy-makers should maintain high expectations of all students, as learners, whilst recognising the diversity of their needs, cultures and identities. A vision for the global academy would surely include diverse perspectives on pedagogies and institutional as well as cultural perspectives. These pedagogies, including inclusive, collaborative or connectionist, critical and personal, would ensure that diverse people's lives across the life course were enhanced.

Universal Access and Dual Regimes of Further and Higher Education (the FurtherHigher Project)

Gareth Parry's team

Objectives

The overall aim of the study was to examine the impact of the division between further and higher education on strategies to widen participation in undergraduate education. We asked:

1   What was the nature and significance of this division and its rationale?
2   What was the impact of this separation on policy formation, organisational development and student participation within and between further and higher education?
3   What kinds of students used what types of further education as a basis for enrolment and study in what forms of higher education, and how was this changing?
4   How important or distinctive has been the contribution of further education colleges to expansion, differentiation and equity in higher education?
5   What meanings and experiences were associated with boundary transitions and transfers between further and higher education?
6   What were the features of an effective cross-sector system of further and higher education?
7   How might policy intelligence, research capacity and practitioner-based research capability be improved across further and higher education?

Methods

We employed a three-level design and analytical framework. Our methods and findings are reported in a set of working papers located on the project website: www.sheffield.ac.uk/furtherhigher/.

Commissioned commentaries

To address research questions 1 and 2, we commissioned four country papers from leading scholars in the USA (Dougherty), Canada (Jones),

Australia (Moodie) and Scotland (Gallacher) plus two contextual papers (Scott and Stanton) on England.

Authors were asked to relate their commentaries to a 20,000-word source paper prepared by the project team and addressed to the role and operation of sectors in English tertiary education. The source paper was based on an analysis of more than 400 policy documents and statistical sources spanning the period 1988–2008 (including unpublished papers).

Policy interviews

Research questions 1, 2 and 4 were investigated using eighteen face-to-face interviews with former and current officials in government and the sector bodies over the period 1988 to 2008.

These included those responsible for drafting and implementing the 1988 and 1992 legislation (which established a two-sector system in England) and the chief executives of the Further Education Funding Council, the Learning and Skills Council (LSC) and the Higher Education Funding Council for England (HEFCE) in office since 1992.

The interviews were recorded and transcribed. The transcriptions were analysed using a framework of themes developed from the review of documentary sources.

Creation of a statistical database

To address research questions 3 and 4, we assembled and analysed a national dataset on individuals studying in further education establishments and higher education institutions in England.

Using data for the most recent years available, we described the movement of students completing one or more learning aims at the level normally required for entry to undergraduate education (level 3) and then beginning a higher education qualification in the following year or the year after. At the same time, the characteristics of the student population were investigated using proxy measures for social class based on postcode and census data.

In order to analyse the contributions of colleges and universities to participation within and between further and higher education we brought together the LSC Individual Learner Records for 2003/04, 2004/05 and 2005/06 with those from the Higher Education Statistics Agency (HESA) for the same years. Under a collaborative agreement with HEFCE, we were provided with a file of unique student identifiers.

Organisational case studies

To illuminate research questions 2 and 4, we undertook case studies of eleven further-higher institutions: ten in England and one in Australia. These were selected to inform a typology of organisational forms.

The institutional case studies centred on in-depth interviews with the chief and second tier executives. Where establishments had complex operating structures, interviews were also sought from senior colleagues responsible for separate or associated sites. A total of thirty-two face-to-face interviews were completed.

The interview data were supplemented by analysis of institutional documentation, including a combination of publicly available materials and unpublished corporate planning documents.

Fieldwork in four partner institutions

Our four partner institutions were the sites of detailed fieldwork studies addressed to research questions 2, 3 and 4. At each institution, a research associate was identified from among the staff and seconded for one day a week to the project. The fieldwork focused on two sets of student transitions: the move from further education at level 3 to higher education at the undergraduate levels; and the move from short-cycle higher education to studies leading to the bachelor degree.

Three cycles of interviews were undertaken in eleven learning sites across the four partner institutions. A total of eighty-two students were interviewed in the first sweep, fifty-three at the point of transition from level 3 to higher education and twenty-nine at the point of transition from short-cycle undergraduate education to the bachelor degree. In the second sweep, undertaken shortly after they had made these transitions, sixty-eight students were interviewed. In the third and final sweep, towards the end of the year after making a transition, fifty-eight students were interviewed. All interviews were conducted face-to-face by members of the fieldwork team. These were recorded, transcribed and analysed using Atlas Ti.

We also interviewed managers responsible for (or working at) the interface between further and higher education and course lecturers involved in teaching at both the further and higher education levels. A total of sixty-nine face-to-face interviews were completed, each recorded and transcribed. In addition, we reviewed an array of materials relating to students, staff, programmes, partnerships and strategies on teaching, learning and widening participation.

Activities

Our synthesis of the international, quantitative and qualitative findings led us to address issues surrounding the effectiveness of current arrangements (research question 6) and the improvement of policy and practice (research question 7).

Alongside capacity-building activities in our partner institutions, we have brought our findings in front of policy-makers, managers of colleges and universities, and tutors and other practitioners. In so doing, we advanced arguments for a steered and staged approach to build quality, ownership and sustainability in the higher education mission of the further education sector.

Widening Participation in Higher Education: A Quantitative Analysis

Anna Vignoles' team

Our analysis uses data from the English National Pupil Database (NPD) and individual student records kept by the Higher Education Statistics Agency (HESA), linked to a third dataset, the Individual Learner Record (ILR) provided by the Learning and Skills Council. Our information on examination results is further enhanced by an additional dataset known as the 'cumulative Key Stage 4 and Key Stage 5' file.

Key Stage tests (from the NPD)

We make use of Key Stage 2 data (age 11) from 1996–97, Key Stage 3 (age 14) data from 1999–00, Key Stage 4 data (age 16) from 2001–02 and Key Stage 5 data (age 18) from 2002–2003 and 2003–04.

To measure attainment at Key Stages 2 and 3, we use the 'raw' information available regarding the tier of each exam sat and the actual marks obtained in English, maths and science. We use an interpolation formula to calculate 'exact' attainment levels (measured on the same scale as the final levels awarded). To illustrate this: children who were awarded level 3 in English at Key Stage 2 would have achieved a mark between 28 and 51 on the English paper. The method we use assigns an attainment level of 3.125 to a child who scored 31, for instance, and 3.917 to a child who scored 50; a child whose score was in the middle of the two thresholds (i.e. 40) is assigned a level of 3.5. At Key Stage 3 the process is complicated somewhat by the existence of different tiers in mathematics and science, which represent different levels of difficulty. Children sitting mathematics at Key Stage 3 could achieve level 5 by scoring above 104 on the lowest tier (3–5) or, alternatively, by scoring between 37 and 42 on the most advanced tier (6–8). According to our method, a child who scores 129 on the Tier 3–5 paper would be assigned an exact level of 5.532, while a child with a mark of 41 on the Tier 6–8 paper would get an exact level of 5.667.

The advantage of our approach is that in producing a more continuous measure of attainment, we are better able to rank pupils in terms of their achievement at each key stage. We then order pupils in terms of their average score by placing them into five evenly sized 'quintile groups' according to Key Stage 2 and Key Stage 3 attainment.

At Key Stage 4 (GCSEs and equivalent), we use the capped total point score: this gives the total number of points accumulated from the student's eight highest GCSE grades. At Key Stage 5, we use the total (uncapped) point score. We divide the population into five evenly sized quintile groups ranked according to their score on these tests.

Cumulative Key Stage 4 and Key Stage 5 dataset

Our second source of Key Stage 4 outcomes – and our only source of Key Stage 5 outcomes for those who do not take A-levels – is a cumulative dataset that captures details of a pupil's highest qualification by age 18. We use an indicator of whether individuals had achieved the National Qualifications Framework (NQF) level 3 threshold (equivalent to two A-level passes at grade A–E) via any route by age 18. Unfortunately, this dataset does not contain more detailed vocational test results.

Pupil Level Annual School Census (PLASC)

This census records pupil-level information – such as date of birth, home postcode, ethnicity, special educational needs, entitlement to free school meals and whether English is an additional language – plus a school identifier. Free school meals can be thought of as a proxy for very low family income. Pupils are eligible for Free School Meals (FSM) if their parents receive Income Support, income-based Jobseeker's Allowance, or Child Tax Credits, with a gross household income of £14,495 (in 2007–08 prices).

HESA

This dataset includes administrative details of the student's institution, subject studied, progression, mode of attendance, qualification aimed for and year of programme. We linked in institution-level average RAE scores from the 2001 RAE exercise. Our measure of HE quality includes all twenty of the research-intensive Russell Group institutions, plus any UK Higher Education Institution (HEI) with an average 2001 RAE rating that exceeds the lowest average RAE found among Russell Group universities. This leads to the definition of a 'high quality' university in Table A2.1.

Control variables

The socio-economic background variables in the administrative datasets we use are extremely limited. In this chapter we make use of the Free School Meal indicator as our measure of socio-economic background. In other

Table A2.1 'High quality' universities (on our definition)

Russell Group universities	2001 RAE > lowest Russell Group university
University of Birmingham	Homerton College
University of Bristol	University of the Arts, London
University of Cambridge	Aston University
Cardiff University	University of Bath
University of Edinburgh	University of Durham
University of Glasgow	University of East Anglia
Imperial College London	University of Essex
King's College London	University of Exeter
University of Leeds	University of Lancaster
University of Liverpool	Birkbeck College
London School of Economics	Queen Mary and Westfield College
& Political Science	Royal Holloway and Bedford New
University of Manchester	College
Newcastle University	Royal Veterinary College
University of Nottingham	School of Oriental and African Studies
Queen's University Belfast	School of Pharmacy
University of Oxford	University of London (Institutes and
University of Sheffield	activities)
University of Southampton	University of Reading
University College London	University of Surrey
University of Warwick	University of Sussex
	University of York
	Courtauld Institute of Art

work we have made use of other measures of socio-economic background, namely, the Index of Multiple Deprivation (IMD) score (derived from Census data on the characteristics of individuals living in their neighbourhood) and neighbourhood level SES and educational attainment from the 2001 Census.

Sample selection

The analysis of HE participation presented in this report is computed on our core estimation sample, which contains 262,516 males and 254,512 females. (The quality of HEI attended is estimated for HE participants only, so the sample is restricted to 46,275 males and 61,216 females.) We use several criteria to select the final estimation sample, namely, the individual must have a valid FSM status and non-missing ethnicity. Finally, we restrict our analysis to those who are in the correct academic year given their age. In total our sample selection criteria exclude around 32,000 individuals (approximately 5.8% of the total PLASC Year 11 cohort) from the analysis.

Socio-Cultural and Learning Experiences of Working-Class Students

Gill Crozier's team

Methods and data sources

The *Socio-Cultural and Learning Experiences of Working-Class Students* project (ESRC RES-139–25–0208) is mainly a qualitative study but also utilised a quantitative questionnaire with a cross-section of students. The focus was on undergraduate students, in years 1 and 2, 18 years and above and took place in four very different higher education institutions. These are: Northern, a post-1992 university; Midland, a pre-1992, civic, university; Southern, which we describe as an elite university; and Eastern College of further education where students were undertaking Foundation Degrees in conjunction with Northern University (see Table A3.1)

It was our intention to look at the same subjects in each university given the hierarchy that exists between subjects but this was not always possible because of difficulties with access. We focused on six disciplinary areas in the three universities – law, engineering, history, chemistry, English, economics – and three Foundation subjects at Eastern College – performing arts, arboriculture, early childhood studies.

Students' social class was determined by: employing the National Office of Statistics (UK) Social and Economic Classifications L7–L14 of parental or mature student occupations, together with information on parents' and

Table A3.1 Participating higher education institutions

HEIs	ONS 4,5,6, 7 %	'Young students' %	State school pupils %
Eastern College	No statistics	No statistics	No statistics
Northern University	39.5	68.9	97.4
Midland University	26	86.9	88.4
Southern University	12.4	95.5	56.8

Source: HESA for 2004–5

immediate family members' education profiles; identifying whether the students were first in their family to attend university; and also whether they received a grant. We attempted to collect this information via the questionnaire but further refined the data on social class backgrounds during the interview process.

The research was in two stages. First, we distributed a questionnaire to all Y1 and Y2 students across the four institutions in the identified subjects at the start of lectures and through the respective university online facilities. The purpose of the questionnaire was to find basic information about the student qualifications, social class, ethnicity, gender, motivation for choice of university, subject, career aspirations; views on their university experience both academic and social; and major challenges facing them on coming to university and through their time there. A total of 1,209 completed questionnaires were analysed. The information gathered allowed us to generalise on certain facets of student views and experiences (Crozier *et al.* 2008). We also used this questionnaire to identify students for follow-up group interviews with students from a range of class backgrounds but more importantly to locate our target group of working-class students.

From the questionnaires we identified eighty-nine students for follow-up interviews (see Table A3.2). Ethnographic semi-structured interviews were used in order to probe and illicit in-depth responses reflecting individual meanings and perspectives (Atkinson *et al.* 2003). We interviewed eighty-nine students: forty-eight middle class and forty-one working class, in groups and one to one. Eight were from minority ethnic backgrounds; fifty-one were women and thirty-eight men. Accessing Black and minority ethnic students was difficult in part because of limited numbers of these students in the elite universities and in the Northern institutions.

In stage 2 we identified twenty-seven working-class students (see Tables A3.3 and A3.4) and followed them across two academic years – years 1 and 2 and years 2 and 3. We interviewed the students at key decision-making moments (Ball *et al.* 2000) such as the beginning and end of term or the start of a new module; before and after assessment periods, and kept in contact with them through e-mail and informal meetings. We aimed to gain insights into the students' perceptions of themselves and whether this changed over time and whether and how this impacted upon their attitude to their studies. We sought to access the social and psychodynamics of student relationships with their institutions and to gain insights into their views and feelings about their university experiences, friendships, learning experiences and their motivations. We spent some time with the students in their environments to contribute to what Skeggs describes as the 'geography of positioning and possibilities' (1994: 72) in this way we aimed to map their cultural and learning experiences, both direct and indirect, and within the time scale of 12–18 months, chart their academic trajectories. We collected data from the students on their

Table A3.2 The 89 students initially interviewed

University	MC SEC L1–6	WC SEC L7–L14	Female	Male	18–21	22–25	26+	Age not known	BME	White	Ethnicity not known	First in family	First in generation	First not known
All	48	41	51	38	65	4	15	5	8	79	2	30	13	9
Eastern	2	10	7	5	5	1	6	0	0	12	0	5	1	0
Northern	9	13	15	7	10	1	8	3	3	19	0	7	8	0
Midland	24	9	19	14	30	1	0	2	5	27	1	9	4	0
Southern	13	9	10	12	20	1	1	0	0	21	1	9	0	9

Table A3.3 The case study students

HEI	Total no. students	Female	Male	18–21	22–25	26+	BME	White	1st in family	1st in generation
Eastern	3	1	2	3				3	3	
Northern	8	6	2	4		4		8	7	1
Midland	7	4	3	7			3	4	6	1
Southern	9	5	4	8		1		9	9	

Table A3.4 Case study students' subjects studied

Subjects studied	Eastern	Northern	Midland	Southern
Performing Arts	2	–	–	–
Early Childhood Studies	1	–	–	–
English	–	–	–	1
History	–	4	2	2
Chemistry	–	–	2	–
Engineering	–	1	–	2
Law	–	3	1	4
Economics	–	–	2	–

progress and asked them to draw a 'mind map' of their social and academic networks.

We undertook a total of 159 interviews: 143 students and sixteen tutors, admissions officers and widening participation officers. In addition we observed twelve lectures and seminars in order to contextualise the interview data. The quantitative data were analysed descriptively but cross-referenced in order to make comparisons regarding gender, class, ethnicity, age, subject discipline, year of study and type of HEI. The qualitative data were coded according to a grounded theory approach (Strauss and Corbin 1990) utilising the Atlas.ti software to manage the data. We complemented this by drawing on a number of theoretical frameworks including Bourdieu's and Bernstein's concepts. All names of place, institution and individuals have been anonymised as agreed with the participants. The researchers abided by the BERA and BSA ethical guidelines as well as their own institutions' requirements.

Degrees of Success: Learners' Transitions from Vocational Education and Training to Higher Education

Geoff Hayward's team

The project aims and design

The *Degrees of Success* project aimed to investigate how people with vocational qualifications make the transition to higher education. The project consisted of three parts which were designed as interlocking elements.

Part 1 analysed large-scale datasets in order both to map the transitional terrain between VET provision and HE and to understand the kinds of factors that have an impact on the conditional probability of transition from VET to HE.

In order to follow up issues that could not be resolved by secondary data analysis alone, *Part 2* compared and contrasted the background of students with vocationally and more academically oriented entry qualifications, and their respective experiences of the learning environments provided by HEIs. One issue that was investigated in this part of the work is the phenomenon of non-linear and so-called 'non-traditional' learning careers (for instance, learners going back to higher or vocational education after a period of work).

Apart from developing a better understanding of transitions from VET to HE, the aim of *Degrees of Success* was also to engage with educational decision-makers and practitioners to enable the results of the quantitative and qualitative investigation to inform thinking about admissions, teaching and learning practice. Therefore, in *Part 3* of the project a continuous discourse with the VET and HE communities was initiated in the form of user forums, to discuss the findings of the first two parts of the study and to make these relevant in practice. The discussions from *Part 3* of the project were used to amend and develop the investigations in the first two parts of the research design.

Questionnaire survey and interviews

The project conducted two questionnaire surveys with the entire intake of students in three subject areas (business, computing and nursing) at five

UK HEIs for the 2006–07 academic year. The five HEIs were selected using the following criteria:

- sufficient enrolment of students with a vocational background;
- appropriate mix of student body in terms of gender;
- relative size and availability of subject groups;
- regional diversity;
- type of institution.

Applying these criteria resulted in the following sample of institutions:

- HEI 1 is a medium-sized new university in south-east England with an intake of students with a varied qualification background and generally low entry standards from a fairly local catchment area.
- HEI 2 is a large, old campus university in the east of England with high entry requirements whose intake is of students from across the UK.
- HEI 3 is a large, new city-based university in Scotland with a predominantly local catchment area and a well-stated widening participation agenda. Some popular subject areas (such as the ones in this project) do not have students with varied qualification backgrounds however, and they have high entry requirements.
- HEI 4 is a small further education college in north-west England which takes students from a fairly local catchment area with very few prior qualifications, and provides opportunities for them to progress through the qualification levels and into HE at the college, in partnership with local universities.
- HEI 5 is a large further education college in Scotland which takes students from the local catchment area with very few prior qualifications, and provides opportunities for them to progress from further to HE within or outside this institution. For further information about the selection of institutions and subjects (see Dunbar-Goddet and Ertl 2007).

One set of student questionnaires was administered at the beginning, and a further set towards the end, of the students' first year of HE studies. The first instrument in our study was an exploratory questionnaire regarding student transition into HE. The second questionnaire looked at the ways in which students describe their experience during their first year of studies. The focus of the contributions from the *Degrees of Success* project in Chapter 3 is the discussion of the first of our two questionnaires: the *Transition to Higher Education Questionnaire*.

The questionnaire was administered by a project researcher, to all first-year students on business, computing and nursing courses at the five institutions, towards the beginning of their HE experience (October 2006–January 2007). In some cases also to students who were admitted to the third or final year of a course because of their prior qualifications. This resulted in 1105 responses, representing a response rate of 64 per cent. For the analysis of the questionnaire, categories of students were created according to their educational background (see Chapter 3 and also Hölscher and Hayward 2008).

The data collected in this questionnaire also allowed the project to identify some particular issues relevant for students with a vocational background; these were followed up in interviews that were carried out over the course of the 2006–07 academic year, with students and staff at each of the institutions. These issues included the students' motivations for studying at HE level, their reasons for choosing to study a) their subject and b) at their current HEI, and the transition from previous to HE studies. Additionally the questionnaire data made it possible to pre-select interesting cases to interview in order to generate in-depth data, for instance, on the ways VET students decide on HE study. At the same time, the first questionnaire was used to identify 'interesting cases', that is, students who came into HE with a vocational background and/or demonstrate a certain degree of reflectiveness regarding their educational pathway. By interviewing students as well as lecturers and admissions staff, complementary data on the transition into, and experience of, different students in higher education was produced. As outlined earlier, the research methods and findings developed in Parts 1 and 2 of the project were triangulated in user forum discussions with experts and practitioners in the field in Part 3. All the interviews conducted were semi-structured, allowing flexibility to follow up the particular insights and areas of expertise of responsibility of interviewees.

Keeping Open the Door to Mathematically Demanding Programmes in Further and Higher Education

Julian Williams' team

Our project aimed to understand how *cultures of learning and teaching* can support learners in ways that help widen and extend participation in mathematically demanding courses in further and higher education (F&HE) (for a general overview see Williams *et al.* 2009). One of its strengths is that it draws on a variety of research methods. It used a large-scale questionnaire survey, case studies, and longitudinal interviews, providing a rich base of data for analysis. The survey involved 1800 students who have been carefully sampled to include a high proportion of students considered 'on the edge' between engagement and disengagement. Specially constructed instruments were used to measure important new learning outcomes including the mathematical self-efficacy of students, their disposition to enter higher education and their dispositions towards studying mathematically demanding subjects in higher education. The students were surveyed at the beginning of their AS year, near the end of their AS year and then again when they were in A2, by that time mostly having applied for university. Generalised linear models were constructed (see Hutcheson 2008a, 2008b) to test hypotheses and measure effects of programme and pedagogy on learning outcomes for different groups of students. This analysis, for instance, showed significant effects as a results of the AS programme followed. Additionally, analyses of background variables revealed effects such as that arising from ethnicity – proportionally more Asian students self-reported a preference for mathematically demanding courses.

Additionally, we constructed a teacher self-report instrument that measures the degree of transmissionist/connectionist practice teachers say they used in each classroom. Validation of these newly constructed instruments using Rasch Measurement suggested robust measures. In particularly we found that students whose teachers self-reported as connectionist were better disposed to choose mathematically demanding courses in HE, although there was no significant relationship found for hard outcome measures (see Pampaka *et al.* 2008).

The hybrid design of the case study and the longitudinal survey of affective and cognitive learning outcomes when combined allowed us to conclude that programme and pedagogy can make significant differences to learning outcomes for these students, and also to offer explanations; for example, the relation between pedagogic culture and disposition for further mathematics study were found in the classroom observations and student interviews (e.g. Wake 2007; Wake and Pampaka 2008). Furthermore this prompted progressive focusing on the contrast between transmissionist and connectionist mathematics classrooms. Additionally the case study analysis enabled a principled and theoretical approach to the construction of the generalised linear models that revealed explanatory models, as well as ensured that our new bespoke measurement instruments were grounded in qualitative data.

Our five case studies took the form of mainly qualitative investigations and involved classroom observations with interviews of students and teachers. The colleges were selected according to the following criteria:

1   HE participation neighbourhood (reflecting parental participation in HE);
2   programme offered (UoM and traditional or only traditional);
3   the institution type FE/sixth form college.

The case studies were designed to gain insight into the complex cultures of teaching and learning. They focused on how these cultures mediate students' learning outcomes, including their disposition(s) to participate mathematically (e.g. in mathematically demanding degree programmes in HE), and how pedagogical cultures position students in crucial ways in regards to how they value learning and mathematics, which we found to relate significantly to drop-out (Davis et al. 2008b).

In each of nine classrooms between four and six students were selected (approx forty-five altogether) on the basis of their GCSE scores, background and subject combinations to provide social diversity, and including numbers from the target social groups (e.g. of low SES, parental education etc.). These case studies were designed to (i) capture the classroom contexts which served to mediate the individual students' participation and their perceptions of participation, (ii) track the various trajectories of participation of the individual students. This approach provided an alternating foregrounding of the classroom activity and the individual students' narratives of participation. Triangulation was also supported by the collection of other college documents and interviews with other stakeholders such as heads of department or college principals (see Williams et al. 2008).

Narrative accounts of these students' experiences of learning mathematics, their aspirations and identification with learning mathematics, within a particular programme and classroom culture were produced. This enabled us to ground theory about how experiences of mathematics in FE and beyond can mediate marginalisation or inclusion in mathematics, and hence students' aspirations, expectations and attitudes towards participation in HE (e.g. Davis et al. 2008b; Wake and Davis 2008).

We also drew upon standard procedures for thematic analysis to contrast the discourses and cultural models of students and how they use these to position themselves as certain kinds of mathematics learners in their various pedagogic practices (e.g. Hernandez *et al.* 2008a). Analysis across the cases compared and contrasted students' narratives of their mathematical identity, aspirations and positioning in relation to background, class, and gender (Davis *et al.* 2008c; Hernandez *et al.* 2008b). A cluster analysis of students positioning with regard to the value of mathematics learning was also undertaken and revealed significantly distinct clusters of student discourses in relation to the value of mathematics (Davis *et al.* 2008a; see also Chapter 4, Section 2 this volume).

Analysis drew on recent developments in the understanding of subjectivity in Cultural Historical Activity Theory, including our own work in this area (see Williams *et al.* 2007), in order to understand the processes by which students can become marginalised or more engaged with learning mathematics. This led to the development of a Marxist labour theory of value for learning (Williams 2008), which offers a theoretical account of the contradiction between exchange- and use-value with regard to students and teachers experiences of learning and teaching mathematics.

Our methodological approach was imbued with the notion of generating practical knowledge in partnership with students and teachers as informed and knowledgeable participants. This partnership approach also provided an ethical (and triangulating) basis for all the empirical, analytical and reporting work. A series of teacher conferences assisted in this respect; for instance, informing our understandings of how different institutions' market positioning can influence their policy on 'access' and hence to widening participation in mathematics. Finally, our warrant was also enriched by the project's advisory group, which consisted of expert academics and practitioners with relevant experience, and who met regularly with the project team. Please note that all papers referenced in this section are freely available at http:www.education.manchester.ac.uk/research/centres/lta/LTAResearch/tlrp/aboutacademicpapers.htm.

Appendix 6

Learning and Teaching for Social Diversity and Difference in Higher Education

Chris Hockings' team

The *Learning and Teaching for Social Diversity and Difference in HE* project was divided into two phases. The first phase was designed to provide an insight into pre-entry students' conceptions and expectations of university. Data were collected from students at four 'pre entry' institutions (one school, a sixth form college and two further education colleges local to the two universities in the study) in the year before they went to university. Each institution had a diverse population in terms of class and ethnicity. Between them they offered a range of entry routes to university including A-level and vocational qualifications. Four broad disciplines were covered: communication and information technology (CIT), science, health and social policy, and business. These subjects provided a mix of science, technology and social sciences as well as academic and vocational subjects. We worked with staff in these institutions to identify suitable groups with whom to work. Teachers encouraged student participation in the project and both students and teachers saw it as an opportunity for students to reflect on entry to HE. In total 225 pre-entry students completed questionnaires; around 100 participated in ten activity-based focus group sessions. From these groups, we interviewed fourteen students either individually or in pairs outside class (see Hockings *et al.* 2007 for an exploration of pre-entry students' expectations of HE. See also Bowl *et al.* 2008b for an exploration of the research process in the early stages of the project). Findings from this phase were compared to the experiences of first-year university students in phase two, and shared with the eight university teachers who would be working with us in phase two to inform the re/development of their first-year modules prior to the start of academic year 2006/7.

Phase two of the research focused on first-year undergraduate students and their university teachers in broadly the same subjects as those chosen for the pre-entry phase (biosciences, business, computing, history, nursing and social work). The main objective for this phase was to see how students' and teachers' identities might be played out in the classroom, and whether they appeared to influence teaching practice and academic engagement. Working in two universities we were also able to explore the

influence of pre- and post-1992 university contexts on academic engagement of diverse students. Four teachers from a pre-1992, and four from a
post-1992 university were encouraged to participate in the study because
they were all teaching first year modules. They were taking or had recently
completed a postgraduate certificate in learning and teaching in HE or
equivalent, and they all had a keen interest in continuing to develop their
own teaching practice and to improve student learning. The eight teachers
(three female, five male) were all white, aged between 25 and 45, and all
but two had middle-class backgrounds (as determined by parents' occupation). We were conscious that this did not reflect the diversity within the
student groups and that this could influence how students and teachers saw
and related to each other (see below, also Housee 2001; Letherby and
Shiels 2001). Nevertheless it did reflect the predominantly white academic
staff population in both institutions.

In this phase we adapted the principles of action research (Carr and
Kemmis 1986) not only to develop the teachers' and researchers' knowledge and understanding of academic engagement in diverse student
settings, but also to act upon it to improve practice and influence policy.
Carr and Kemmis (1986) suggest a typology of action research: technical,
where the role of the researcher is as outside 'expert'; practical, where the
role of the researcher is to work alongside the practitioner to encourage participation and reflection on practice; and emancipatory, where
researcher and practitioner are collaborators with equal responsibility in
the research process. In practice, these distinctions are not as clear-cut as
they appear and we found ourselves moving between roles as we worked
with different teachers at different stages of the research.

Over semester one of the academic year 2006/7 we observed and video-
recorded at least three classroom sessions per module (around fifty hours
of video data). Following these sessions, the observer would hold and
record a debriefing meeting with individual teachers to explore issues
arising from the session with regard to the research questions and to
consider changes in practice. Where possible, changes discussed in these
sessions were observed in subsequent sessions. Teachers from both
institutions paired up, by subject, and reviewed their own as well as their
partner's video-recorded sessions to compare approaches to teaching, the
teaching environment and their respective groups of students. They also
participated in inter-university meetings to consider the implications of the
research findings for their practice. At the end of the second semester the
teachers completed an open-ended questionnaire in which they reflected
on the influences of their participation of the project.

Data were also gathered from the first-year students before, during and
after observed sessions. Within the first five weeks of the year over 290
students completed a questionnaire providing details of themselves and
their families, their conceptions of higher education, their chosen subject,
the learning and teaching they had experienced so far, and their ways of

knowing. They also described ways in which they felt the same as or different from other students in the group. In addition we held thirty-four semi-structured interviews with students from across the participating module groups. We invited individuals to talk to us who had appeared engaged or disengaged at some point during the lesson.

Taking as the unit of analysis the interplay between the individual and the (classroom) community (Wenger 1998), we began observing lessons. As we did so, we developed and refined our understanding of what it is to be engaged and disengaged and became sensitive to the circumstances surrounding such incidents. Careful not to rely on observational data alone, wherever possible we used other methods (including interviewing students who had seemed disengaged in the session immediately after the session or during breaks) to triangulate our interpretations and explore how and why students had become engaged or disengaged. Some of these students also participated in the focus group meetings that were set up for each module part way through the semester.

Since we did not have the facility to code video data, we needed to create text documents from the DVDs to allow the reader to 'experience a sense of event, presence and action' and also to be able to check on the inter-pretation offered by the researcher (Kochman 1972 cited in Furlong and Edwards 1986: 54). Thick descriptions (Geertz 1973) of selected engage-ment and disengagement episodes from the video recordings were made, and associated classroom talk, captured with the aid of discrete desk microphones, were transcribed. These recorded data were combined with the 'live' (Delamont and Hamilton 1986: 38) researchers' observational field notes, contextual data and analytical memos to form one composite document per classroom observation.

All phase two data, including the composite documents, student and teacher interviews, focus group transcripts and questionnaire responses, were subsequently grouped by module, combed through for instances where students appeared, or spoke about being, academically engaged or disengaged and subsequently written up as subject case studies (e.g. Hockings *et al.* 2008b). Nvivo 7 was used to code and analyse all textual forms of qualitative data, a web-based questionnaire package (Surveyor by Object Planet) was used to capture and analyse quantitative data. These tools combined with our detailed knowledge developed in the field allowed us to make connections between subjects, approaches to teaching, and institutions, and to see how these influenced academic engagement of students from diverse and different backgrounds.

'Non-participation' in Higher Education: Decision-making as an Embedded Social Practice

Alison Fuller's team

Research design and methodological challenges

This project had two phases. In phase one, we reviewed quantitative literature on educational participation and explored the characteristics of 'non-participants' through secondary analysis of Labour Force Survey (LFS) and Youth Cohort Study (YCS) data. We also conducted thirty-two interviews with key informants from the local, regional and national widening participation arena. Phase one provided a broader context for the subsequent qualitative fieldwork. Secondary analysis of LFS data allowed us to explore the characteristics of the level 3 population nationally and enabled us to compare our sample with the national picture. Analysis of YCS data focused on the little used HE module and enabled us to compare non-participation amongst 'standard age' potential recruits with non-participation amongst our older target group. The key informant interviews provided useful insights into the local, regional and national policy context.

The second phase consisted of a qualitative exploration of sixteen case study networks, spiralling out from sixteen potentially recruitable individuals, defined for our research as those whose current highest level of qualification is at level 3 and who have subsequently neither participated in HE nor are currently applying to do so. An initial interview was conducted with each of these individuals (the 'entry point') to explore their educational and career histories and their broader networks. These individuals then nominated members of their networks (mainly relatives, partners and friends) to participate in our research. Individual interviews were then conducted with network members, exploring their own educational and employment histories and their decision-making in these realms, as well as their perceptions of how they might have influenced, and in turn been influenced by, the 'entry point' individual. In total, we interviewed ninety-one network members across the sixteen networks. A second more detailed interview was subsequently held with fifteen out of the initial sixteen individuals to explore themes and issues which had emerged within their network.

We faced various sampling challenges. Our level 3 target population is not an easily identifiable group, coming from diverse socio-economic groups and encompassing all kinds of educational backgrounds, ages, life stages, geographical locations and employment histories. Nor are there any obvious sampling frames for this group. We also encountered confusion concerning what 'counts' as a level 3 qualification, particularly with regard to vocational awards and changes to qualifications over time. Many potential participants may not have known whether or nor they were eligible to participate in our research. Access was nonetheless achieved via several routes, including local FE colleges, training providers, employers, community groups, personal contacts, requests for volunteers through (e)mail shots to various groups. announcements in various newsletters, and postcards in shop windows.

Various levels of filtering occurred in gaining access to broader network members: our entry points initially had to be willing to introduce us to their networks, they then chose who to nominate, and we were then reliant on people's willingness to participate. The number of network members we interviewed (ranging from three to thirteen people, with an average of six) did not always reflect the actual size of an individual's network, or the quality of relationships within them. Some networks were large and close, yet contained few individuals who were willing to participate. In other cases, people who had been key influences on the entry point person were unavailable because of infirmity or death. The influence of 'missing members' was explored through the second interview with entry points and, although aware that we did not hear their voices directly, the rapport we had developed by the second interview allowed us to explore the influence of the 'missing members'. Despite these challenges, we generated a diverse sample in terms of key socio-economic characteristics and in line with our purposive sampling strategy. The achieved sample also enabled us to look in some detail at the characteristics, experiences and perceptions of a potentially recruitable group that extended beyond our entry point individuals, as twenty-eight broader network members also met our criteria of 'potentially recruitable'.

The design of our interview schedule also posed challenges in finding ways of talking about 'non-participation' in HE within networks where participation is not the norm. In particular, we were concerned not to imply that non-HE pathways are somehow inferior to HE pathways. Accordingly we structured our interviews around the more neutral topics of 'educational and employment decision-making', which allowed interviewees to provide their own accounts, reflections and values on the pathways they have taken, and which invariably provided a powerful counterpoint to the policy assumption that participation in HE is always and necessarily 'a good thing'.

Our analysis proceeded in several identifiable stages. The early analysis based on the initial entry point interviews was very much at the level of individual cases and comparisons between different individuals. We sub-sequently moved towards analyses which focused on individual networks as the primary unit of analysis, in some cases comparing two or more networks. Our third level of analysis is cross-network analysis, which seeks to compare and contrast different networks and to identify common themes and patterns across our entire dataset. We also developed a range of helpful tools such as policy timelines and graphical representations of network characteristics. Given the nature of our network data, we were particularly mindful of the need to preserve confidentiality within each network and our informed consent procedures included a guarantee that we would not pass on information from interviewee to interviewee.

Sample profiles

Overall totals:
Entry point interviewees = 16
Network interviewees = 91
Total number of interviewees = 107

Table A7.1 Sample profile by gender

Gender	Entry point interviewees	Network interviewees
Male	7	35
Female	9	56

Table A7.2 Sample profile by age

Age	Entry point interviewees	Network interviewees
Up to and including 16	0	4
17–20	0	1
21–30	2	15
31–40	3	18
41–50	4	14
51–60	4	19
61–65	3	6
Over 65	0	14

Table A7.3 Sample profile by ethnicity

Ethnicity	Entry point interviewees	Network interviewees
White British	15	88
Other	1	3

Table A7.4 Sample profile by lifestage

Lifestage	Entry point interviewees	Network interviewees
With own parents and without children	2	11
Independent of parents and without children	1	9
With children: youngest child up to age 10	3	20
With children: youngest child is 11 or more	5	19
Children are grown up and have left home	5	32

Table A7.5 Sample profile by employment status

Employment status	Entry point interviewees	Network interviewees
Full-time	10	38
Part-time	2	20
Self-employed	1	5
Not in paid work	2	6
Retired	1	17
Full-time student	0	5

Table A7.6 Sample profile by geographical location

Geographical location	Entry point interviewees	Network interviewees
Southampton	5	15
Portsmouth	1	6
Isle of Wight	5	22
Other Hampshire	5	18
Other	0	30

Table A7.7 Sample profile by disability

Disability	Entry point interviewees	Network interviewees
Yes	5	33
No	11	57

Table A7.8 Sample profile by highest qualification

Highest qualification	Entry point interviewees	Network interviewees
Not applicable as aged under 16	0	4
No qualifications	0	8
Level 1	0	11
Level 2	0	9
Level 3	13	21
Trade apprenticeship	3	7
Level 4+	0	31

Table A7.9 Sample profile by social class

Social class	Entry point interviewees	Network interviewees
1	1	17
2	6	14
3	5	19
4	1	6
5	1	2
6	1	10
7	0	10
8	1	13

References

Acemoglu, D. (1998) Why do new technologies complement skills? Directed technical change and wage inequality. *Quarterly Journal of Economics*, 113 (4): 1055–1089.

Admissions to Higher Education Review (2004) *Fair Admissions to Higher Education: Recommendations for Good Practice*. London: Department for Education and Skills.

Ainley, P. (1999) *Learning Policy: Towards the Certified Society*. New York: St Martin's Press.

Apple, M. (1986) *Teachers and Texts: A Political Economy of Class and Gender Relations in Education*. London: Routledge & Kegan Paul.

Archer, L. (2008) The new neoliberal subjects? Young/er academics' constructions of professional identity. *Journal of Education Policy*, 23 (3): 265–285.

Archer, L. and Hutchings, M. (2000) 'Bettering yourself?' Discourses of risk, cost and benefit in ethnically diverse, young working class non-participants' constructions of higher education. *British Journal of Sociology of Education*, 21 (4): 555–574.

Archer, L. Hutchings, M. and Ross, A. (eds) (2003) *Higher Education and Social Class: Issues of Exclusion and Inclusion*. London: Routledge/Falmer.

Arnot, M., David, M.E. and Weiner, G. (1999) *Closing the Gender Gap: Postwar Education and Social Change*. Cambridge: Polity Press.

Arum, R. and Shavit, Y. (1993) *Another Look at Tracking, Vocational Education and Social Reproduction*. Florence: European University Institute.

Ashwin, P. and McLean, M. (2004) Towards a reconciliation of phenomenographic and critical pedagogy perspectives in higher education through a focus on academic engagement. *Improving Student Learning Symposium*, Birmingham Jury's Hotel.

Askew, M., Brown, M., Rhodes, V., Johnson, D. and Wiliam, D. (1997) Effective teachers of numeracy (final report). London: King's College.

Atkinson, P. *et al.* (2003) *Key Themes in Qualitative Research*. Walnut Creek, CA: Altamira Press.

Bakhtin, M. (1981) Discourse in the novel. In M. Holquist (ed.) *The Dialogic Imagination*. Trans. C. Emerson and M. Holquist. Austin, TX: University of Texas Press.

Ball, S. (2003a) The teacher's soul and the terrors of performativity. *Journal of Education Policy*, 18 (2): 215–228.

Ball, S.J. (2003b) *Class Strategies and the Education Market. The Middle Classes and Social Advantage*. London: Routledge.

Ball, S. and Vincent, C. (1998) 'I heard it on the grapevine': 'hot' knowledge and school choice. *British Journal of Sociology of Education*, 19 (3): 377–400.

Ball, S.J., Maguire, M. and Macrae, S. (2000) *Choice, Pathways and Transitions Post-16*. London and New York: Routledge/Falmer.

Bamber, J. and Tett, L. (2001) Ensuring integrative learning experiences for non-traditional students in higher education. *Widening Participation and Lifelong Learning*, 3 (1): 8–16.

Barnett, R. (1990) *The Idea of Higher Education*. Milton Keynes: Society for Research into Higher Education and Open University Press.

Bartky, S.L. (1990) *Femininity and Domination: Studies in the Phenomenology of Oppression*. New York: Routledge.

Bastedo, M.N. and Gumport, P.J. (2003) Access to what? Mission differentiation and academic stratification in US public higher education. *Higher Education*, 46: 341–359.

Bathmaker, A.M. and Avis, J. (2005) Becoming a lecturer in further education in England: the construction of professional identity and the role of practice. *Journal of Education for Training*, 31 (1): 1–17.

Bathmaker, A.M. and Thomas, W. (2009) Positioning themselves: an exploration of the nature and meaning of transitions in the context of dual sector FE/HE institutions in England. *Journal of Further and Higher Education*, 3 (2) 119–130.

Beck, J. (2002) The sacred and the profane in recent struggles to promote pedagogic identities. *British Journal of Sociology of Education*, 23 (4): 617–626.

Bekhradnia, B. (2003) Widening participation and fair access: an overview of the evidence. Report from the Higher Education Policy Institute.

Belenky, M., Clinchy, B., Goldberger, N. and Tarule, J. (1997) *Women's Ways of Knowing*. New York: Basic Books.

Belley, P. and Lochner, L. (2007) The changing role of family income and ability in determining educational achievement. *Journal of Human Capital*, 1 (1): 37–89.

Bennett, R. (2003) Determinants of undergraduate student drop out rates in a university business studies department. *Journal of Further and Higher Education*, 27 (2): 123–141.

Bernstein, B. (1975) *Class, Codes and Control*. 2nd edn. London: Routledge & Kegan Paul.

Bernstein, B. (1996) *Pedagogy, Symbolic Control and Identity. Theory, Research Critique*. London and Philadelphia: Taylor & Francis.

Bernstein, B. (2000) *Pedagogy, Symbolic Control and Identity* (rev. edn). Lanham, MD: Rowman & Littlefield.

Bhaba, H. (1996) Cultures in between. In S. Hall and P. Du Gay (eds) *Cultural Identity*. London and California: Sage.

Blair, T. (2007) Our Nation's Future – the role of work. Online: www.number10. gov.uk/output/Page11405.asp (accessed 26 November 2007).

Blanden, J. and Gregg, P. (2004) Family income and educational attainment: a review of approaches and evidence for Britain. *Oxford Review of Economic Policy*, 20: 245–263.

Blanden, J. and Machin, S. (2004) Educational inequality and the expansion of higher education. *Scottish Journal of Political Economy* (Special Issue on the Economics of Education), 51 (2): 230–249.

Blossfeld, H.-P. and Shavit, Y. (1991) *Persisting Barriers: Changes in Educational Opportunities in Thirteen Countries*. Florence: European University Institute.

Bourdieu, P. (1976) The school as a conservative force: scholastic and cultural inequalities. In R. Dale *et al.* (eds) *Schooling and Capitalism: A Sociological Reader*. London: Routledge.

Bourdieu, P. (1977) *Reproduction in Education, Society and Culture*. London: Sage.

Bourdieu, P. (1986) The forms of capital. In J.G. Richardson (ed.) *The Handbook of Theory: Research for the Sociology of Education*. New York: Greenwood Press.

Bourdieu, P. (1988) *Homo Academicus*. Cambridge: Polity Press.

Bourdieu, P. (1990a) *The Logic of Practice*. Cambridge: Polity Press.

Bourdieu, P. (1990b) *In Other Words: Essays Towards a Reflexive Sociology*. Cambridge: Polity Press.

Bourdieu, P. (2000) *Pascalian Meditations*. Cambridge: Polity Press.

Bourdieu, P. (2005) Habitus. In J. Hillier and E. Rooksby (eds) *Habitus: A Sense of Place*. Aldershot: Ashgate.

Bourdieu, P. and Wacquant, L. (1992*) An Invitation to Reflexive Sociology*. Chicago: University of Chicago Press.

Bowl, M. (2006) *Non-Traditional Entrants to Higher Education*. Stoke-on-Trent: Trentham Books.

Bowl, M., Cooke, S. and Hockings, C. (2008a) Home and away? Issues of student 'choice', living arrangements and what it means to be a student. *Widening participation and lifelong learning,* 10 (1): 4–13.

Bowl, M., Cooke, S. and Hockings, C. (2008b) Researching across boundaries and borders: challenges for research. *Educational Action Research*, 16 (1): 85–95.

Brennan, J., Mills, J., Shah, T. and Woodley, A. (1999) Part-time students and employment: report of a survey of students, graduates and diplomates. London: QSC, The Open University.

Brint, S. and Karabel, J. (1989) *The Diverted Dream. Community Colleges and the Promise of Educational Opportunity in America, 1900–1985*. New York: Oxford University Press.

Broecke, S. and Nicholls, T. (2007) Ethnicity and degree attainment. London: Department for Education and Skills Research Report RW92.

Brooks, R. (2005) *Friendship and Educational Choice*. Basingstoke: Palgrave Macmillan.

Brunsden, V., Davies, M., Shevlin, M. and Bracken, M. (2000) Why do HE Students Drop Out? A test of Tinto's model. *Journal of Further and Higher Education*, 24 (3): 301–310.

Bryson, C. and Hand, L. (2007) The role of engagement in inspiring teaching and learning. *Innovations in Education and Teaching International*, 44 (4): 349–362.

Burke, P. (2004) Women accessing education: subjectivity, policy and participation, *Journal of Access Policy and Practice*, 1 (2): 100–118.

Bynner, J. and Roberts, K. (eds) (1991) *Youth and Work: Transition to Employment in England and Germany*. London: Anglo-German Foundation.

Callender, C. (2003) Student financial support in higher education: access and exclusion. In M. Tight (ed.) *Access and Exclusion: International Perspectives on Higher Education Research*. London: Elsevier Science.

Cannon, R. and Newble, D. (2000) *A Guide to Improving Teaching Methods: A Handbook for Teachers in University and Colleges*. London: Kogan Page.

Carneiro, P. and Heckman, J. (2002) The evidence on credit constraints in post-secondary schooling. *Economic Journal*, 112: 705–734.

Carneiro, P. and Heckman, J. (2003) Human capital policy. In J. Heckman, A. Krueger and B. Friedman (eds) *Inequality in America: What Role for Human Capital Policies?* Cambridge, MA: MIT Press.

Carr, W. and Kemmis, S. (1986) *Becoming Critical: Education, Knowledge and Action Research*. Basingstoke: Falmer Press.

Chapman, K. (1996) Entry Qualifications, degree results and value-added in UK universities. *Oxford Review of Education*, 22: 251–262.

Charlesworth, S.J, Gilfillan, P. and Wilkinson, R. (2004) Living Inferiority. *British Medical Bulletin*, 69: 49–60.

Cheung, S.Y. and Egerton, M. (2007) Great Britain: higher education expansion and reform – changing educational inequalities. In Y. Shavit, R. Arum and A. Gamoran (eds) *Stratification in Higher Education. A Comparative Study*. Stanford: Stanford University Press.

Chevalier, A. and Conlon, G. (2003) Does it pay to attend a prestigious university? CEE Discussion Paper No. 33.

Chowdry, H., Crawford, C., Dearden, L., Goodman, A. and Vignoles, A. (2008a) Widening participation in higher education: analysis using linked administrative data. Institute for Fiscal Studies Report No. R69, mimeo.

Chowdry, H., Crawford, C., Dearden, L., Goodman, A., and Vignoles, A. (2008b) Understanding the determinants of participation in higher education and the quality of institute attended: analysis using administrative data. Institute of Fiscal Studies, working paper.

Clancy, D. and Fazey, J. (2008) Knowledge and knowing in higher education: valuing a socialised habitus of academic personal epistemologies (SHAPE). Society for Research into Higher Education annual conference, Liverpool.

Clayton, J., Crozier, G. and Reay, D. (forthcoming) Home and away: risk, familiarity and the multiple geographies of the higher education experience.

Clegg, S. (2008) Academic identities under threat? *British Educational Research Journal,* 34 (3): 329–345.

CMPO (2006) Family background and child development up to age 7 in the Avon Longitudinal Survey of Parnets and Children (ALSPAC). DfES Research Report No. RR808A.

Coffield, F. and Vignoles, A. (1997) Widening participation in higher education by ethnic minorities, women and alternative students. Report 5 National Committee of Inquiry into Higher Education. London: NCIHE.

Coffield, F., Edward, S., Finlay, I., Hodgson, A., Spours, K. and Steer, R. (2008) *Improving Learning, Skills and Inclusion. The impact of policy on post-compulsory education*, Abingdon: Routledge.

Cole, M., Engestrom, Y. and Vasquez, O.A. (eds) (1977) *Mind, Culture and Activity: Seminal Papers from the Laboratory of Comparative Human Cognition*. Cambridge: Cambridge University Press.

Coleman, J. (1988) Social capital in the creation of human capital. *Americam Journal of Sociology,* 94:, 95–120.

Colley, H., James, D., Tedder, M. and Diment, K. (2003) Learning as becoming in vocational education and training: class, gender and role of vocational habitus. *Journal of Vocational Education and Training,* 55 (4): 471–496.

Committee on Higher Education (1963) Higher Education. Report of the Committee appointed by the Prime Minister under the Chairmanship of Lord Robbins. Cmnd 2154. London: HMSO.

Connor, H. and Dewson, S. with Tyers, C., Eccles, J., Regan, J. and Aston, J. (2001) Social class and higher education: issues affecting decisions on participation by lower social class groups. DfES Research Report No. 267.

Connor, H., Tyers, C., Modood, R. and Hillage, J. (2004) Why the difference? A closer look at higher education minority ethnic students and graduates. DfES Research Report No. 552.

Connor, H., Burton, R., Pearson, R., Pollard, E. and Regan, J. (1999) *Making the Right Choice: How Students Choose University and Colleges.* London: IES.

Cooke-Sather, A. and Youens, B. (2007) Repositioning students in initial teacher preparation. A comparative descriptive analysis of learning to teach for social justice in the United States and in England. *Journal of Teacher Education,* 58 (1): 62–75.

Corrigan, M.E. (2003) Beyond access: persistence challenges and the diversity of low-income students. *New Directions for Higher Education,* 121: 25–34.

Cranton, P. and Carusetta, E. (2004) Perspectives on authenticity in teaching. *Adult Education Quarterly,* 55 (1): 5–22.

Cristofoli, L. and Watts, M. (2005) *The Role of Regional Further Education Colleges in Delivering Higher Education in the East of England.* Cambridge: Association of Universities in the East of England.

Crozier, G. and Reay, D. (2008) Capital accumulation: working class students learning how to learn in HE. SRHE Special Interest Group Seminar Presentation. London Metropolitan University. June.

Crozier, G., Reay, D., Clayton, J., Colliander, L. and Grinstead, J. (2008) Different strokes for different folks: diverse students in diverse institutions – experiences of higher education. *Research Papers in Education* (Special issue on challenges of diversity for widening participation in UK higher education), 23 (2): 167–177.

Crozier, G. Reay, D. and Clayton, J. (forthcoming) Border crossings and cultural fusions: constructing hybrid social identities in higher education.

Cunha, F. and Heckman, J. (2007) The technology of skill formation. *American Economic Review,* 92 (2): 31–47.

Cunha, F., Heckman, J., Lochner, L. and Masterov, D. (2006) Interpreting the evidence on life cycle skill formation. In E. Hanushek and F. Welch (eds) *Handbook of the Economics of Education,* Amsterdam: Elsevier, pp. 697–812.

David, M.E. (2007) Equity and diversity: towards a sociology of higher education for the twenty-first century? *British Journal of Sociology of Education,* 28 (5): 675–690.

David, M.E. (2008a) Introduction. *Research Papers in Education* (Special issue on challenges of diversity for widening participation in UK higher education), 23 (2): 111–113.

David, M. (2008b) Social diversity and equality: challenges and implications for policies, pedagogies and practices in UK post-compulsory and lifelong learning. In G. Copeland, D. Sachdev and C. Flint (eds) *Unfinished Business in Widening Participation: The End of the Beginning*. London: Learning and Skills Network. Online: www.LSNeducation.org.uk.

David, M. (2008c) Social inequalities, gender and lifelong learning: a feminist, sociological review of work, family and education. *International Journal of Sociology and Social Policy* (Special issue on processes of social inequality), 28 (7 and 8): 260–272.

David, M. (2009) Social diversity and democracy in higher education in twenty-first century. *Higher Education Policy* (special issue), 22 (2): 61–79.

David, M. with Clegg, S. (2008) Power, pedagogy and personalisation in global higher education: the occlusion of second wave feminism? *Discourse, The Cultural Politics of Education* (Special issue on second wave feminism) 29 (4): 483–498.

David, M.E, West, A. and Ribbens, J. (1994) *Mother's Intuition? Choosing Secondary Schools*. London: Falmer Press.

Davies, P. (1999) Half full, not half empty: a positive look at part-time higher education. *Higher Education Quarterly,* 53 (2): 141–55.

Davis, P. (2009) The place of maths in a different 'space': value of mathematics in student narratives of an imagined future in higher education. Paper presented at the AERA Conference, San Diego. Online: www.education.manchester.ac.uk/research/centres/lta/LTAResearch/tlrp/about/academicpapers/.

Davis, P., Pampaka, M., Hutcheson, G., Black, L., Hernandez-Martinez, P., Nicholson, S., Wake, G. and Williams, J.S. (2008a) Making decisions about Higher Education: aspirations, subject choice and maths drop out. TLRP-WP-Maths working paper. Online: www.education.manchester.ac.uk/research/centres/lta/LTAResearch/tlrp/about/academicpapers/ (accessed 15 December 2008).

Davis, P., Williams, J.S., Black, L., Hernandez-Martinez, P., Hutcheson, G., Nicholson, S., Pampaka, M. and Wake, G. (2008b) Renegotiating identities: mediation of troubling AS Level mathematics. TLRP-WP-Maths working paper. Online: www.lta.education.manchester.ac.uk/TLRP/academicpapers.htm (accessed 15 December 2008).

Davis, P., Williams, J.S., Pampaka, M., Wake, G., Nicholson, S., Hutcheson, G., Hernandez-Martinez, P. and Black, L. (2008c) Participating differently in mathematics: the role of an exchange/use value dialectic. TLRP-WP-Maths working paper. Online: www.education.manchester.ac.uk/research/centres/lta/LTAResearch/tlrp/about/academicpapers/ (accessed 15 December 2008).

Dearden, L., Fitzsimons, E. and Wyness, G. (2008) The impact of up-front fees and student support on university participation. Institute of Education, unpublished mimeo.

Dearing, R. (1997) Higher education in the learning society. Report of the National Committee of Inquiry into Higher Education. London: HMSO. Online: https://bei.leeds.ac.uk/Partners/NCIHE.

Delamont, S. and Hamilton, D. (1986) Revisiting classroom research: a continuing cautionary tale. In Hammersley, M. (ed.) *Controversies in Classroom Research*. 2nd edn. Milton Keynes: Open University Press.

Denham, J. (2008) Be fair to adults as well as young people. *The Guardian*, 16 September.

DES (Department of Education and Science) (1966) A plan for polytechnics and other colleges. Higher education in the further education system. Cmnd 3006. London: HMSO.

DES (1985) The development of higher education into the 1990s. Cmnd 9524. London: HMSO.

DES (1987) Higher education. Meeting the challenge. Cm 114. London: HMSO.

DES (1991) Higher education. A new framework. Cm 1541. London: HMSO.

DfEE (Department for Education and Employment) (1998a) Higher education for the twenty-first century. Response to the Dearing Report. London: DfEE.

DfEE (1998b) Learning to succeed: response to the Kennedy Report. London: DfEE.

DfEE (1999) Learning to succeed. A new framework for post-16 learning. Cm 4392. London: HMSO.

DfEE (2000a) The excellence challenge. The government's proposals for widening participation of young people in higher education. London: DfEE.

DfEE (2000b) Foundation degrees. Consultation paper. London: DfEE.

DfEE (2003) The future of higher education. Cm 5735. London: DfES.

DfES (Department for Education and Skills) (2003) Widening participation in higher education. London: HMSO. Online: www.dfes.gov.uk/hegateway/uploads/EWParticipation.pdf.

DfES (2006a) Higher education funding 2006–07. Grant letter to the HEFCE, 31 January.

DfES (2006b) Widening participation in higher education. London: HMSO. Online: www.dcsf.gov.uk/hegateway/uploads/6820-DfES-WideningParticipation2.pdf.

Department for Innovation, Universities and Skills (2007) World class skills: implementing the Leitch review of skills in England. Cm 7181. Norwich: HMSO.

Dolton, P. and Vignoles, A. (2000) The incidence and effects of overeducation in the graduate labour market. *Economics of Education Review*, 19: 179–198.

Dougherty, K.J. (1994) *The Contradictory College. The Conflicting Origins, Impacts, and Features of the Community College*. Albany: State University of New York.

Doughney, L. (2000) Universal tertiary education: how dual-sector universities can challenge the binary divide between TAFE and higher education – the case of Victoria University of Technology. *Journal of Higher Education Policy and Management*, 22 (1): 59–72.

Duke, C. (2005) The crab's progress: approaching a tertiary system for lifelong learning. In C. Duke (ed.) *The Tertiary Moment. What Road to Inclusive Higher Education*. Leicester: National Institute of Adult Continuing Education, pp. 1–12.

Dunbar-Goddet, H. and Ertl, H. (2007) *Research o the Transition from Vocational Education and Training to Higher Education*. Online: www.tlrp.org.proj.Higher.html.

Dunbar-Goddet, H. and Ertl, H. (2008) *Investigating the Transition to Higher Education: Descriptive analysis of a questionnaire survey*. Online: www.tlrp.org/pfoj/Higher.html.

Dunkin, M. (1983) A review of research on lecturing, *Higher Education Research and Development*, 2: 63–78.

Education and Employment Committee (2001) Higher education: access. Fourth report. London: HMSO.

Edwards, R. (1993) *Mature Women Students: Separating or Connecting Family and Education*. London: Taylor & Francis.

Engestrom, R. (1995) Voice as communicative action. *Mind, Culture and Activity*, 2 (3): 192–214.

Ertl, H. and Dunbar-Goddet, H. (2008) *Investigating the learning experience of HE students with a vocational pathway: findings from a questionnaire survey*. Online: www.tlrp.org/project%20sites/degrees/download.html.

Feinstein, L. (2003) Inequality in the early cognitive development of British children in the 1970 cohort. *Economica*, 70 (277): 73–98.

Felstead, A., Gallie, D., Green, F. and Zhou, Y. (2007) Skills at work, 1986 to 2006. Nottingham: DfES.

Fordham, S. and Ogbu, J. (1986) Black students' success: coping with the burden of acting white. *Urban Review*, 18: 176–206.

Forsyth, A. and Furlong, A. (2003) Access to higher education and disadvantaged young people. *British Educational Research Journal*, 29 (2): 205–225.

Foskett, R. and Johnston, B. (forthcoming) 'A uniform seemed to be the obvious thing': the impact of careers, information, advice and guidance on potential HE participants.

Fuller, A. (2001) Credentialism, adults and part-time higher education in the United Kingdom: an account of rising take up and some implications for policy, *Journal of Education Policy*, 16 (3): 233–248.

Fuller, A. (2007) Mid-life transitions to higher education: developing a multi-level explanation of increasing participation. *Studies in the Education of Adults*, 39 (2): 217–235.

Fuller, A. and Heath, S. (2008) Participation in HE across the life-course: illustrations from two cohort generations. Paper presented at Society for Research in Higher Education, Annual Conference, Liverpool, 9–11 December.

Fuller, A. and Paton, K. (2008) Widening participation in higher education: mapping and investigating the stakeholder landscape. *Journal of Access, Policy and Practice*, 2 (2): 140–160.

Fuller, A., Hodkinson, H., Hodkinson, P. and Unwin, L. (2005) Learning as peripheral participation in communities of practice: a reassessment of key concepts in workplace learning. *British Educational Research Journal*, 31 (1): 49–68.

Fuller, A., Paton, K., Foskett, R. and Maringe, F. (2008) 'Barriers' to participation in higher education?: Depends who you ask and how. *Widening Participation and Lifelong Learning*, 10 (2): 6–17.

Fuller, A., Foskett, R., Johnston, B. and Paton, K. (forthcoming) 'Getting by' or 'getting ahead'? Gendered educational and career decision-making in networks of intimacy. In S. Jackson, I. Malcolm, T. Springer (eds).

Furlong, V. and Edwards, A. (1986) Language in classroom interaction: theory and data. In Hammersley, M. (ed.) *Controversies in Classroom Research*. 2nd edn. Milton Keynes: Open University Press.

Gallacher, J. (2002) Parallel lines? Higher education in Scotland's colleges and higher education institutions. *Scottish Affairs*, 40: 123–139.

Gallacher, J. (2005) Complementarity or differentiation? The role of further education colleges and higher education institutions in Scotland's higher education system. In J. Gallacher and M. Osborne (eds) *A Contested Landscape. International Perspectives on Diversity in Mass Higher Education*. Leicester: National Institute of Adult Continuing Education, pp. 153–177.

Gallacher, J. (2006) Widening access or differentiation and stratification in higher education in Scotland,EDITED TO HERE *Higher Education Quarterly*, 60 (4): 349–369.

Gallacher, J. and Osborne, M. (eds) (2005) *A Contested Landscape. International Perspectives on Diversity in Mass Higher Education*. Leicester: National Institute of Adult Continuing Education.

Garrod, N. and Macfarlane, B. (2007) Scoping the duals: structural challenges of combining further and higher education in post-secondary institutions. *Higher Education Quarterly*, 61 (4): 578–596.

Garrod, N. and Macfarlane, B. (eds) (2009) *Challenging Boundaries. Managing the Integration of Post-Secondary Education*, Oxford: Routledge.

Gayle, V., Berridge, D. and Davies, R. (2002) Young people's entry into higher education: quantifying influential factors. *Oxford Review of Education*, 28 (1): 5–20.

Geertz, C. (1973) Thick description: toward an interpretive theory of culture. In C. Geertz (ed.) *The Interpretation of Cultures*. New York: Basic Books.

Gibbons, S. and Chevalier, A. (2008) Assessment and age 16+ education participation. *Research Papers in Education* (Special issue on challenges of diversity for widening participation in UK higher education), 23 (2): 113–125.

Gibbs, G. (1982) *Twenty Terrible Reasons for Lecturing*. Oxford: Educational Methods Unit, Oxford Polytechnic.

Giele, J. and Elder, G. (eds) (1998) *Methods of Life Course Research: Qualitative and Quantitative Approaches*. London: Sage.

Gillies, V. and Lucey, H. (2006) 'It's a connection you can't get away from': brothers, sisters and social capital. *Journal of Youth Studies*, 9 (4): 479–493.

Glennerster, H. (2001) United Kingdom education 1997–2001. Centre for the Analysis of Social Exclusion (CASE) Working Paper No. 50.

Gokulsing, K., Ainley, P. and Tysome, T. (1996) *Beyond Competence: The National Council for Vocational Qualifications Framework and the Challenge to Higher Education in the New Millennium*. Aldershot: Avebury.

Goodwin, L.L. (2006) *Graduating Class. Disadvantaged Students Crossing the Bridge of Higher Education*. New York: SUNY Press.

Gorard, S. (2000) *Education and Social Justice: The Changing Composition of Schools and Its Implications*. Cardiff: University of Wales Press.

Gorard, S., Smith, E., May, H., Thomas, L., Adnett, N. and Slack, K. (2006) Review of widening participation research: addressing the barriers to participation in higher education. A report to HEFCE by the University of York, Higher Education Academy and Institute for Access Studies. Bristol: HEFCE. Online: www.hefce.ac.uk/pub.

Granovetter, M. (1973) The strength of weak ties. *American Journal of Sociology*, 78 (6): 1360–1380.

Green, F. and Zhu, Y. (2008) Overqualification, job dissatisfaction, and increasing dispersion in the returns to graduate education. Studies in Economics 0803, Department of Economics, University of Kent.

Grossberg, L. (1996) Identity and cultural studies – is that all there is? In S. Hall. and P. Du Gay (eds) *Cultural Identity*. London and California: Sage.

Grubb, W.N. (2006) Vocationalism and the differentiation of tertiary education: lessons from the US community colleges. *Journal of Further and Higher Education*, 30 (1): 27–42.

Haggis, T. (2003) Constructing images of ourselves? A critical investigation into 'approaches to learning' research in higher education. *British Educational Research Journal*, 29 (1): 89–104.

Haggis, T. (2006) Pedagogies for diversity: retaining critical challenge amidst fears of 'dumbing down'. *Studies in Higher Education*, 31 (5): 521–535.

Haggis, T. and Pouget, M. (2002) Trying to be motivated: perspectives on learning from younger students accessing higher education. *Teaching in Higher Education*, 7 (3): 323–336.

Haraway, D. (1991) *Simians, Cyborgs and Women: The Reinvention of Nature*. New York: Routledge.

Harris, S. (2005) Rethinking academic identities in neo-liberal times. *Teaching in Higher Education*, 10 (4),): 421–433.

Harvey, L., Drew, S. and Smith, M.(2006) *The First Year Experience: A Review of the Literature for the Higher Education Academy*. York: HEA.

Haveman, R. and Wolfe, B. (1995) The determinants of children's attainments: a review of methods and findings. *Journal of Economic Literature*, 33 (4): 1829–1878.

Haveman, R. and Wilson, K. (2005) Economic inequality in college access, matriculation and graduation. Paper presented to the Maxwell School Conference on Economic Inequality and Higher Education: Access, Persistence and Success, September 23–24. mimeo.

Hayward, G. (2005) *A Systems Analysis of the English VET System*. London: Learning and Skills Development Agency.

Hayward, G., Hodgson, A., Johnson, J., Keep, E., Oancea, A., Pring, R., Spours, K. and Wilde, S. (2004) Nuffield 14–19 review annual report. Oxford: OUDES.

Heath, S., Fuller, A. and Johnston, B. (forthcoming) Chasing shadows? Exploring network boundaries in qualitative social network analysis. *Qualitative Research* (Special issue), 9 (5).

Heath, S., Fuller, A. and Paton, K. (2008) Networked ambivalence and educational decision-making: a case study of 'non-participation' in higher education. *Research Papers in Education* (Special issue on challenges of diversity for widening participation in UK higher education), 23 (2): 219–231.

Heath, S. and Cleaver, E. (2003) *Young, Free and Single? Twenty-Somethings and Household Change*. New York: Palgrave.

Heenan, D. (2002) Women, access and progression: an examination of women's reasons for not continuing in higher education following the completion of the Certificate in Women's Studies. *Studies in Continuing Education*, 24 (1): 40–55.

HEFCE (Higher Education Funding Council for England) (1996) Widening access to higher education. A report by the HEFCE's advisory group on access and participation. 9/96. Bristol: HEFCE.

HEFCE (1997) *Response to the Dearing Report*. Bristol: HEFCE.

HEFCE (1998) Widening participation in higher education: funding proposals. 98/39. Bristol: HEFCE.

HEFCE (1999) *Performance Indicators in Higher Education*. Guide 99/66. Bristol: HEFCE.

HEFCE (2000) *Performance Indicators in Higher Education in the UK*. London: HEFCE.

HEFCE (2004) Lifelong learning networks. Joint letter from HEFCE and the Learning and Skills Council. 12/2004. Bristol: HEFCE.

HEFCE (2005a) *Young Participation in Higher Education*. Bristol: HEFCE. Online: www.hefce.ac.uk/pubs/hefce/2005/05_03/05_03.pdf.

HEFCE (2005b) *Higher Education Admissions: Assessment of Bias*. Bristol: HEFCE.

HEFCE (2006a) Higher education in further education colleges. Consultation on HEFCE policy. 2006/48. Bristol: HEFCE.

HEFCE (2006b) Review of widening participation research: addressing the barriers to participation in higher education. A report to HEFCE by the University of York, Higher Education Academy and Institute for Access Studies. Bristol: HEFCE.

HEFCE (2006c) Widening participation: a review. Report to the Minister of State for Higher Education and Lifelong Learning by the Higher Education Funding Council for England. Bristol: HEFCE.

HEFCE (2008a) Foundation degrees. Key statistics 2001–02 to 2007–08. 2008/16. Bristol: HEFCE.

HEFCE (2008b) Policy development HEFCE widening participation and fair access research strategy 2008 update. February 2008/10. Online: www.hefce.ac.uk/pubs/hefce/2008/08_10/.

HEFCE (2008c) Strategic Plan for 2006–2011 revised in May 2008. Online: www.hefce.ac.uk/pubs/hefce/2008/08_15/.

Hernandez-Martinez, P., Black, L., Davis, P., Hutcheson, G., Nicholson, S., Pampaka, M., Wake, G., and Williams, J.S. (2008a) Students' experiences of transition from GCSE to AS level mathematics. TLRP-WP-Maths working paper. Online: www.education.manchester.ac.uk/research/centres/lta/LTAResearch/tlrp/about/academicpapers/ (accessed 15 December 2008).

Hernandez-Martinez, P., Black, L., Davis, P., Hutcheson, G., Nicholson, S., Pampaka, M., Wake, G., and Williams, J.S. (2008b) Students' perceptions of coursework in mathematics AS level. TLRP-WP-Maths working paper. Online: www.education.manchester.ac.uk/research/centres/lta/LTAResearch/tlrp/about/academicpapers/ (15 December 2008).

Hernandez-Martinez, P., Black, L., Williams, J.S., Davis, P., Pampaka, M. and Wake, G., (2008c) Mathematics students' aspirations for higher education: class, ethnicity, gender and interpretative repertoire styles. *Research Papers in Education* (Special Issue on Challenges of diversity for widening participation in UK higher education), 23 (2),): 153–165.

HERO (2006) Online: www.hero.ac.uk/uk/home/index.cfm (accessed 7 March 2006).

Hockings, C. (2009) Reaching the students that student-centred learning cannot reach. *British Educational Research Journal*, 35 (1): 83–99.

Hockings, C., Cooke, S. and Bowl, M. (2007) 'Academic engagement' within a widening participation context – a 3D analysis. *Teaching in Higher Education* 12 (5–6): 721–734.

Hockings, C., Cooke, S. and Bowl, M. (2008a) Learning and teaching for social diversity and difference in higher education: towards more inclusive learning environments. *Research Briefing 41*. London, TLRP.

Hockings, C., Cooke, S., Yamashita, H., McGinty, S. and Bowl, M. (2008b) Switched off? A study of disengagement among computing students at two universities. *Research Papers in Education* (Special issue on challenges of diversity for widening participation in UK higher education) 23 (2): 191–203.

Hockings, C., Cooke, S., Yamashita, H. McGinty, S. and Bowl, M. (forthcoming) 'I'm neither entertaining nor charismatic. . .' Negotiating university teacher identity within diverse student groups. *Teaching in Higher Education* (Special issue on purpose, knowledge and identities).

Hodge, M. (2002) Labour's plans for lifelong learning in the second term. Speech by Margaret Hodge, MP at the Social Market Foundation, London, 11 April.

Hölscher, M. (2008) Success in HE of students from vocational and general academic background. Conference proceedings of SRHE conference, December, Liverpool), London: SRHE.

Hölscher, M. and Hayward, G. (2008) Analysing access to HE for students with different educational backgrounds: preliminary descriptive results. Online: www.tlrp.org/project%20sites/degrees/download.html.

Hölscher, M., Hayward, G., Ertl, H. and Dunbar-Goddet, H. (2008) The transition from vocational education and training: a successful pathway. *Research Papers in Education* (Special issue on challenges for diversity for widening participation in UK higher education), 23 (2): 139–153.

Hogarth, T., Maguire, M., Pitcher, J., Purcell, K. and Wilson, R. (1997) *The Participation of Non-traditional Students in Higher Education*, HEFC Research Series. Warwick: Institute for Employment Research.

Hoskins, S.L., Newstead, S.E. and Dennis, I. (1997) Degree performance as a function of age, gender, prior qualifications and discipline studied. *Assessment and Evaluation in Higher Education*, 22: 317–28.

Housee, S. (2001) Insiders and outsiders: black female voices from the academy. In P. Anderson and J. Williams (eds) *Identity and Differences in Higher Education: Outsiders within*. Aldershot: Ashgate.

Hussain, Y. and Bagguley, P. (2007) *Moving on Up: South Asian Women and Higher Education*. Stoke on Trent: Trentham Books.

Hutcheson, G.D., Black, L., Davis, P., Hernandez, P., Nicholson, S., Pampaka, M., Wake, G. and Williams, J.S. (2008a) ASTrad and UoM courses: factors influencing enrolment. TLRP working paper. Online: www.lta.education. manchester.ac.uk/TLRP/academicpapers.htm (accessed 15 December 2008).

Hutcheson, G.D., Black, L., Davis, P., Hernandez, P., Nicholson, S., Pampaka, M., Wake, G., Williams, J.S. (2008b) Dispositions towards mathematically-demanding subjects. TLRP working paper. Online: www.education.manchester. ac.uk/research/centres/lta/LTAResearch/tlrp/about/academicpapers (accessed 15 December 2008).

Iftikhar, H., McNally, S. and Telhaj, S. (2008) University quality and graduate wages in the UK. Centre for Economics of Education mimeo, output from ESRC/TLRP project *Widening Participation in Higher Education: A Quantitative Analysis*.

Jenkins, A., Greenwood, C. and Vignoles, A. (2007) *The Returns to Qualifications in England: Updating the Evidence Base on Level 2 and Level 3 Vocational Qualifications*. Centre for the Economics of Education DP89. London: London School of Economics.

Johnes, G. and McNabb, R. (2004) Never give up on the good times: student attrition in the UK. *Oxford Bulletin of Economics and Statistics*, 66: 23–47.

Johnes, J. (1990) Determinants of student wastage in higher education. *Studies in Higher Education*, 15 (1),): 87–99.

Johnes, J. and Taylor, J. (1989) Undergraduate non-completion rates: differences between UK universities. *Higher Education*, 18: 209–225.

Keating (2006) Post-school articulation in Australia: a case of unresolved tensions, *Journal of Further and Higher Education,* 30 (1): 59–74.

Keep, E. and Mayhew, K. (2004) The economic and distributional implications of current policies on Higher Education. *Oxford Review of Economic Policy*, 20 (2): 298–314.

Kelly, K. and Cook, S. (2007) Full-time young participation by socio-economic class: a new widening participation measure in higher education. DfES Research Report RR806.

Krueger, A. and Lindahl, M. (2001) Education for growth: Why and for whom? *Journal of Economic Literature*, December, 1101–36.

Lammers, W. and Murphy, J. (2002) A profile of teaching techniques used in the university classroom. *Active Learning in Higher Education*, 3 (1): 54–68.

Lave, J. and McDermott, R. (2002) Estranged labor learning. *Outlines,* 4 (1): 19–48.

Lave, J. and Wenger, E. (1991) *Situated Learning*. Cambridge: Cambridge University Press.

Learning and Skills Council (LSC) (2007) Review of further education provision within HE institutions. Report. Coventry: LSC.

Leathwood, C. and O' Connell, P. (2003) 'It's a struggle': the construction of the 'new student' in higher education. *Journal of Education Policy*, 18 (6): 597–615.

Leitch, S. (2006) Prosperity for all in the global economy – world class skills (The Leitch Report). London: HM Treasury.

Leont'ev, A.N. (1981) *Problems of the Development of Mind.* Moscow: Progress Publishers.

Letherby, G. and Shiels, J. (2001) 'Isn't he good, but can we take her seriously?': Gendered expectations in higher education. In P. Anderson and J. Williams (eds) *Identity and Difference in Higher Education.* Aldershot: Ashgate, pp. 121–132.

Machin, S. and A. Vignoles (2004) Educational inequality: the widening socio-economic gap. *Fiscal Studies*, 25: 107–128.

Malcolm, J. and Zukas, M. (2001) Bridging pedagogic gaps: conceptual discontinuities in higher education. *Teaching in Higher Education*, 6 (1): 33–42.

Malcolm, J. and Zukas, M. (2007) Poor relations. Exploring discipline, research and pedagogy in academic identity. In M. Osborne, M. Houston and N. Toman (eds) *The Pedagogy of Lifelong Learning: Understanding Effective Teaching and Learning in Diverse Contexts*. Oxford: Routledge.

Mann, S. (2001) Alternative perspectives on the student experience: alienation and engagement. *Studies in Higher Education* 26 (1): 7–19.

Mann, S. (2008) *Study, Power and the University*. Maidenhead: Society for Research in Higher Education.

Marks, A. (2002) '2+2' = 'Access': working towards a higher education and further education overlap to facilitate greater adult participation. *Teaching in Higher Education,* 7 (1): 113–116.

Marshall, D. and Case, J. (2005) Approaches to learning research in higher education: a response to Haggis. *British Educational Research Journal,* 31 (2): 257–267.

Marton, F., Hounsell D. and Entwistle, N. (eds) (1997) *The Experience of Learning. Implications for Teaching and Studying in Higher Education*. 2nd edn. Edinburgh: Scottish Academic Press.

Marton. F. and Booth. S. (1997) *Learning and Awareness*. Mahwah, NJ: Lawrence Erlbaum and Associates.

Massey, D. (1996) A global sense of place. In S. Daniels and R. Lee (eds) *Exploring Human Geography*. London: Arnold.

McDonnell, L. M. and Grubb, W.N. (1991) *Education and Training for Work: The Policy Instruments and the Institutions*. Santa Monica and Berkeley: RAND and National Center for Research in Vocational Education, University of California at Berkeley.

McDonough, P. and Fann, A. (2007) The study of inequality. In P. Gumport (ed.) *Sociology of Higher Education*. Baltimore: Johns Hopkins University.

McGivney, V. (1996) Staying or *Leaving the Course: Non-Completion and Retention of Mature Students in Further and Higher Education*. Leicester: National Institute of Adult Continuing Education.

McIntosh, S. (2005) Evidence on the balance of supply and demand for qualified workers. In S. Machin and A. Vignoles (eds) *What's the Good of Education? The Economics of Education in the United Kingdom*. Princeton: Princeton University Press.

McNabb, R., Pal, S. and Sloane, P. (2002) Gender differences in educational attainment: the case of university students in England and Wales. *Economica,* 69 (275),): 481–50.

Meghir, C. and Palme, M. (2005) Educational reform, ability, and family background, *American Economic Review,* 95 (1): 414–424.

Miller, R.L. (2000) *Researching Life Stories and Family Histories*. London: Sage.

Mirza, H. (2008) *Race, Gender and Educational Desire: Why Black Women Succeed and Fail*. London: Routledge.

Modood, T. and Shiner, M. (1994) *Ethnic Minorities and Higher Education*. London: Policy Studies Institute/Universities and Colleges Admissions Services.

Molinero, C. and Portilla, L. (1993) An evaluation of a degree classification system. *Education Economics,* 1 (2): 137–152.

Moodie, G. (2008) *From Vocational to Higher Education. An international Perspective*. Maidenhead: Society for Research into Higher Education and Open University Press.

Moogan, Y.J., Baron, S. and Harris, K. (1999) Decision-making behaviour of potential higher education students. *Higher Education Quarterly,* 53 (3): 211–228.

Morley, L. (2002) A comedy of errors: quality and power in higher education. In P. Trowler (ed.) *Higher Education Policy and Institutional Change.* Miilton Keynes: Society for Research into Higher Education and Open University Press, pp. 126–141.

Morley, L. and David, M. (2009) Celebrations and challenges: gender in higher education introduction. *Higher Education Policy,* 22 (1): 1–2.

Mussellbrook, K. and Dean, J. (2003) Students' experiences of first year at university. Southeast of Scotland Access Forum. Online: http://snap.ac.uk/seswarf/studexepinterimreport.pdf.

National Audit Office (2007) *Staying the Course: The Retention of Students in Higher Education.* London: HMSO.

National Audit Office (2008) Widening participation in higher education. Report by the Comptroller and Auditor General HC 725 Session 2007–2008 25 June 2008. Online: www.nao.org.uk/publications/nao_reports/07–08/0708725.pdf.

Nayak, A. (2003) *Race, Place and Globalization.* Oxford and New York: Berg.

Nicholl, K. and Harrison, R. (2003) Constructing the good teacher in higher education: the discursive work of standards. *Studies in Continuing Education,* 25 (1): 23–35.

Nora, A. (2004) The role of habitus and cultural capital in choosing a college, transitioning from high school to higher education and persisting in college among minority an nonminority students. *Journal of Hispanic Higher Education,* 3 (2): 180–208.

O'Leary, N.C. and Sloane, P.J. (2004) The return to a university education in Great Britain. IZA Working Paper, No. 1199.

O'Leary, N.C. and Sloane, P.J. (2007) Rates of Return to Degrees across British Regions. Online: www.swan.ac.uk/sbe/welmerc/papers/2006_01.pdf (accessed 27 May 2009)

Osborne, M., Marks, A. and Turner, E. (2004) Becoming a mature student: how adult applicants weigh the advantages and disadvantages of higher education. *Higher Education: The International Journal of Higher Education and Educational Planning,* 48 (3): 291–315.

Palmer, J. (2001) Student drop-out: a case study in new managerialist policy. *Journal of Further and Higher Education,* 25 (3): 349–357.

Pampaka, M., Williams, J., Davis, P. and Wake, G. (2008) Measuring pedagogic practice: a measure of 'teacher-centrism'. Paper presented at The American Educational Research Association annual conference (AERA).

Parry, G. (2003) Mass higher education and the English: wherein the colleges? *Higher Education Quarterly,* 57 (4): 308–337.

Parry, G. (2005) British higher education and the prism of devolution. In T. Tapper and D. Palfreyman (eds) *Understanding Mass Higher Education. Comparative Perspectives on Access.* Oxford: RoutledgeFalmer.

Parry, G. (2007) The English experiment. *Journal of University Studies,* 35: 95–110.

Pascarella, E.T. and Terenzini, P.T. (2005) *How College Affects Students. A third decade of Research.* San Francisco: Josey-Bass.

Patiniotis, J. and Holdsworth, C. (2005) 'Seize that chance!' Leaving home and transitions to higher education. *Journal of Youth Studies,* 8 (1): 81–95.

Payne, J. (2003) Vocational pathways at age 16–19. DfES Research Report RR501. Nottingham: DfES.

Pennell, H. and West, A. (2005) The impact of increased fees on participation in higher education in England. *Higher Education Quarterly*, 59 (2): 127–137.

Polanyi, M. (2002/1958) *Personal Knowledge: Towards a Post-critical Philosophy*. London: Routledge.

Pollard, E., Bates, P., Hunt, W. and Bellis, A. (2008) University is not just for young people: working adults' perceptions of, and orientation to, higher education. Research Report 0806, Department for Innovation, Universities and Skills.

Polytechnics and Colleges Funding Council (PCFC) (1992) Widening participation in higher education. Report of a study of polytechnics and colleges of higher education in England. London: PCFC.

Powdthavee, N. and Vignoles, A. (2008) The socio-economic gap in university drop out. Institute of Education, mimeo.

Power, M. (1997) *The Audit Society: Rituals of Verification*. Oxford: Oxford University Press.

Pratt, J. (1997) *The Polytechnic Experiment 1965–1992*. Milton Keynes: Society for Research into Higher Education and Open University Press.

Professional Standards Framework for Teaching and Learning Support in Higher Education. Online: www.heacademy.ac.uk/ourwork/policy/framework (accessed 22 December 2008).

Prosser, M. and Trigwell, K. (1999) *Understanding Learning and Teaching: The Experience in Higher Education*. Milton Keynes: Society for Research into Higher Education and Open University Press.

Pugsley, L. (2004) *The University Challenge. Higher Education Markets and Social Stratification*. Aldershot: Ashgate.

Purcell, K., Elias, P., Davies, R. and Wilton, N. (2005) The class of '99: a study of the early labour market experience of recent graduates. Department for Education and Skills Research Report RR691.

Putnam, R. (2000) *Bowling Alone: The Collapse and Revival of American Community*. New York: Simon and Schuster.

Quinn, J. (2004) Understanding working-class 'drop-out' from higher education through a socio-cultural lens: cultural narratives and local contexts. *International Studies in Sociology of Education*, 14 (1): 57–74.

Raffe, D., Croxford, L., Iannelli, C., Shapira, M. and Howieson, C. (2006) *Social-class Inequalities in Education in England and Scotland*. Edinburgh: Centre for Educational Sociology, University of Edinburgh,

Ramsden, P. (1992) *Learning to Teach in Higher Education*. London: Routledge.

Raphael Reed, L., Croudace, C., Harrison, N., Baxter, A. and Last, K. (2007) *Young Participation in HE: A Socio-cultural Study of Educational Engagement*. Bristol: University of West of England and a HEFCE funded project.

Read, B., Archer, L. and Leathwood, C. (2003) Challenging cultures? Student conceptions of 'belonging' and 'isolation' at a post-1992 university. *Studies in Higher Education* 28 (3): 261–77.

Reay, D. (1998) 'Always knowing' and 'never being sure': familial and institutional habituses and higher education. *Journal of Educational Policy* 13 (4): 519–29.

Reay, D. (2003) A risky business? Mature working-class women students and access to higher education. *Gender and Education*, 15 (3): 301–17.

Reay, D., Crozier, G.and Clayton, J. (2009) 'Fitting in' or 'standing out': working class students in higher education. *British Educational Research Journal*, pp. 1–18.

Reay, D. Crozier, G. and Clayton, J. (forthcoming) Strangers in paradise? Working-class students in elite universities. *Sociology*.

Reay. D, David, M. and Ball, S. (2005) *Degree of Choice: Social Class, Race and Gender in Higher Education*. Stoke on Trent: Trentham Books.

Research Briefings 38–44. Online: www.tlrp.org/pub/research.html:
No. 38 – Keeping Open the Door to Mathematically Demanding Programmes in Further and Higher Education
No. 39 – Widening Participation in Higher Education: A Quantitative Analysis
No. 40 – Combining Policy, Organisation and Progression in Further and Higher Education
No. 41 – Learning and Teaching for Diversity and Difference in Higher Education: Towards more Inclusive Learning Environments
No. 42 – Degrees of Success: Learners' Transitions from Vocational Education and Training to Higher Education
No. 43 – Non-Participation in Higher Education: Decision-Making as an Embedded Social Practice
No. 44 – The Socio Cultural and Learning Experiences of Working Class Students in Higher Education

Rhoads, R.A. and Torres, C.A. (eds) (2006) *The University, State, and Market. The Political Economy of Globalization in the Americas*. Stanford, CA: Stanford University Press.

Richardson, J.T.E. and Woodley, A. (2003) Another look at the role of age, gender and subject as predictors of academic attainment in higher education. *Studies in Higher Education*, 28 (4): 475–493.

Robbins L. (1963) Higher education, report and appendices. Cmnd 2154. London: HMSO.

Robertson, D. and Hillman, J. (1997) Widening participation in higher education from lower socio-economic groups and students with disabilities. Report 6 National Committee of Inquiry into Higher Education. London: NCIHE.

Rose, D. and O'Reilly, K. (1998) The ESRC review of government social classifications: Final report. London: HMSO.

Sammons, P. (1995) Gender, ethnic and socio-economic differences in attainment and progress: a longitudinal analysis of student achievement over 9 years. *British Educational Research Journal*, 21 (4): 465–485.

Schuller, T., Preston, J., Hammond, C., Brassett-Grundy, A. and Bynner, J. (2004) *The Benefits of Learning: The Impact of Education on Health, Family Life and Social Capital*. Oxford: RoutledgeFalmer.

Scott, P. (1995) *The Meanings of Mass Higher Education*. Milton Keynes: Society for Research into Higher Education and Open University Press.

Sharp, P.R. (1987) *The Creation of the Local Authority Sector of Higher Education*. Lewes: Falmer Press.

Shavit, Y., Arum, R. and Gamoran, A. (eds) (2007) *Stratification in Higher Education. A Comparative Study*. Stanford: Stanford University Press.

Shepherd, J. (2007) Working class student numbers fall, *The Guardian*, 20 February.

Silver, H. and Brennan, J. (1988) *A Liberal Vocationalism*. London: Methuen.

Silver, H., Stennett, A. and Williams, R. (1995) *The External Examiner System: Possible Futures*. London: Higher Education Quality Council.

Skeggs, B. (1994) Situating the production of feminist ethnography. In M. Maynard and J. Purvis (eds) *Researching Women's Lives from a Feminist Perspective*. London and Philadelphia: Taylor and Francis.

Skeggs, B. (1997) *Formations of Class and Gender*. London, Thousand Oaks and New Delhi: Sage.

Slaughter, S. and Rhoades, G. (2004) *Academic Capitalism and the New Economy. Markets, State and Higher Education*. Baltimore, MA: The Johns Hopkins University Press.

Smith, E. and Gorard, S. (2007) Who succeeds in teacher training? *Research Papers in Education*, 19 (4): 465–482.

Smith, J.P. and Naylor, R.A. (2001) Dropping out of university: a statistical analysis of the probability of withdrawal for UK university students. *Journal of Royal Statistical Society: Series A*, 164: 389–405.

Stewart, D. (2008) Being all of me: black students negotiating multiple identities. *The Journal of Higher Education*, 79 (2): 183–207.

Strand, S. (1999) Ethnic group, sex and economic disadvantage: associations with pupil's educational progress from baseline to the end of key stage 1. *British Educational Research Journal*, 25 (2): 179–202.

Strauss, A. and Corbin, J. (1990) *Basics of Qualitative Research: Grounded Theory Procedures and Techniques*. California and London: Sage.

Stubbs, W.H. (1988) The polytechnics and colleges funding council. Speech to the Association of Colleges for Further and Higher Education, June.

Sutton Trust (2000) *Entry to Leading Universities*. London: Sutton Trust.

Sutton Trust (2004) *Missing 3000*. London: Sutton Trust.

Sutton Trust (2005) *State School Admissions to our Leading Universities. An Update to 'The Missing 3000'*. London: Sutton Trust.

Sutton Trust (2007) *University Admissions by Individual Schools* London: Sutton Trust.

Sutton Trust (2008) University admissions by individual schools. Report first published September 2007, republished February 2008. Online: www.sutton trust.com/reports/UniversityAdmissions.pdf.

Swan, M. (2006) Designing and using research instruments to describe the beliefs and practices of mathematics teachers. *Research in Education*, 75: 58–70.

Thomas, L. and Quinn, J. (2007) *First Generation Entry into Higher Education*. Milton Keynes: Open University Press.

Thomas, L. (2002) Student retention in higher education: the role of institutional habitus. *Journal of Education Policy*, 17 (4): 423–442.

Times Higher Education (2007) The best, the brightest and the brutal truth. 21 September, p. 12.

Times Higher Education (2008) Academics split over value of access funding: Some say initiative will pay off, others say it is best to invest in schools, 24 July. Online: www.timeshighereducation.co.uk/story.asp?sectioncode=26&storycode=402938.

Tinto, V. (1993) *Leaving College: Rethinking the Causes and Cures of Student Attrition*. 2nd edn. Chicago: University of Chicago Press.

Tinto, V. (1996) Reconstructing the first year at college. *Planning for Higher Education*, 25 (1): 1–6.

Tomalin, E. (2007) Supporting cultural and religious diversity in higher education: pedagogy and beyond. *Teaching in Higher Education*, 12 (5–6): 621–634.

Tomlinson, S. (2001) Some success, could do better: education and race 1976–2000. In R. Phillips and J. Furlong (eds) *Education, Reform and the State: Twenty-five Years of Politics, Policy and Practice*. London: Routledge, pp. 192–206.

Trow, M. (2005) Reflections on the transition from elite to mass to universal access: forms and phases of higher education in modern societies since WWII. In P. Altbach (ed.) *International Handbook of Higher Education*. Dordrecht: Kluwer.

UUK (2007) *Variable Tuition Fees in England: Assessing their Impact on Students and Higher Education Institutions*. London: Universities UK.

Vermunt, J. (1998) The regulation of constructive learning experiences. *British Journal of Educational Psychology*, 68 (2): 149–171.

Wake, G. (2009) What is the value of mathematics in an institutional culture of performance management? Paper presented to AERA Conference, San Diego. Online: www.education.manchester.ac.uk/research/centres/lta/LTAResearch/tlrp/about/academicpapers/.

Wake, G.D. and Davis, P. (2008) Renegotiating identities: mediation of troubling AS Level mathematics. Paper presented at the Society for Research in Higher Education conference (SHRE).

Wake, G. and Pampaka, M. (2008) The central role of the teacher – even in student centred pedagogies. *Proceedings of the Joint Meeting of the 32nd Conference of the International Group for the Psychology of Mathematics Education (PME)*. Michoacan, Mexico: Morelia.

Wake, G., Williams, J.S., Black, L., Davis, P., Hernandez-Martinez, P. and Pampaka, M. (2007) Pedagogic practices and interweaving narratives in AS Mathematics classrooms. Paper presented at BERA 2007. Online: www.education.manchester.ac.uk/research/centres/lta/LTAResearch/tlrp/about/academicpapers/. (accessed 15 December 2008).

Walker, I. and Zhu, Y. (forthcoming) The college wage premium, over education and the expansion of higher education in the UK. *Scandinavian Journal of Economics*.

Watson, D. (2006) How to think about widening participation in UK higher education. Discussion paper for HEFCE. Bristol: HEFCE.

Weiler, K. and David, M. (2008) The personal and political: second wave feminism and educational research: introduction. *Discourse, Studies in the Cultural Politics of Education*, 29 (4): 433–435.

Wenger, E. (1998) *Communities of Practice. Learning Meaning and Identity*. Cambridge: Cambridge University Press.

Wheelahan, L. (2009) Do dual-sector institutions contribute to social justice? In N. Garrod and B. Macfarlane (eds) *Challenging Boundaries: Managing the Integration of Post-Secondary Education*. London: Routledge, pp. 29–44.

White, J. (2009) Further and higher education: a philosophical divide? In N. Garrod and B. Macfarlane (eds) *Challenging Boundaries. Managing the Integration of Post-Secondary Education*. Oxford: Routledge.

Widdowson, J. (2005) Implications for the mixed economy colleges. In C. Duke, and G. Layer (eds) *Widening Participation. Which way forward for English Higher Education?* Leicester: NIACE, pp. 36–44.

Wilde, S. and Hölscher, M. (2007) *Missed Opportunities? Non-placed applicants (NPA) in the UCAS data.* Oxford and Cheltenham: UCAS.

Wilde, S., Wright, S., Hayward, G., Johnson, J. and Skerrett, R. (2006) Nuffield review higher education focus groups. Online: www.nuffield14–19review.org.uk/files/documents106–1.pdf.

Williams, J.S. (2008) The cultural historical mediation of a professional identity. Paper presented at ISCAR Symposium, San Diego. Online: www.education.manchester.ac.uk/research/centres/lta/LTAResearch/tlrp/about/academic papers/.

Williams, J.S. (2009) Towards a political economic theory of value in education. Paper presented to AERA conference, San Diego. Online: www.education.manchester.ac.uk/research/centres/lta/LTAResearch/tlrp/about/academic papers/.

Williams, J., Davis, P. and Black, L. (eds) (2007) Subjectivities in school: socio-cultural and activity theory perspectives. *International Journal of Educational Research* (Special Issue on Sociocultural and Cultural-Historical Activity Theory Perspectives and Subjectivities and Learning in Schools and other Educational Contexts), 46 (1–2): 1–107.

Williams, J., Hernandez-Martinez, P., Black, L., Davis, P., Pampaka, M. and Wake, G. (2008) Transition into post-compulsory (mathematics) education. TLRP working paper. Online: www.education.manchester.ac.uk/research/centres/lta/LTAResearch/tlrp/about/academicpapers/ (accessed 15 December 2008).

Williams, J.S., Black, L., Hernandez-Martinez, P., Davis, P., Pampaka, M. and Wake, G. (2009) Narratives, cultural models and identity. In M. César and K. Kumpulainen (eds) *Social Interactions in Multicultural Settings*. Rotterdam: Sense Publishers.

Wilson, D., Burgess, S. and Briggs, A. (2005) The dynamics of school attainment of England's ethnic minorities. CMPO Working Paper No. 05/130.

Wingate, U. and Macaro, E. (2004) From sixth form to university: motivation and transition among high achieving sate school language students. *Oxford Review of Education,* 30 (4): 467–488.

Woolcock, M. (1998) Social Capital and Economic Development: Toward a theoretical synthesis and policy framework. *Theory and Society,* 27 (1): 151–208.

Working papers available online:
www.tlrp.org/proj/wphe/wp_crozier.html
www.tlrp.org/proj/wphe/wp_fuller.html
www.tlrp.org/proj/wphe/wp_hayward.html
www.tlrp.org/proj/wphe/wp_hockings.html
www.tlrp.org/proj/wphe/wp_vignoles.html
www.tlrp.org/proj/wphe/wp_williams.html
www.tlrp.org/proj/wphe/wp_parry.html

Yorke, M. and Longden, B. (2004) *Retention and Student Success in Higher Education.* Milton Keynes: Open University Press.

Yorke, M. (1998) Non-completion of undergraduate study: some implications for policy in higher education. *Journal of Higher Education Policy and Management*, 20 (2): 189–201.

Yorke, M. (2007) *Grading Student Achievement in Higher Education: Signals and Shortcomings*. London: Routledge/Taylor & Francis.

Young, M. (2006) Further and higher education: a seamless or differentiated future? *Journal of Further and Higher Education*, 30 (1): 1–10.

Zepke, N. and Leach, L. (2007) Improving student outcome in higher education: New Zealand teachers' views on teaching students from diverse backgrounds. *Teaching in Higher Education*, 12 (5–6): 655–668.

Index

Note: *italic* page numbers denote references to figures/tables.